中国桥梁

Bridges in China (2003-2013)

李国豪 题

人民交通出版社
China Communications Press

编辑委员会

主任委员	范立础
副主任委员	邓文中　林元培　郑皆连　秦顺全
委　　员	王用中　王伯惠　王昌将　王武勤　王福敏　车宇琳
	牛　斌　凤懋润　包琦玮　吉　林　庄卫林　刘正光
	许志豪　李关寿　李守善　李怀峰　杨志刚　张喜刚
	陈　阵　邵长宇　罗世东　周世忠　周　良　孟凡超
	胡建华　顾安邦　徐升桥　徐恭义　高宗余　常兴文
	韩振勇　谢邦珠　楼庄鸿
	（以姓氏笔画为序）

编写组

顾　　问	范立础　金成棣　林长川　郑信光
	陆宗林　袁国干　詹蓓蓓　陆　楸
主　　编	项海帆
副 主 编	葛耀君　肖汝诚　杨志刚
分篇负责人	
跨海大桥	葛耀君　朱乐东　杨詠昕
悬索桥	肖汝诚　程　进　孙　斌
斜拉桥	徐利平　邵长宇　阮　欣　孙利民
拱式桥	吴定俊　石雪飞
梁式桥	李国平　徐　栋
城市桥梁	陈艾荣　韩振勇　马如进　孙　智
特约翻译	Paul Gauvreau

编辑统筹

责任编辑	孙玺　曲乐　王文华　卢俊丽　郭海龙
美术编辑	李燕

Editorial Committee

Chairman: Fan Lichu
Vice-chairman: M. C. Tang　　Lin Yuanpei
　　　　　　　　Zheng Jielian　Qin Shunquan
Members: Wang Yongzhong　Wang Bohui　　Wang Changjiang
　　　　　Wang Wuqin　　　Wang Fumin　　Che Yulin
　　　　　Niu Bin　　　　　Feng Maorun　　Bao Qiwei
　　　　　Ji Lin　　　　　Zhuang Weilin　Liu Zhengguang
　　　　　Xu Zhihao　　　　Li Guanshou　　Li Shoushan
　　　　　Li Huaifeng　　　Yang Zhigang　　Zhang Xigang
　　　　　Chen Zhen　　　Shao Changyu　　Luo Shidong
　　　　　Zhou Shizhong　Zhou Liang　　　Meng Fanchao
　　　　　Hu Jianhua　　　Gu Anbang　　　Xu Shengqiao
　　　　　Xu Gongyi　　　Gao Zongyu　　　Chang Xingwen
　　　　　Han Zhenyong　Xie Bangzhu　　Lou Zhuanghong

Compilation Board

Consultants: Fan Lichu　　　Jin Chengdi　　Lin Changchuan
　　　　　　　Zheng Xinguang　Lu Zonglin　　Yuan Guogan
　　　　　　　Zhan Beibei　　Lu Qiu
Compiler-in-chief: Xiang Haifan
Deputy Compiler-in-chief: Ge Yaojun　Xiao Rucheng　Yang Zhigang
Compliers:
　　Sea-crossing bridge: Ge Yaojun　Zhu Ledong　Yang Yongxin
　　Suspension bridge: Xiao Rucheng　Cheng Jin　Sun Bin
　　Cable-stayed bridge: Xu Liping　Shao Changyu　Ruan Xin　Sun Limin
　　Arch bridge: Wu Dingjun　Shi Xuefei
　　Girder bridge: Li Guoping　Xu Dong
　　Urban Bridge: Chen Airong　Han Zhenyong　Ma Rujin　Sun Zhi
Contributing Translator: Paul Gauvreau

Managing Editor

Editor in Charge: Sun Xi　Qu Le　Wang Wenhua　Lu Junli　Guo Hailong
Art Editor: Li Yan

李国豪（1913-2005）

中国桥梁
Bridges in China
(2003-2013)

前 言

2005年2月23日元宵节，敬爱的李国豪老师永远离开了我们。当时，他曾积极参与前期规划工作并日夜关心的上海东海大桥即将建成，苏通长江大桥和杭州湾大桥已投入紧张的施工，舟山连岛工程的关键工程西堠门大桥也即将动工建设。2013年4月13日是李老师的百年诞辰，我们通过遴选将进入21世纪以来的最近十年间新建桥梁中的100座具有代表性的中国桥梁汇编成册，献给李老师以及已故的桥梁界许多前辈，用以报答他们曾经给予的教诲和奠定的基础，也表达我们后辈对他们的崇高敬意和永久怀念之情。

中国桥梁在21世纪初又出现了一个新高潮。由于国家财力日渐充裕，为了发展中西部地区的经济，投入了巨额的交通设施建设费，沿海发达地区也继续提高交通设施水平，加密路网，以适应日益增长的交通需求，加上高速铁路建设的兴起，桥梁建设呈现出全国遍地开花的兴旺景象。然而，巨额投资也滋长了浮躁心态和好大喜功的不良倾向，出现了少数盲目追求"第一"和"之最"，不顾经济合理性的工程。这不仅违背了设计基本原则，也遭到国际同行的质疑，已引起有责任心的管理者、技术人员的警觉和反思。

本画册共分六篇，分别收集了跨海大桥、悬索桥、斜拉桥、拱桥、梁式桥和城市桥梁六类共100座桥梁。每座桥除精美的图片外均附有中英文的简单说明，以着重介绍该桥不同一般的特点、难点和亮点。每篇各撰写一简短的引言，对所收编的桥梁进行综合评述，简述有特殊意义的创新技术成果和存在的不足，并指出今后努力的方向。

从1993年为纪念李校长的80寿辰出版的第一本《中国桥梁》，2003年为纪念他90寿辰的第二本《中国大桥》，到2013年的这本画册，共同记录了新中国成立以来六十余年间中国桥梁从学习和追赶、跟踪和提高到有所创新和超越的奋斗历程。李国豪老师作为中国桥梁在改革开放以来通过自主建设取得进步的首要功臣和领路人，建立了不朽的功勋。

今天，我们纪念他的百年诞辰，一定要牢记他"理论联系实际，发展桥梁科技"的教导，勇于创新，用创新的成果提高国际竞争力，克服不足，走出误区，为实现从桥梁大国走向桥梁强国的目标而继续努力。

项海帆　范立础
2013年1月

Preface

On February 23, 2005, the date of Chinese Lantern Festival, our respected and beloved teacher Prof. Li Guohao left us forever. At the time of his passing, the Shanghai East Sea Bridge was nearly complete. The Sutong Bridge over the Yangtze River and the Hangzhou Bay Bridge, two bridges of great importance to Prof. Li which had benefitted from his personal involvement in the preliminary planning stage, were under construction. Construction was about to begin on the Xihoumen Bridge, the key project of the Zhoushan Island connection. April 13, 2013 is the one hundredth anniversary of Prof. Li's birth. To coincide with this date, we have compiled this book to showcase one hundred Chinese bridges built between 2003 and 2013. We dedicate this book to Prof. Li and other eminent experts for their contributions to bridge engineering in China. Through the publication of this book, we recognize their teaching and guidance, and express our deepest gratitude, utmost respect, and everlasting remembrance.

The beginning of 21st century ushered in a new boom in bridge construction in China as a result of the great success of Chinese economy. The central and western regions of China received major investments in new infrastructure while the developed coastal areas saw further expansion of existing highway networks to keep pace with the rapid growth of transportation. The demand for new bridges was further intensified by the development of China's high speed railway network. Together, these factors enabled bridge construction to flourish in China during the past decade. The unprecedented scale of infrastructure investment during the past ten years may result in making aggressive and impetuous decisions. In the most serious cases, officials took advantage of the power associated with their rank. As a consequence, several recent record-breaking projects actually achieved their status by violating basic rules of good design and economy. These projects have been questioned by international colleagues and criticized within China by responsible government officials, engineers, and professors.

This book presents a total of 100 bridges organized into six chapters, each representing one type of bridge: sea-crossing bridges, suspension bridges, cable-stayed bridges, arch bridges, girder bridges, and urban bridges. For each bridge, there are photographs as well as a brief explanation in both Chinese and English describing unique features and challenges. Each chapter begins with an introduction that gives a comprehensive appraisal of each type of bridge, recommending applications of technology that are associated with significant creative achievements, as well as pointing out insufficiencies and suggested directions for future improvement.

The first book *Bridges in China* was published in 1993 to commemorate Prof. Li's 80th birthday. The second book *Major Bridges in China(2003)* commemorated his 90th birthday. The current book, to be published in 2013, together with the previous two books, record the history of bridges in China over the past 60 years since the foundation of the People's Republic of China. These volumes bear witness to the progress made in bridge engineering in China, which began with a period of learning from international bridge engineering practice, followed by a period of adaptation and enhancement of international practice, to the current period in which Chinese bridge engineers have demonstrated the capacity to innovate and have assumed a position of leadership that is recognized worldwide. Since the beginning of China's economic reform and opening-up policy in 1978, Prof. Li Guohao became the pre-eminent bridge engineer in China, serving the profession through leadership inspired by a spirit of self-reliance.

Today, as we commemorate his one hundredth birthday, we must remain mindful of the primary elements of Prof. Li's teaching: to "combine theory with practice to develop bridge technology", to be bold in innovation, and to use the achievements of innovation to be competitive on the international stage, overcome shortcomings, and to avoid past mistakes. Under his guidance, we will strive to transform China from a nation of large bridges to a nation of strong bridges.

Xiang Haifan, Fan Lichu
January, 2013

目 录　INDEX

第一篇　跨海大桥　　　　　　　　　　Chapter 1　Sea-crossing Bridges

引言	2	Introduction
澳门西湾大桥	4	West Bay Bridge in Macao
东海大桥	6	East Sea Bridge
湛江海湾大桥	12	Zhanjiang Bay Bridge
深圳湾大桥	14	Shenzhen Bay Bridge
杭州湾跨海大桥	16	Hangzhou Bay Bridge
金塘大桥	20	Jintang Bridge
平潭海峡大桥	24	Pingtan Straits Bridge
青岛海湾大桥	26	Qingdao Bay Bridge
宁波象山港公路大桥	30	Xiangshan Harbor Bridge in Ningbo
厦漳跨海大桥	34	Xiazhang Sea-crossing Bridge

第二篇　悬索桥　　　　　　　　　　Chapter 2　Suspension Bridges

引言	40	Introduction
润扬长江公路大桥南汊桥	42	Runyang Highway Bridge over Southern Branch of the Yangtze River
湘江三汊矶大桥	44	Sanchaji Bridge over the Xiangjiang River
佛山平胜大桥	46	Pingsheng Bridge in Foshan
阳逻长江公路大桥	48	Yangluo Highway Bridge over the Yangtze River
镇胜公路北盘江大桥	50	Zhensheng Highway Bridge over the Beipan River
广州珠江黄埔大桥南汊桥	52	Huangpu Bridge over Southern Branch of the Pearl River in Guangzhou
杭州江东大桥	54	Jiangdong Bridge in Hangzhou
恩施四渡河大桥	56	Enshi Bridge over the Sidu River
贵州坝陵河大桥	58	Balinghe Bridge in Guizhou
西堠门大桥	60	Xihoumen Bridge
矮寨大桥	66	Aizhai Bridge
柳州双拥大桥	68	Shuangyong Bridge in Liuzhou
泰州长江大桥	70	Taizhou Bridge over the Yangtze River
南京长江第四大桥	74	The Fourth Nanjing Bridge over the Yangtze River
马鞍山长江公路大桥	78	Ma'anshan Highway Bridge over the Yangtze River

第三篇 斜拉桥 | Chapter 3 Cable-stayed Bridges

引言	82	Introduction
舟山桃夭门大桥	84	Taoyaomen Bridge in Zhoushan
安庆长江大桥	86	Anqing Bridge over the Yangtze River
南京长江第三大桥	88	The Third Nanjing Bridge over the Yangtze River
奉节长江大桥	92	Fengjie Bridge over the Yangtze River
香港昂船洲大桥	94	Stonecutters Bridge in Hong Kong
苏通长江大桥	100	Sutong Bridge over the Yangtze River
康家沱长江大桥	106	Kangjiatuo Bridge over the Yangtze River
上海闵浦大桥	108	Minpu Bridge in Shanghai
观音岩长江大桥	112	Guanyinyan Bridge over the Yangtze River
天兴洲长江大桥	114	Tianxingzhou Bridge over the Yangtze River
上海长江大桥	120	Shanghai Bridge over the Yangtze River
鄂东长江大桥	126	Edong Bridge over the Yangtze River
荆岳长江大桥	128	Jingyue Bridge over the Yangtze River
宜宾长江大桥	130	Yibin Bridge over the Yangtze River
上海闵浦二桥	132	The Second Minpu Bridge in Shanghai
郑州黄河公铁两用桥	134	Zhengzhou Highway and Railway Bridge over the Yellow River
武汉二七长江大桥	136	Erqi Bridge over the Yangtze River in Wuhan
宁波清水浦大桥	140	Qingshuipu Bridge in Ningbo
新疆果子沟大桥	142	Guozigou Bridge in Xinjiang
安庆长江铁路大桥	144	Anqing Railway Bridge over the Yangtze River
嘉绍大桥	146	Jiashao Bridge
郴州赤石大桥	150	Chishi Bridge in Chenzhou
九江长江大桥	152	Jiujiang Bridge over the Yangtze River
粉房湾长江大桥	154	Fenfangwan Bridge over the Yangtze River
宁波甬江铁路大桥	156	Ningbo Railway Bridge over the Yong River
台州椒江二桥	158	The Second Jiao River Bridge in Taizhou

第四篇 拱式桥 | Chapter 4　Arch Bridges

引言	162	Introduction
卢浦大桥	164	Lupu Bridge
巫山长江大桥	170	Wushan Bridge over the Yangtze River
重庆万州长江大桥	172	Wanzhou Bridge over the Yangtze River in Chongqing
广州新光大桥	174	Xinguang Bridge in Guangzhou
茅草街大桥	176	Maocaojie Bridge
东平大桥	178	Dongping Bridge
太平湖大桥	180	Taiping Lake Bridge
菜园坝长江大桥	182	Caiyuanba Bridge over the Yangtze River
支井河大桥	188	Zhijinghe Bridge
小河大桥	190	Xiaohe Bridge
朝天门大桥	192	Chaotianmen Bridge
南京大胜关长江大桥	196	Dashengguan Bridge over the Yangtze River in Nanjing
巫山大宁河大桥	200	Wushan Bridge over the Daning River
宜万铁路宜昌长江大桥	202	Yiwan Railway Bridge over the Yangtze River in Yichang
宁波明州大桥	204	Mingzhou Bridge in Ningbo
广元昭化嘉陵江大桥	206	Zhaohua Bridge over the Jialing River in Guangyuan
肇庆南广铁路西江特大桥	208	Nanguang Railway Bridge over the West River in Zhaoqing
波司登合江长江大桥	210	Bosideng Hejiang Bridge over the Yangtze River

第五篇 梁式桥 | Chapter 5　Girder Bridges

引言	216	Introduction
云南红河大桥	218	Honghe Bridge in Yunnan
福建宁德下白石大桥	220	Xiabaishi Bridge in Ningde
广州琶洲珠江大桥	222	Pazhou Bridge over the Pearl River in Guangzhou
广州海心沙珠江大桥	224	Haixinsha Bridge over the Pearl River in Guangzhou
重庆石板坡长江大桥复线桥	226	Shibanpo Parallel Bridge over the Yangtze River in Chongqing
滨州黄河公铁两用大桥	230	Binzhou Railway-Highway Bridge over the Yellow River
重庆嘉华嘉陵江大桥	232	Jiahua Bridge over the Jialing River in Chongqing
四川汉源大树大渡河大桥	234	Dashu Bridge over the Dadu River in Hanyuan
广珠城际容桂水道铁路桥	236	Guangzhu Intercity Railway Bridge over the Ronggui Water Channel
重庆鱼洞长江大桥	238	Yudong Bridge over the Yangtze River in Chongqing
山东鄄城黄河公路大桥	240	Juancheng Bridge over the Yellow River in Shandong
崇启大桥	242	Chongqi Bridge
雅泸高速腊八斤大桥	244	Labajin Bridge on Ya'an-Lugu Expressway
雅泸高速黑石沟大桥	246	Heishigou Bridge on Ya'an - Lugu Expressway

INDEX　目　录

第六篇　城市桥梁　　　　**Chapter 6　Urban Bridges**

引言	250	Introduction
复兴大桥	252	Fuxing Bridge
长沙洪山大桥	254	Hongshan Bridge in Changsha
天津大沽桥	256	Dagu Bridge in Tianjin
舟山新城大桥	258	Xincheng Bridge in Zhoushan
开封黄河大桥	260	Kaifeng Bridge over the Yellow River
青藏铁路拉萨河大桥	262	Qinghai-Tibet Railway Bridge over the Lhasa River
广州猎德大桥	266	Liede Bridge in Guangzhou
福建三明台江大桥	268	Sanming Bridge over the Taijiang River in Fujian
宁波外滩大桥	270	Waitan Bridge in Ningbo
重庆嘉悦嘉陵江大桥	272	Jiayue Bridge over the Jialing River in Chongqing
太原跻汾桥	274	Jifen Bridge in Taiyuan
塘沽响螺湾海河开启桥	276	Xiangluowan Movable Bridge over the Haihe River in Tanggu
大鹏湾桥	280	Dapeng Bay Bridge
九堡大桥	282	Jiubao Bridge
社子大桥	286	Shezi Bridge
东水门长江大桥	288	Dongshuimen Bridge over the Yangtze River
千厮门嘉陵江大桥	290	Qiansimen Bridge over the Jialing River

出版后记　　292　　**Afterword**

第一篇　跨海大桥
Chapter 1　Sea-crossing Bridges

引言

世界跨海大桥（包括跨越湾口）的先声是1890年苏格兰福思湾的铁路桥，而最著名的应是建于1937年跨越美国旧金山湾口的金门大桥。连接佛罗里达Keys岛（美国东南部珊瑚群岛）和迈阿密的跨海铁路高架桥是一座最早的跨海连岛桥梁，这座高架桥建于1910年，后被改建为跨海公路桥（美国1号公路Keys岛段），1935年被"Labor Day"飓风摧毁。此外，佛罗里达Keys长桥和1935年建成的丹麦公铁两用小海带老桥也是跨海桥梁的先驱，其中，小海带老桥公路桥梁的功能被1970年建成的一座新悬索桥所代替。20世纪世界最长的连岛工程是由荷兰在80年代承建的长25km的巴林和沙特之间的巴林海峡大桥。丹麦和日本两个岛国于60年代开始起步建设连岛工程，日本从关门大桥起步，于20世纪末建成明石大桥和多多罗大桥，实现了三条本四联络线的跨海连岛工程。丹麦则于1997年建成大海带桥，完成了连岛工程，并且还和瑞典合作建成了连接两国之间的厄勒海峡大桥。

中国的跨海大桥建设可以从20世纪90年代的汕头海湾大桥算起。接着，在香港回归前为连接新机场建成了青马大桥、汲水门桥及汀九桥三座连岛大桥。此时，舟山连岛工程也已开始起步，从本岛向大陆逐步连岛推进。其他沿海城市的一些连岛工程也开始前期规划。中国第一座在广阔海域的跨海连岛工程是2005年建成的上海东海大桥，它将上海市与洋山深水港连接起来，全长32.5km。东海大桥为以后的杭州湾大桥、上海崇明桥隧工程和广东珠江口的港珠澳大桥以及规划中的渤海海峡、琼州海峡和台湾海峡等未来跨海工程建设提供了宝贵经验。其中，杭州湾大桥全长36km，已于2008年北京奥运会前建成通车，上海长江桥隧工程也于2010年上海世博会前建成通车。

本画册入选的十座跨海大桥中还有澳门西湾大桥（2004年）、湛江海湾大桥（2006年）、深圳西部通道深圳湾大桥（2007年）、舟山金塘大桥（2009年）、平潭海峡大桥（2010年）、青岛海湾大桥（2010年）、宁波象山港大桥（2012年）和厦漳跨海大桥（2013年）。其中最长的是41.58km的青岛海湾大桥。

跨海工程往往存在桥隧之争。在公路隧道中过长时间行车人会感到不安全；超过10km的隧道需建造通风井，再加上应急逃生方面的不利因素，这都降低了隧道工程的竞争力。跨越海峡的公路宜寻找能避开深水的绕行路线，建造更为经济合理的长桥，如舟山连岛工程中的金塘大桥。但是，跨海桥梁与隧道相比，也存在非全天候运营的劣势，大风、大雾等恶劣天气会导致桥上交通关闭。

随着斜拉桥跨越能力的提高，为避免悬索桥水中锚碇的技术难度和昂贵造价，应采用连续多跨千米级斜拉桥的方案，既能满足分孔通航要求，又能降低造价。相信未来的琼州海峡、渤海海峡和台湾海峡工程都能用多孔千米级斜拉桥组成的公路长桥（或公铁两用桥）加以实现。

Introduction

Built in 1890, the Forth Railway Bridge in Scotland is the first of the world's major bridges to cross seas and bays. The Golden Gate Bridge which crosses San Francisco Bay, built in 1937, remains the most famous. The Overseas Railway Trestles, a series of bridges connecting the Florida Keys (a coral archipelago in southeast United States) to Miami, is most likely the first true bridge to cross the sea by linking islands. This structure was built in the early 1910s. After its destruction by the Labor Day Hurricane in 1935, it was replaced with the Overseas Highway (the Florida Keys section of U.S. Highway 1). The Old Little Belt Bridge, a combined highway and railway truss bridge built in 1935 over the Little Belt Strait in Denmark, is another precursor of modern sea-crossing bridges. Its highway function was eventually assumed by the New Little Belt Bridge, a suspension bridge built in 1970. The longest island-linking work of engineering in the last century was the 25km-long King Fahd Causeway linking Bahrain to Saudi Arabia across the Gulf of Bahrainw, which was constructed by Dutch contractors in the 1980s. Since 1960, the island nations of Denmark and Japan both completed several significant island-linking projects. Japan's program began with Kanmonkyo Bridge and culminated with the construction of three expressways connecting the islands of Shikoku and Honshu at the end of the 20th century, which incorporated the Akashi Kaikyo Bridge and the Tatara Bridge. Denmark completed the Great Belt Bridge in 1997, and constructed, in cooperation with Sweden, the Öresund Strait Bridge connecting the two countries.

The construction of sea-crossing bridges in China began with the Shantou Bay Bridge built in 1990s. Following this, three island-linking bridges, the Tsing Ma Bridge, Kap Shui Mun Bridge, and Ting Kau Bridge, were successively completed in the late 1990s to provide access to the new Hong Kong International Airport on Lantau Island. Construction of the Zhoushan island-linking project began in the late 1990s and progressed gradually from Zhoushan Island towards the mainland at Ningbo. At the same time, preliminary plans for island-linking projects in other coastal cities were made. China's first island-linking project crossing a wide expanse of ocean was the 32.5km-long Shanghai East Sea Bridge, completed in 2005, which connects the Yangshan Deep-Water Port to the mainland at Shanghai. The successful construction of this bridge provided valuable experience to guide the design and construction of subsequent sea-crossing projects, such as the 36km-long Hangzhou Bay Bridge completed before the Beijing Olympic Games in 2008, the Shanghai Chongming Bridge-Tunnel completed before the Shanghai EXPO in 2010, the Hong Kong-Zhuhai-Macao Bridge crossing the Pearl River Estuary in Guangdong, as well as the planning of future crossings of the Bohai Strait, the Qiongzhou Strait, and the Taiwan Strait.

The following ten sea-crossing bridges have been selected for this book: the Shanghai East Sea Bridge (2005), Hangzhou Bay Bridge (2008), West Bay Bridge in Macao (2004), Zhanjiang Bay Bridge (2006), Shenzhen Bay Bridge (2007), Jintang Bridge (2009), Pingtan Straits Bridge (2010), Qingdao Bay Bridge (2010), Xiangshan Harbor Bridge in Ningbo (2012), and the Xiazhang Sea-crossing Bridge (2013). The Qingdao Bay Bridge, with a total length of 41.58km, is the longest bridge in this group.

There has been competition between bridges and tunnels on sea-crossing projects. Motorists and passengers during long drives through highway tunnels feel unsafety. The need for vent wells in tunnels longer than 10km and difficulties associated with providing emergency egress also weaken the competitive advantage of tunnels. For highways crossing straits, it is feasible to choose a circuitous route and construct a more economic bridge of reasonable length to avoid deep water areas, which was done for the Jintang Bridge in the Zhoushan island-linking project. Nevertheless, tunnels tend to have a better capacity for all-weather operation than bridges, which may need to be closed to traffic during strong winds and thick fog.

Following recent increases in the feasible span length of cable-stayed bridges, it has been suggested to use continuous multi kilometer-span cable-stayed bridges in sea-crossing projects to avoid the technical difficulties and high cost associated with the construction of underwater anchorages for suspension bridges. Continuous multi-span cable-stayed bridges are not only able to satisfy requirements for multiple navigation spans with relative ease, but are also relatively economical. It is therefore expected that future sea-crossing projects over the Qiongzhou Straits, the Bohai Strait, and the Taiwan Strait will incorporate long highway bridges or amphibious bridges for highway and railway incorporating multi kilometer-span cable-stayed bridges.

澳门西湾大桥
West Bay Bridge in Macao

澳门西湾大桥是为了缓解澳门南北向交通压力并建立海上全天候交通通道所建设的澳门第三座跨海大桥。大桥全长1825m，由斜拉桥主桥和两端引桥组成。桥面宽度分左右双幅对称布置，上层每幅桥面宽14.55m，在箱梁顶面布置三车道，下层每幅宽8m，在箱梁内设机动车和轻轨各一个车道。

主桥采用分离双幅的双塔四索面预应力混凝土斜拉桥，跨径布置为110m+180m+110m=400m，混凝土箱梁单箱单室，其顶板和底板上双层行车，斜拉索采用竖琴式稀索布置，主塔为三柱式钢筋混凝土结构，采用钻孔桩基础。引桥为四联60m跨径等高度预应力混凝土连续箱梁。

澳门西湾大桥为了满足多车道和台风期不中断行车的使用要求，将斜拉桥主梁箱梁布置成顶面和底面双层桥面，采用了特殊的箱梁横隔板技术，研制了合理的主梁预制节段剪力键及梁段分离技术。

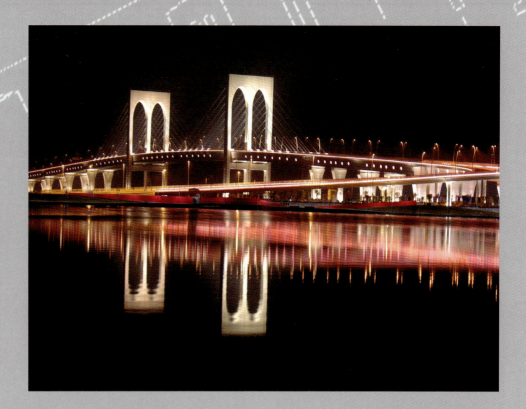

West Bay Bridge in Macao with an overall length of 1825m is comprised of a cable-stayed main bridge and two side approach bridges. The bridge has two separate box decks arranged symmetrically. Each deck has a single one-room box cross section, and its top plate is 14.55m wide and contains three traffic lanes while its bottom plate is 8m wide and contains one traffic lane and one track of Light Rail Transit in the box.

The main bridge is a PC cable-stayed bridge with a pair of separated box decks, double three-column towers, four harp-like cable planes and three spans of 110m+180m+110m=400m. The towers are supported by bored piles foundations. The approach bridges are composed of four multiple 60m-span PC continuous box beam bridges with constant girder depth.

 A special diaphragm technique was adopted to realize the traffic in the deck box. Moreover, a kind of reasonable shear key and a separating technique of girder segments were developed for the precast construction.

桥　名：澳门西湾大桥
桥　型：预应力混凝土箱梁斜拉桥
　　　　四联等高度预应力混凝土连续梁桥
长　度：1825m
桥　址：澳门
完成日期：2004年
设计单位：中铁大桥勘测设计院有限公司
施工单位：中铁（澳门）有限公司
　　　　中铁大桥局集团有限公司

Name: West Bay Bridge in Macao
Type: Cable-stayed bridges with PC box deck
　　　　Four PC continuous beam bridges with even girder depth
Length: 1825m
Location: Macao
Completion: 2004
Designer(s): China Railway Major Bridge Reconnaissance & Design Institute Co., Ltd.
Contractor(s): China Railway (Macao) Co., Ltd.
　　　　China Railway Major Bridge Engineering Group Co., Ltd.

东海大桥
East Sea Bridge

东海大桥起于上海南汇芦潮港，跨越杭州湾东北部海域，在洋山岛登陆，是上海国际航运中心洋山深水港区唯一陆路集疏运通道。大桥全长32.5km，包括陆上段3.7km、海上段25.3km、港桥连接段3.5km。其中，海上段平面线形设计主要考虑桥轴线与海流的夹角、航道位置和走向、路线最短和投资最小等因素。大桥标准桥宽31.5m，分上下行双幅桥面，设双向六车道加紧急停车带。

主通航孔桥采用双塔单索面结合梁斜拉桥，跨径布置为73m+132m+420m+132m+73m=830m，混凝土桥面板与单箱三室钢梁结合，斜拉索采用扇形密索布置，主塔为150m高的钻石形钢筋混凝土结构，主塔和边墩分别采用钻孔桩和钢管桩基础。颗珠山桥采用双塔双索面结合梁斜拉桥，跨径布置为50m+139m+332m+139m+50m=710m，混凝土桥梁面板与两个分离钢箱结合，主塔为96m高的门式钢筋混凝土结构。三个辅通航孔桥统一采用四跨一联预应力混凝土连续箱梁，通航孔分别为120m、140m和160m，下部结构统一采用预制式钢筋混凝土空心墩。全桥非通航孔统一采用多跨一联等高度预应力混凝土连续箱梁，跨径有30m、50m、60m和70m等。

东海大桥是我国第一座真正意义上的跨外海桥梁。通过全方位的结构耐久性设计研究，提出并实施了保证100年设计基准期的防腐蚀综合技术。大桥施工采用大规模桥墩和主梁构件预制吊装，最大整孔吊装跨径70m，促进了我国大型预制构件施工技术的发展，从而极大提高了我国跨海大桥的建设技术。

East Sea Bridge starts at Luchao Harbor of Nanhui District of Shanghai, and lands at the Yangshan Island after crossing the northeastern sea area of Hangzhou Bay. It is the sole landway channels of gathering and distributing transportation of the Yangsan Deep-Water Port of Shanghai International Shipping Center. The bridge is 32.5km in all, including a 3.7km-long land part, a 25.3km-long sea-crossing part and a 3.5km-long link park to the port zone. The major factors considered in the alignment design of the sea-crossing part includes the inclination angle between the bride axis and the ocean current, the location and direction of sea-route, shortest bridge route and lowest investment, etc. The bridge has six traffic lanes plus two emergency lanes in dual directions. Its typical width is 31.5m, including the up and down dual decks.

The bridge over the main navigable passage is a double-tower composite-girder cable-stayed bridge with five spans of 73m+132m+420m+132m+73m=830m, and single fan-shaped cable-plane. Its main girder is composed of RC deck plate and a single-box three- room steel girder. The diamond- shaped RC tower is 150m in height. The bridge towers and piers are supported by the bored pile foundations and the steel-pipe foundations, respectively.

The Kezhushan Bridge is also a double-tower composite-girder cable-stayed bridge, but with five spans of 50m+139m+332m+139m+ 50m=710m, and double parallel fan-shaped cable-planes. Its main girder is composed of RC deck plate and two separate steel box girders. Its two 96m-high towers are of portal-shaped RC structure.

The structures of four-span PC continuous box beam are used for all the bridges over three auxiliary navigable passages with the main spans of 120m, 140m and 160m, respectively. Their substructures are of precast RC hollow piers. The structures of multi-span PC continuous box beam with constant girder depths are employed for all the non-navigable spans with the various span lengths of 30m, 50m, 60m and 70m etc.

East Sea Bridge is the first real bridge crossing open sea in China. Through comprehensive research and design on the structural durability, an integrated anticorrosive technique was presented and implemented to ensure the 100-year design service life. The extensive hoisting of precast pier and girder components was carried out in the bridge construction, with the largest span length of the entire-span hoisting reaching 70m. The construction techniques of large precast components and sea-crossing bridges of our country were thus promoted greatly.

桥　　名：东海大桥
桥　　型：结合梁斜拉桥两座
　　　　　预应力混凝土连续梁桥多联
长　　度：32.5km
桥　　址：上海
完成日期：2005 年
设计单位：上海市政工程设计研究总院
　　　　　中铁大桥勘测设计院有限公司
　　　　　中交第三航务勘察设计院有限公司
施工单位：中铁大桥局集团有限公司
　　　　　上海建工（集团）公司
　　　　　中国交通建设集团有限公司
　　　　　上海城建（集团）公司

Name: East Sea Bridge
Type: Two cable-stayed bridges with composite decks
　　　　Some PC continuous box beam bridges
Length: 32.5km
Location: Shanghai
Completion: 2005
Designer(s): Shanghai Municipal Engineering Design Institute
　　　　　China Railway Major Bridge Reconnaissance & Design Institute Co., Ltd.
　　　　　CCCC Third Harbor Consultants Co., Ltd.
Contractor(s): China Railway Major Bridge Engineering Group Co., Ltd.
　　　　　Shanghai Construction Group Co., Ltd.
　　　　　China Communications Construction Company Limited
　　　　　Shanghai Urban Construction (Group) Corporation

湛江海湾大桥
Zhanjiang Bay Bridge

湛江海湾大桥位于粤西雷州半岛东北侧。大桥全长 3.981km，由主桥斜拉桥和两端引桥组成。桥面宽度 28.5m，设双向四车道，远期考虑六车道规划。

主桥采用双塔双索面混合梁斜拉桥，跨径布置为 60m+120m+480m+120m+60m=840m，主梁为流线型闭口混合箱梁，中间 761.4m 长为钢箱梁，两侧各 61.8m 长为预应力混凝土箱梁，斜拉索采用扇形密索布置，主塔为钻石形钢筋混凝土结构，采用钻孔桩基础。引桥为预应力混凝土简支梁和连续梁。

湛江海湾大桥采用混合梁体系，最大限度地改善了结构受力性能，塔墩采用浮式柔性消能防船撞设施，不仅可以削弱船舶撞击的能量，保护桥墩，而且对船舶和防撞设施本身都能起到保护作用。

Located in the northeastern part of Leizhou Peninsula of West Guandong, the Zhanjiang Bay Bridge is comprised of a cable-stayed main bridge and two side approach bridges, with a total length of 3.981km. The 28.5m-wide deck contains four traffic lanes or six traffic lanes in future, which are divided into dual directions.

The main bridge is a double-tower compounded-deck cable-stayed bridge with five spans of 60m+120m+480m+120m+60m=840m and double inclined cable planes. The steel box girder is used for the middle 761.4m-long deck while the PC box girder is used for each 61.8m-long side deck. The box girder has a curved streamline bottom plate. The dense and fan-shaped arrangement is adopted for the stay cables. The two diamond-shaped RC towers are supported by bored pile foundations. The approach bridges are comprised of some PC simply-supported beams and continuous beams.

The mechanics behavior of the bridge is improved by the greatest extent via the adoption of the compounded deck system. Float and flexible steel anticollision devices are adopted to protect the towers and piers as well as the colliding ships and the anticollision devices themselves from the damage or destruction due to the ship collisions by energy dissipation.

桥　　名：湛江海湾大桥
桥　　型：混合梁斜拉桥主桥
　　　　　预应力混凝土简支梁和连续桥引桥
长　　度：3.981km
桥　　址：广东省湛江市
完成日期：2006 年
设计单位：中铁大桥勘测设计院有限公司
施工单位：广东省长大公路工程有限公司
　　　　　中铁山桥集团有限公司

Name: Zhanjiang Bay Bridge
Type: Cable-stayed bridges with compounded box deck
　　　　Some PC simply-supported and continuous beam bridges
Length: 3.981km
Location: Zhanjiang, Guangdong Province
Completion: 2006
Designer(s): China Railway Major Bridge Reconnaissance & Design Institute Co., Ltd.
Contractor(s): Guangdong Provincial ChangDa Highway Engineering Co., Ltd.
　　　　　　　　China Railway Shanhaiguan Bridge Group Co., Ltd.

深圳湾大桥
Shenzhen Bay Bridge

深圳西部通道深圳湾大桥始于深圳湾口岸，横跨深圳湾（香港称后海湾），在香港新界鳌磡石着陆后连接后海湾干线。大桥全长5.5km，其中香港段3.5km、深圳段2km。桥面净宽33.1m，设双向共六车道。

香港段主桥为独塔单索面钢箱梁斜拉桥，跨径布置为76.4m+99m+210m=385.4m，主塔是高159m的钢筋混凝土结构，采用钻孔桩基础；引桥采用等高度预应力混凝土连续刚构，平均跨径75m。深圳段主桥为倾斜式独塔单索面钢箱梁斜拉桥，跨径布置为180m+90m+75m=345m，倾斜主塔高140m、中心斜率1：5.7；引桥与香港段基本相同。

深圳湾大桥两个主桥都采用了单索面、钢箱梁，箱宽达到38.6m。设计使用寿命为120年，采取了一系列措施提高和保证桥梁结构的耐久性。

Shenzhen Bay Bridge is also called Hong Kong-Shenzhen Western Corridor. It crosses the Shenzhen Bay (also called Deep Bay in Hong Kong) between Shenzhen Bay Port of Shenzhen and Ngau Hom Shek of New Territory of Hong Kong with a S-shaped alignment. The total length of the bridge is 5.5km, where the Hong Kong part is 3.5km long and the Shenzhen part is 2km long. The net width of the bridge deck is 33.1m, containing six traffic lanes in dual directions.

The main bridge of the Hong Kong part is a steel box cable-stayed bridge with a single 159m-high RC tower supported by bored piles, a single cable plane and three spans of 76.4m+99m+210m=385.4m. The main bridge of the Shenzhen part is also a steel box cable-stayed bridge, but with a inclined 140m-high RC tower, a single cable plane and three spans of 180m+90m+75m=345m. The incline ratio of the tower central axis is 1：5.7.

The widths of the box girders of the both main bridges are 38.6m. The approach bridge of the Hong Kong part is of PC continuous bridge with integral piers, with an average span of 75m and a constant girder depth. The approach bridge of the Shenzhen part is similar to that of the Hong Kong one. The design service life of the bridge is 120 years, therefore, a series of measures were adopted to enhance and ensure the bridge durability.

桥　　名：深圳湾大桥
桥　　型：两座独塔单索面钢箱梁斜拉桥
　　　　　等高度预应力混凝土连续刚构多联
长　　度：5.5km
桥　　址：深圳和香港
完成日期：2007 年
设计单位：奥雅纳工程顾问公司（香港段）
　　　　　中交公路规划设计院有限公司（深圳段）
施工单位：金门—斯坎雅—中铁大桥局（香港段）
　　　　　广东省长大公路工程有限公司（深圳段）
　　　　　中铁四局集团有限公司等（深圳段）

Name: Shenzhen Bay Bridge
Type: Two cable-stayed bridges with steel box girder
　　　　Some PC continuous bridges with integral piers, with constant girder depth
Length: 5.5km
Location: Shenzhen and Hong Kong
Completion: 2007
Designer(s): ARUP Engineering Consultant Co. (Hong Kong part)
　　　　　　　CCCC Highway Consultants Co.,Ltd. (Shenzhen part)
Contractor(s): Gammon-Skanska-MBEC Joint Venture (Hong Kong part)
　　　　　　　　Guangdong Provincial ChangDa Highway Engineering Co., Ltd. (Shenzhen part)
　　　　　　　　China Tiesiju Civil Engineering Group Co., Ltd. (Shenzhen part)

杭州湾跨海大桥
Hangzhou Bay Bridge

杭州湾跨海大桥北起浙江嘉兴海盐县，横跨杭州湾，南止宁波慈溪市。大桥全长36km，包括北引桥、北航道桥、北高墩区引桥、中引桥、南航道桥、南高墩区引桥、南深水区引桥、南滩涂区引桥、南陆地区引桥等九大部分。大桥桥面宽度33m，设双向六车道加紧急停车带。

北航道桥采用双塔双索面钢箱梁斜拉桥，跨径布置为70m+160m+448m+160m+70m=908m，斜拉索采用扇形密索布置，主塔为钻石形钢筋混凝土结构、钻孔桩基础。南航道桥采用独塔双索面钢箱梁斜拉桥，跨径布置为80m+160m+318m=558m，主塔为A字形钢筋混凝土结构。与南、北航道桥相邻的高墩区引桥、中引桥和南深水区引桥均采用70m跨径等高度预应力混凝土连续箱梁，南滩涂区引桥为50m跨径等高度预应力混凝土连续箱梁，北引桥和南陆地区引桥采用30～80m跨径等高度预应力混凝土连续箱梁，引桥基础分别采用钢管桩和钻孔桩。

杭州湾跨海大桥工程规模大、自然环境恶劣、施工制约因素多，50m跨径箱梁采用了"梁上运架设"技术，研发了抵抗氯离子侵蚀为主的海工耐久混凝土以及其他混凝土和钢管桩防腐措施。

Located in Zhejiang Province, the Hangzhou Bay Bridge starts in Haiyan County of Jiaxing in the north, and ends in Cixi County of Ningbo in the south after crossing the Hangzhou bay. The total length of the bridge is 36km including the following nine parts: the northern approach bridge, the northern sea-route bridge, the northern high-pier zone approach bridge, the middle approach, the southern sea-route bridge, the southern high-pier zone approach bridge, the southern deep-water zone approach bridge, the southern intertidal zone approach bridge and the southern land approach bridge. The deck width of the bridge is 33m, containing six traffic lanes plus two emergency lanes in dual directions.

The northern sea-route bridge is a double-tower steel box girder cable-stayed bridge with five spans of 70m+160m+448m+160m+70m=908m, and two inclined cable-planes. The cables are arranged densely with fan-shape. Its diamond-shaped RC towers are supported by bored piles. The southern sea-route bridge is a single-tower steel box girder cable-stayed bridge with three spans of 80m+160m+318m=558m, and two inclined cable-planes. Its tower is of A-shaped RC structure. The PC continuous box beams with constant girder depth are adopted for the approach bridges. The span length is 70m for the high-pier zone and middle approach bridges adjacent to the northern and southern sea-route bridges, and the southern deep-water zone approach bridge. The span length is 50m for the southern intertidal zone approach bridge. The span lengths of the northern and southern land approach bridges are between 30m and 80m. The steel-pipe pile and bored pile foundations are adopted for the piers of the approach bridges.

Hangzhou Bay Bridge is not only a colossal scale engineering project, but also located in an atrocious natural environment. Its construction was affected by many factors. In this connection, the technique of transporting and erecting of precast girder on the erected girders was employed during the construction of the 50m-span box girders. A kind of marine durable concrete was excogitated to mainly resist the chloride ion corrosion. In addition, other measures were also developed for the anticorrosion of concrete and steel-pipe piles.

桥　　名	杭州湾跨海大桥
桥　　型	钢箱梁斜拉桥两座
	等高度预应力混凝土连续梁桥多联
长　　度	36km
桥　　址	浙江省海盐县至慈溪市
完成日期	2008 年
设计单位	中交公路规划设计院有限公司
	中铁大桥勘测设计院有限公司
	中交第三航务勘察设计院有限公司
施工单位	中交第二航务工程局有限公司
	中铁大桥局集团有限公司
	路桥建设股份有限公司
	广东长大公路工程有限公司等

Name: Hangzhou Bay Bridge
Type: Two cable-stayed bridges with steel box girder
　　　　Some PC continuous beam bridges with constant girder depth
Length: 36km
Location: Haiyan County to Cixi, Zhejiang Province
Completion: 2008
Designer(s): CCCC Highway Consultants Co.,Ltd.
　　　　China Railway Major Bridge Reconnaissance & Design Institute Co., Ltd.
　　　　CCCC Third Harbor Consultants Co., Ltd.
Contractor(s): CCCC Second Harbor Engineering Company Ltd.
　　　　China Railway Major Bridge Engineering Group Co., Ltd.
　　　　Road & Bridge International Co., Ltd.
　　　　Guangdong Provincial ChangDa Highway Engineering Co., Ltd.

金塘大桥
Jintang Bridge

舟山大陆连岛工程金塘大桥始于浙江宁波镇海区，跨越灰鳖洋，在金塘岛沥港镇登陆。大桥全长18.27km，包括金塘侧引桥、东通航孔桥、东段非通航孔桥、主通航孔桥、中段非通航孔桥、西通航孔桥、西段非通航孔桥、浅水区引桥、镇海侧引桥等九大部分。桥面宽度26.5m，设双向四车道加紧急停车带。

主通航孔桥采用双塔双索面钢箱梁斜拉桥，跨径布置为77m+218m+620m+218m+77m=1210m，主梁采用全宽30.1m的扁平钢箱梁，斜拉索采用扇形密索布置，主塔为钻石形钢筋混凝土结构、钻孔桩基础。东、西两座通航孔桥分别为122m+216m+122m=460m 和 87m+156m+87m=330m 变高度预应力混凝土连续刚构，其他非通航孔桥为30~60m等高度预应力混凝土连续梁桥，另有70m+10×118m+70m=1320m 和 45m+72m+45m=162m 两联变高度预应力混凝土连续梁桥，基础分别采用钢管桩和钻孔桩。

金塘大桥主通航孔斜拉桥索塔端锚固采用新型钢牛腿钢锚梁组合结构，可以有效锚固4根空间拉索。确定10级大风为桥面通车最高设计风速，依据风洞试验、数值分析和现场实测结果，在70%长度的桥面两侧设置了三种不同形式的风障，以保证桥面行车的安全性和适用性。

Jintang Bridge of the island-linking engineering between Zhoushan Island and the mainland starts at Zhenhai District of Ningbo of Zhejiang Province. It crosses the Huibie Ocean and lands at the Ligang Town on the Jintang Island. The bridge is 18.27km long and comprised of the following nine parts: the approach bridge at Jintang side, the east navigable channel bridge, the east non-navigable channel bridge, the main navigable channel bridge, the middle non-navigable channel bridge, the west navigable channel bridge, the west non-navigable channel bridge, the approach bridge over shallow-water zone and the approach bridge at Zhenhai side. The bridge deck is 26.5m wide containing four traffic lanes plus two emergency lanes in dual directions.

The main navigable channel bridge is a steel box girder cable-stayed bridge with two towers, two cable planes and five spans of 77m+218m+620m+218m+77m=1210m. The main girder is of flat steel box cross section and is 30.1m wide. The cables are densely arranged in fan shape. The diamond-shaped towers are supported by bored pile foundations. The east and west navigable channel bridges are of PC continuous structures with integral piers with variant girder depth, and with spans of 122m+216m+122m=460m and 87m+156m+87m=330m, respectively. The other non-navigable channel bridges are of PC continuous beam structures with constant girder depths and spans from 30m to 60m. In addition, there are two PC continuous beam bridges with variant girder depth and spans of 70m+10×118m+70m=1320m and 45m+72m+45m=162m, respectively. The steel-pipe and bored piles are used for the foundations of these auxiliary navigable channel and approach bridges, respectively.

The cables of the main navigable channel bridge of Jintang Bridge are anchored on the tower through a new type of combined structure of steel bracket and steel anchor box. Each of the new type anchor devices can efficiently anchor four spatial cables. The wind speed of 10th grade is determined as the maximal design wind speed for the safe driving of vehicles on the bridge. According to the results of wind tunnel test, numerical analysis and field measurement, three different types of wind barriers were excogitated and mounted on the two sides of the bridge deck within the range of 70% total length of the bridge deck, to ensure the safety and serviceability of vehicle driving on the bridge deck.

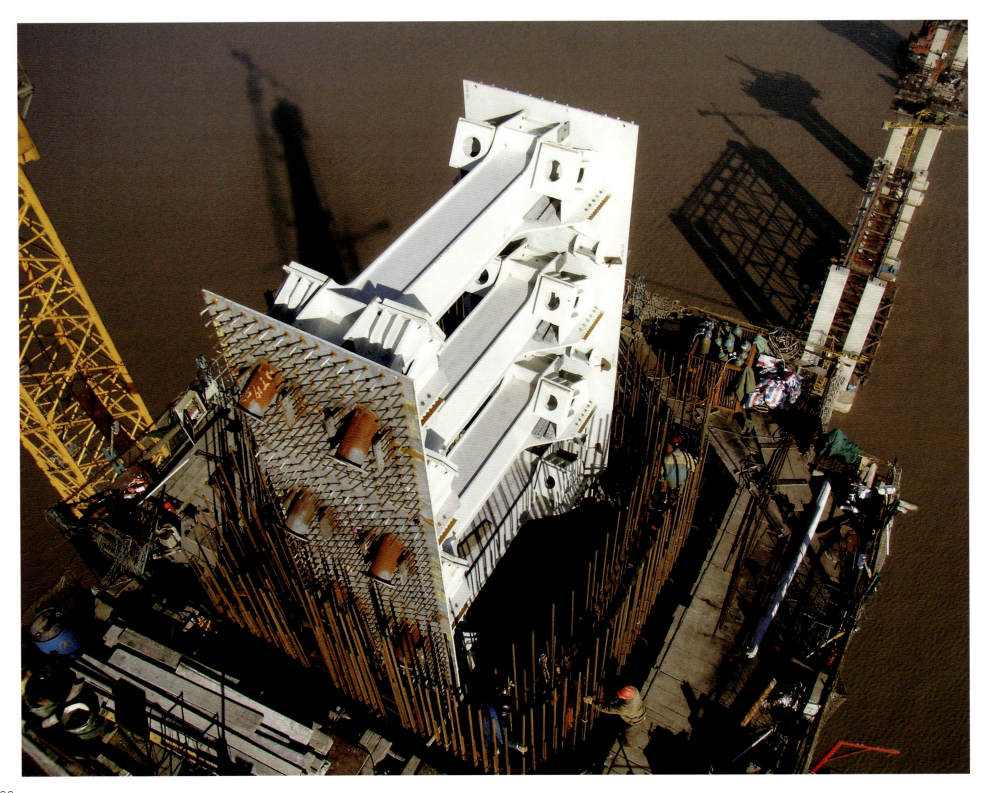

桥　　名：	金塘大桥
桥　　型：	钢箱梁斜拉桥
	等高度和变高度预应力混凝土刚构和连续梁多联
长　　度：	18.27km
桥　　址：	浙江省镇海区至沥港镇
完成日期：	2009年
设计单位：	中交公路规划设计院有限公司
	浙江省交通规划设计研究院
	中铁大桥勘测设计院有限公司
施工单位：	中交第二航务工程局有限公司
	中铁四局集团第二工程有限公司
	中铁宝桥集团有限公司

Name: Jintang Bridge

Type: Cable-stayed bridges with steel box deck
　　　Some PC continuous bridges with integral piers, with constant and variant girder depth
　　　Two PC continuous bridges with integral piers, with variant girder depth

Length: 18.27km

Location: Zhenhai District to Ligang Town, Zhejiang Province

Completion: 2009

Designer(s): CCCC Highway Consultants Co.,Ltd.
　　　Zhejiang Provincial Institute of Communications Planning, Design and Research
　　　China Railway Major Bridge Reconnaissance and Design Institute Co., Ltd.

Contractor(s): CCCC Second Harbor Engineering Company Ltd.
　　　The Second Construction Co.,Ltd of CTCE Group
　　　China Railway Baoji Bridge Group Co., Ltd.

平潭海峡大桥
Pingtan Straits Bridge

平潭海峡大桥起于福清市小山东，跨越海坛海峡，经北青屿，终于平潭县娘宫，全长3510m（含两侧桥台），设双向共四车道。

通航孔主桥为四跨变高度预应力连续刚构桥，桥跨布置为100m+180m×2+100m=560m。主梁采用单箱单室直腹板箱梁，宽17m，高3.5～11m，采用悬浇法施工。三个主墩采用双肢薄壁实心墩，单肢截面尺寸8.5m×2.0m。两个边墩采用矩形空心墩，截面尺寸8.5m×3.6m，壁厚80cm。五个桥墩均采用变直径钻孔灌注桩基础，并设消能防撞套箱。

引桥为采用移动模架现浇的多联多跨等截面预应力混凝土连续箱梁，东西引桥跨布置分别为：5×50m+2×(4×50)m+(3×50+40)m 和 8×(4×50)m+2×(5×50)m。单箱单室斜腹板箱梁宽17m，高3.1m。现浇墩身，钻孔灌注桩基础。海洋防腐抗震型球形支座。所有桥墩采用25%粉煤灰混凝土，以降低水化热、控制墩身微裂缝。

Pingtan Straits Bridge crosses the Haitan Straits between Xiaoshandong of Fuqing City and Nianggong of Pingtan County via the North Qingyu islet. It has a total length of 3510m including the two end abutments, and four traffic lanes in all in dual direction.

The main bridge over the navigable passage is a four-span continuous bridge with integral piers, with twin thin-leg piers and a variant depth PC box-girder. Its span arrangement is 100m+180m×2+100m=560m. The bridge deck is of a single-box girder with single room and vertical webs. The deck, constructed by using the cast-in-cantilever method, is 17m wide and 3.5m to 11m in depth. The structure of twin thin rectangular legs is used for the three main piers with a cross section of a single leg being 8.5m×2.0m, whilst the two side piers are of rectangular hollow structure with a cross section of 8.5m×3.6m and a wall thick of 80cm. Each of the five piers is supported by a bored pile foundation with a variant diameter and protected with a dissipating anti-collision cofferdam.

The approach bridges are comprised of some multi-span PC continuous beams with a constant depth, and cast in-situ on movable formworks. The span arrangements of the eastern and western approach bridges are 5×50m+2×(4×50) m+(3×50+40)m and 8×(4×50)m+ 2×(5×50)m, respectively. The girders are of a single-box cross section with single room and inclined webs, and are 17m wide and 3.1m in depth. Their piers are cast in situ and each of them is supported by a bored pile foundation. The marine-corrosion-preventing and aseismatic spherical bearings are used in the continuous beams, and a special kind of concrete containing 25% pulverized coal ash is applied to the all piers of the bridge to drop the hydration heat and control the micro-crack of the piers.

桥　名：	平潭海峡大桥
桥　型：	四跨双支薄壁墩预应力箱梁连续刚构桥 多联多跨预应力混凝土连续梁桥
长　度：	3.51km
桥　址：	福建省福清市至平潭县
完成日期：	2010年
设计单位：	福建省交通规划设计院 中交公路规划设计院有限公司
施工单位：	中交第二航务工程局有限公司

Name: Pingtan Straits Bridge
Type: Four-span continuous bridge with integral piers, with twin thin-leg piers
　　　　Some multi-span PC continuous beam bridges with constant girder depth
Length: 3.51km
Location: Fuqing City to Pingtan County, Fujian Province
Completion: 2010
Designer(s): Fujian Communications Planning and Design Institute
　　　　　　 CCCC Highway Consultants Co., Ltd.
Contractor(s): CCCC Second Harbor Engineering Company Ltd.

青岛海湾大桥
Qingdao Bay Bridge

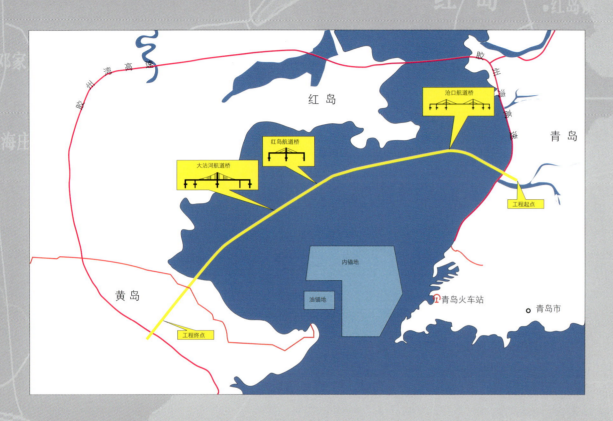

青岛海湾大桥跨越胶州湾北部，连接青岛、黄岛和红岛，含二期接线工程全长41.58km，一期跨海大桥全长25.881km，包括沧口、红岛、大沽河三个航道桥以及红岛海上和李村河海陆互通立交、非通航孔桥和陆域引桥，设双向六车道加两条紧急停车带。

大沽河航道桥为独塔自锚式悬索桥，跨径布置为80m+260m+190m+80m=610m；采用中央开槽钢箱梁主梁，槽宽11.4m，全宽47m，高3.6m，两根主缆呈空间布置；塔高149m，采用哑铃形变截面单柱结构和钻孔灌注桩基础。

沧口航道桥为半飘浮分离平行双幅双塔钢箱梁斜拉桥，跨径布置为80m+90m+260m+90m+80m=600m；两幅桥中心距30.5m，索塔完全分离，高107.5m，采用H形钢筋混凝土结构和整体钻孔灌注桩基础，外设消能防撞设施；单幅梁内外两侧均设风嘴，底板水平，宽24m，中心高3.5m；稀疏竖琴式平行双索面斜拉索，在塔和梁上分别采用鞍式和锚箱锚固。

红岛航道桥为半飘浮分离平行双幅独塔钢箱梁斜拉桥，跨径布置为2×120m=240m，两幅桥中心距20.5m；索塔和钢箱梁结构形式与沧口航道桥类似，塔高72.5m，梁全宽24m，中心高3.3m。水中区引桥总长15.9km，采用整孔预制吊装、先简支后连续的60m跨径预应力混凝土连续梁，西岸滩涂区引桥总长5km，采用移动模架浇筑的4至5孔一联50m跨径连续梁；红岛互通立交主线长1.98km，为50m跨径预应力混凝土连续箱梁；李村河互通立交采用变梁高预应力混凝土连续箱梁。

Qingdao Bay Bridge crosses the northern part of Jiaozhou Bay in Shandong Province, and connects Qingdao, Huangdao and Hongdao. Its total length including the 2nd phase linking project is 41.58km, The 1st phase sea-crossing bridge is 25.881km in length, including the Cangkou navigable channel bridge, the Hongdao navigable channel bridge, the Daguhe navigable channel bridge, the Hongdao maritime interchange bridge, the Licunhe interchange bridge over the boundary zone from sea to land, the non-navigable channel bridge and land approach bridge. The bridge contains six traffic lanes plus two emergent lanes in dual directions.

The Daguhe navigable channel bridge is a single-tower self-anchored suspension bridge with four spans of 80m+260m+190m+80m= 610m. The steel box girder with a 11.4m-wide central slot is adopted for the bridge deck. The overall deck width is 47m and the deck depth is 3.6m. Its two cables are spatially arranged. It 149m-high tower is of single-column structure with a dumbbell-shaped cross section and supported by a bored pile foundation.

The Cangkou navigable channel bridge is comprised of separated twin parallel semi-floating cable-stayed bridges. Each of them is with two 107.5m-high H-shaped RC towers and a steel box deck. The span arrangement is 80m+90m+260m+90m+80m=600m. The central distance between the two decks is 30.5m. The superstructures of towers of the two parallel bridges are completely separated, but share a whole bored pile foundation with energy- dissipating anticollision devices. Wind fairings are mounted at both the inner and outer sides of the single deck, which has a horizontal bottom plate. The width and the height of the single deck is 24m and 3.5m, respectively. The parallel double cable planes are adopted for the bridge cables, which are arranged in the sparse harp form. The cables are anchored on the towers with anchor saddles and on the deck with anchor boxes.

The Hongdao navigable channel bridge is also comprised of separated twin parallel semi-floating cable-stayed bridges with steel box decks. However, each of them has merely single 72.5m-high H-shaped bridge tower. The span arrangement is 2×120m=240m and the central distance between the two decks is 20.5m. The structural configurations of its towers and box decks are similar to those of the Cangkou navigable-span bridge. The width and the height of the single deck is 24m and 3.3m, respectively.

The maritime approach bridge has a total length of 15.9km, and is comprised of a series of 60m-span PC continuous box beams. It was constructed through a whole span hoisting method in conjunction with a system transformation from the simply-supported beam to continuous beam.

The west intertidal zone approach bridge is 5km long in all, and comprised of a series of 50m-span continuous beams with 4~5 spans for each, and was cast on movable formworks. The Hongdao maritime interchange bridge is comprised of a series of 50m-span PC continuous box beams and has a 1.98km-long principal line. The PC continuous box beams with variant depth are employed in the Licunhe interchange.

Name: Qingdao Bay Bridge
Type: Self-anchored suspension bridge with single tower and slotted steel box girder
  Separated twin double-tower cable-stayed bridges with steel box girder
  Separated twin single-tower cable-stayed bridges with steel box girder
  A series of PC continuous box beam bridges
Length: 25.881km
Location: Qingdao, Huangdao and Hongdao, Shandong Province
Completion: 2010
Designer(s): CCCC Highway Consultants Co.,Ltd.
  Shandong Provincial Communications Planning and Design Institute
  Jiangsu Provincial Communications Planning and Design Institute Co., Ltd.
Contractor(s): Shandong Luqiao Group Co., Ltd.
  Road & Bridge International Co., Ltd.
  CCCC Third Highway Engineering Co., Ltd.

宁波象山港公路大桥
Xiangshan Harbor Bridge in Ningbo

宁波象山港公路大桥是浙江省沿海高速公路（甬台温复线）关键工程之一，采用双向共四车道，全长6.723km，在鄞州咸祥镇山岩岭和象山县贤庠镇小蔚庄之间跨越象山港。主桥为双塔双索面钢箱梁斜拉桥，跨径布置为82m+262m+688m+262m+82m=1376m。钻石形索塔总高度226.500m，桥面以上173.134m，下、中塔柱为普通钢筋混凝土结构，上塔柱、上中塔柱结合段、横梁为预应力混凝土结构，基础采用钻孔灌注桩和整体式承台，并设置防撞套箱及柔性防撞设施。扁平流线型封闭钢箱主梁采用较尖的40°风嘴，以提高大桥的颤振临界风速、减轻涡激共振，箱梁中心高3.5m，含风嘴全宽34.0m。平行钢丝斜拉索在塔、梁上均采用钢锚箱锚固，表面架螺旋线，近主梁侧设外置阻尼器。

南、北引桥全长5.356km，采用分离双幅多联多跨等截面预应力混凝土连续箱梁，单幅桥采用斜腹板单箱单室截面，宽12.25m，两幅间缝隙用隔离带混凝土板覆盖。跨径有60m和46m两种，其中60m跨径六孔一联，中心梁高3.5m，采用整孔预制、吊装施工，为方便内模脱卸，墩顶处未设横隔板，仅作局部加厚处理。46m跨径箱梁中心高2.7m，采用移动模架施工，纵向按全预应力混凝土结构设计，墩顶处设横隔板，其中北岸和南岸引桥分别位于半径2500m及2300m的圆曲线上。

为改善行车风环境，跨海大桥上全线设置曲线形格栅风障，其中桥塔附近局部风障为变高度和变透风率风障。

Xiangshan Harbor Bridge in Ningbo is one of the key projects of the Zhejiang costal motorway (2nd Yong-Tai-Wen motorway). It is 6.723km long in all and contains four traffic lanes in dual directions. It crosses the Xiangshan Harbor between Xianxiang Town of Yinzhou District and Xianyang Town of Xiangshan County. The main bridge is a double-tower steel box deck cable-stayed bridge with two inclined cable planes. Its span arrangement is 82m+262m+688m+262m+82m=1376m. The diamond-shaped towers are 226.500m high in all and has a 173.134m-high part above the bridge deck. Its lower and middle columns are of RC structure and its upper column, composite segment between the upper and middle columns and transverse beam are of PC structures. Each of its foundations is comprised of some bored piles and a whole bearing platform, and is protected with anticollision steel box cofferdam and flexible anticollision devices. Two wind fairings with 40° nose angle are mounted at the two side of the flat closed box deck to improve the flutter critical wind speed, reduce the vortex-excited resonances of the bridge. The steel box deck has thus a overall width of 34.0m and a central height of 3.5m. Its stay cables comprised of parallel steel wires are anchored with steel anchor boxes on both the towers and the deck. To mitigate the cable vibration, spiral strings are added on the cable surfaces and dampers are installed on the cables at the locations near to deck.

The southern and northern approach bridges are 5.356km long in all, and are comprised of some separated twin-deck PC continuous box beams of multi-spans with constant girder depth. The single deck has a cross section of single box with single room, and is 12.25m in width. The gap between the two adjacent decks is covered with concrete plates of central isolation belt. There are two kinds of spans. i.e., 60m and 46m. Each of the 60m-span continuous beams has six spans with a constant girder central depth of 3.5m, and was constructed with the method of whole span precasting, hoisting and installation. To facilitate dismounting the inner moulding plates of the precast box girders, the girder parts over piers are stiffened only via thickening the box plates locally, but without any diaphragm. The 46m-span continuous beams has a constant girder central depth of 2.7m, and were constructed with the method of movable formworks. In the span-wise direction, it was designed as a full prestressed concrete structure. A diaphragm is set in the box girder at the pier top. The alignments of the northern and southern bank approach bridges are circularly curved with the radiuses of 2500m and 2300m, respectively.

To improve the conditions of vehicle driving on the bridge deck, curve-type grid wind barriers were excogitated through numerical analysis in conjunction with wind tunnel test, and installed on the bridge deck with the whole sea-crossing part, where, the wind barriers around the bridge towers are variant in both the height and the ventilation ratio.

46m 跨引桥移动模架施工
Construction of 46m-span approaching bridges with the movable formworks method

46m 跨引桥移动模架施工
Construction of 46m-span approaching bridges with the movable formworks method

桥　　名：宁波象山港公路大桥
桥　　型：双塔双索面斜拉桥
　　　　　预应力混凝土连续梁
长　　度：6.723km
桥　　址：浙江省宁波市至象山县
完成日期：2012 年
设计单位：中交公路规划设计院有限公司
施工单位：中交第二公路工程局有限公司
　　　　　中铁大桥局集团有限公司
　　　　　中交第二航务工程局有限公司等

Name: Xiangshan Harbor Bridge in Ningbo
Type: Double-tower cable-stayed bridge
　　　　 PC continuous beam bridges
Length: 6.723km
Location: Ningbo City to Xiangshan County, Zhejiang Province
Completion: 2012
Designer(s): CCCC Highway Consultants Co.,Ltd.
Contractor(s): CCCC Second Highway Engineering Co., Ltd.
　　　　　　　 China Railway Major Bridge Engineering Group Co., Ltd.
　　　　　　　 CCCC Second Harbor Engineering Company Ltd.

厦漳跨海大桥
Xiazhang Sea-crossing Bridge

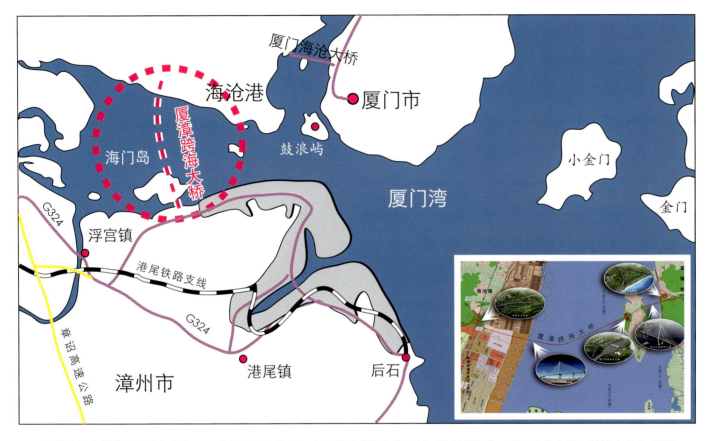

厦漳跨海大桥位于九龙江入海口，北连厦门海沧区，南接漳州龙海市沙坛村，途经海门岛，双向共六车道，路线全长9.3354km，桥长8.5464km，包括南、北汊两主桥及其引桥、海门岛和漳州岸接线和互通立交。

北汊主桥为双塔双索面半飘浮钢箱梁斜拉桥，跨径布置为95m+230m+780m+230m+95m＝1430m；钻石形钢筋混凝土索塔总高227m，采用钻孔灌注桩基础；主梁中心高3.5m，含风嘴梁宽38m，每侧风嘴外另设1.2m宽水平分流板；塔梁之间设竖向支座、横向抗风支座和纵向黏滞阻尼器；平行钢丝斜拉索在塔、梁上分别采用钢锚梁和锚拉板锚固，表面附加螺旋线，近梁侧设阻尼器。

南汊主桥为双塔双索面半飘浮叠合梁斜拉桥，跨径布置为135m+300m+135m＝570m；H形钢筋混凝土桥塔高137m；主梁为π形截面钢混凝土叠合梁，外侧设检修道和平置L形导流板，全宽40m，中心高3.435m；基础形式、塔梁间约束、拉索结构及锚固方式和阻尼器设置与北汊主桥类似，但拉索表面压制规则花纹。

引桥采用多联多跨分离双幅预应力混凝土连续箱梁，中间缝隙约1m宽，用2m宽隔离带混凝土板覆盖，总宽33m。北汊北引桥跨径50m，北汊南引桥有50m、67.7m和70m三种跨径，南汊北引桥跨径45m，南汊南引桥有30m、40m和60m三种跨径。南汊南引桥采用落地支架施工，北汊南引桥67.7m和70m跨径部分采用短线法节段预制拼装施工，其余采用移动模架施工。

桥　名:	厦漳跨海大桥
桥　型:	钢箱梁斜拉桥
	叠合梁斜拉桥
	预应力混凝土连续箱梁
长　度:	9.3354km
桥　址:	福建省厦门市至漳州市
完成日期:	2013年
设计单位:	招商局重庆交通科研设计院有限公司
	福建省交通规划设计院
	中交第一公路勘察设计研究院有限公司
施工单位:	中铁大桥局集团有限公司
	中交第二航务工程局有限公司
	中交第一公路工程局有限公司等

Name: Xiazhang Sea-crossing Bridge
Type: Cable-stayed bridge with steel box deck and two diamond-shaped RC towers
　　　　Cable-stayed bridge with π-shaped composite deck and two H-shaped RC towers
　　　　Several PC continuous box beam bridges
Length: 9.3354km
Location: Xiamen to Zhangzhou, Fujian Province
Completion: 2013
Designer(s): China Merchants Chongqing Communications Research & Design Institute Co., Ltd.
　　　　　　Fujian Communications Planning and Design Institute
　　　　　　CCCC First Highways Consultants Co., Ltd.
Contractor(s): China Railway Major Bridge Engineering Group Co., Ltd.
　　　　　　　CCCC Second Harbor Engineering Company Ltd.
　　　　　　　CCCC First Highway Engineering Co., Ltd.

Xiazhang Sea-crossing Bridge crosses the estuary of the Jiulong River between Haicang District of Xiamen and Shatan Village of Longhai City of Zhangzhou, Fujian Province by the way of Haimen Island. It contains six traffic lanes in dual directions and its total lengths of route and bridge are 9.3354km and 8.5464km, respectively. It includes the two main bridges over the southern and northern channels of Jiulong River, respectively, and the approach bridge, the link routes on Haimen Island and the bank at the Zhangzhou side, and the interchange.

The Northern Channel Main Bridge is a semi-floating cable-stayed bridge with a steel box girder and two 227m-high diamond-shaped RC towers. Its span arrangement is 95m+230m+780m+230m+95m=1430m. The bored pile foundations are used in the bridge. The deck central depth is 3.5m, and the overall width including wind fairings is 38m. In addition, an 1.2m-wide horizontal flow-splitting plate is installed at the outer side of each of the two wind fairings. The vertical bearings, lateral anti-wind bearings and longitudinal viscous damper are mounted between the towers and the deck. Its stay cables comprised of parallel steel wires are anchored on the towers with steel anchor boxes and on the deck with tensile anchor plates. To mitigate the cable vibration, spiral strings are added on the cable surfaces and dampers are installed on the cables at the locations near to deck.

The Southern Channel Main Bridge is a semi-floating cable-stayed bridge with a π-shaped composite deck and two 137m-high H-shaped RC towers. Its span arrangement is 135m+300m+135m =570m. An cantilever overhaul and maintenance path is installed at each of the two side edge of the deck. A L-shaped flow-guide plate stretches horizontally from the outer edge of each overhaul and maintenance path, with its short flange at outer side and being downward. The overall width of the whole deck is 40m, and its central depth is 3.435m. The foundation type, the constraint relations between the tower and the deck, the structure and anchor ways of the cables and the set of the dampers of the Southern Channel Main Bridge are similar to those of the Northern Channel Main Bridge. However, the surfaces of cables are empaistic with regularly distributed dimples.

The approach bridge is comprised of a series of separated twin-deck PC continuous box beams of multi-spans with constant or variant girder depths.The central gap between two adjacent decks is 1m wide and covered with a 2m-wide concrete plates of central isolation belt. The overall width of the whole bridge deck is 33m. The span lengths are, respectively, 50m for the northern approach bridge of the Northern Channel Main Bridge, 50m, 67.7m and 70m for the southern approach bridge of the Northern Channel Main Bridge, 45m for the northern approach bridge of the Southern Channel Main Bridge, 30m, 40m and 60m for the southern approach bridge of the Southern Channel Main Bridge. The southern approach bridge of the Southern Channel Main Bridge was constructed using the landing falseworks. The 67.7m-span and 70m-span parts of the southern approach bridge of the Northern Channel Main Bridge were assembled the girder segments precast by short-line matching method. The rest parts of the approach bridges were cast in situ on movable formworks.

第二篇　悬索桥
Chapter 2　Suspension Bridges

引言

自 1883 年第一座现代悬索桥——纽约布鲁克林桥问世至今，现代悬索桥经历了 130 年的发展。虽然其构造基本上还是 130 年前 Reobling 父子所创造的形式，但英国在 20 世纪 70 年代创造了钢箱梁的加劲梁和钢筋混凝土桥塔；日本在 20 世纪 70 年代推广美国技术，将主缆从纺缆改为预制索股，并在 90 年代创造了除湿防腐装置；中国在 21 世纪将分体桥面的抗风措施应用于小宽跨比的大跨度悬索桥等都是对悬索桥的重大革新。

20 世纪 90 年代初，在已经成功建成许多斜拉桥的鼓舞下，中国桥梁界开始酝酿建造现代悬索桥，以填补空白。广东汕头海湾大桥是第一次尝试。虽然跨度仅 452m 的汕头海湾大桥理应采用斜拉桥方案，但桥梁界试建悬索桥愿望强烈，以李国豪为组长的专家组一致支持了这种愿望。大桥局担负了这项任务，通过出国考察和精心设计施工，于 1994 年建成此桥。紧接着，中国接连建成了西陵长江大桥、虎门珠江大桥、厦门海沧大桥和江阴长江大桥四座悬索桥。其中 1999 年建成的江阴长江大桥跨度突破了千米。中国桥梁界用不足十年时间赶上了欧美发达国家百余年的发展进程，实现了中国的悬索桥梦想。进入 21 世纪后，中国迎来了新一轮的交通建设高潮，在短短十年间（2003~2013 年），中国建成了 20 座以上的大跨度悬索桥，并且在悬索桥结构体系、施工工法、锚碇与基础形式等方面有诸多改进，推动了悬索桥的发展。

悬索桥是跨越能力最强的桥梁结构形式。大跨度悬索桥大多建在海峡、海湾和河口的深水航道上，而在跨越内河航道和山谷时则很少采用。中国进入 21 世纪后，有些地区滋长了追求跨度的浮躁心态，误认为悬索桥代表高水平而忽视了经济性，使得一些通航等级不高、基础难度较小的内河航道以及跨谷桥本可以用经济合理、施工方便的斜拉桥或拱桥方案，却纷纷选用大跨度悬索桥方案，出现了一股建造大跨度悬索桥的热潮。这是一个误区，不能认为悬索桥就代表高水平，而放弃更经济合理的斜拉桥或拱桥方案。

选入本画册的 15 座悬索桥中，除 3 座自锚式悬索桥和一座较小跨径的地锚式悬索桥由于在主缆索面数量、空间索形等方面各具特色而入选外，其余 11 座均为大跨悬索桥。其中 4 座跨越山谷的悬索桥在主梁架设方面各有特点；泰州长江大桥、马鞍山长江公路大桥为双主跨悬索桥，采用了不同的结构方案克服中塔主缆抗滑移问题；润扬长江公路大桥、阳逻长江大桥、广州珠江黄埔大桥、南京长江四桥等在结构构造、锚碇基础和施工方面各具特色；西堠门大桥第一次采用了分体箱梁的抗风措施。但是，在这 11 座大跨度悬索桥中，也存在有跨度与通航要求不相称等情况，在跨度和桥型选择的经济性和合理性方面值得总结和反思。

Introduction

The development of modern suspension bridges began with the Brooklyn Bridge, built in New York in 1883. Although the basic elements of the structural system used in recent suspension bridges differ little from those created by John Roebling and his son Washington Roebling 130 years ago, there have nevertheless been significant developments since the Brooklyn Bridge, such as steel box stiffening girders and reinforced concrete bridge towers introduced by the British in 1970s, prefabricated strands replacing air-spun wire cables introduced by Americans and then popularized by the Japanese in 1970s, cable dehumidification systems invented by the Japanese in 1990s, and the twin separated box girder with central slot developed by Chinese in the 21st century as a wind-resistance measure for long span suspension bridges of small width to span ratio.

Since the early 1990s, the success of cable-stayed bridges in China has inspired Chinese bridge engineers to construct modern suspension bridges. The first modern suspension bridge in China was the Shantou Bay Bridge. Designed and built on the basis of prior domestic and overseas experience, the bridge was completed in 1994 and has a main span of 452m. This was followed by the Xiling Bridge over the Yangtze River, the Humen Bridge over the Pearl River, and the Haicang Bridge in Xiamen. The Jiangyin Bridge over the Yangtze River, completed in 1999, was the first Chinese bridge with span greater than 1000m. To accommodate the rapid development of China's transportation system in the 21st century, more than twenty suspension bridges were constructed between 2003 and 2013. During this period, many significant improvements have been introduced, such as structural system layout, construction techniques, and systems for anchorages and foundations, which encourage the further development of suspension bridge technology.

Suspension bridges have the longest spanning capacity of all the structural systems used for bridges. They are generally the preferred option for the deep-water channel of straits, bays, and estuaries. Although they are generally not economical for crossings of inland waterways and valleys, in recent years they have been increasingly proposed in China for these situations. This is due to a mistaken assumption that, because suspension bridges have the longest span capacity, they must be the most advanced type of bridge technology. Although span capacity is one important characteristic of bridges, it is always preferable to choose the type of bridge to achieve economy and ease of construction. On this basis, it is generally preferable to build cable-stayed bridges or arch bridges for most crossings of inland waterways and valleys.

This chapter introduces fifteen suspension bridges constructed in the last decade. Four of them are bridges with main span length less than 500m. Three of these are self-anchored suspension bridges and one is earth-anchored. Although their spans are not long, they are worthy of inclusion due to unique characteristics such as the number of main cables or cable-planes, or three-dimensional cable profile. The remaining eleven bridges have main spans in excess of 500m. Within this group, four bridges over valleys have been included to highlight unique features of the erection of the main girders. Two suspension bridges with double main spans, the Taizhou Bridge over the Yangtze River and the Ma'anshan Highway Bridge over the Yangtze River, have been included due to special details provided to overcome slip of the main cables at the central tower. The Runyang Highway Bridge over the Yangtze River, Yangluo Highway Bridge over the Yangtze River, the Huangpu Bridge over the Pearl River at Guangzhou, or the Fourth Nanjing Bridge over the Yangtze River all have unique structural details, anchorages, foundations, or construction methods. The Xihoumen Bridge has been included because it is the first suspension bridge to incorporate a twin separated box girder with central slot to improve wind resistance. All eleven of these long-span bridges, however, exhibit some degree of disharmony between span length and navigation clearance requirements. It is important to learn from these problems to enable more reasonable and economic selection of bridge type on future projects.

润扬长江公路大桥南汊桥
Runyang Highway Bridge over Southern Branch of the Yangtze River

润扬长江公路大桥位于长江江苏河段，北起扬州，南接镇江，全长35.66km，桥面净宽32.5m，设双向六车道。

南汊桥主桥为单跨吊钢箱梁悬索桥，主跨跨径1490m。钢箱梁总宽38.7m，梁中心高3.0m。主缆跨径为470m+1490m+470m，主跨垂跨比1/10，采用127ϕ5.3mm预制平行钢丝索股，每根主缆184股。吊索纵向间距16.1m，采用平行钢丝束索股。桥塔采用钢筋混凝土门式框架结构，塔高210m，采用钻孔灌注桩基础。南、北锚碇均为重力式锚碇、预应力锚固系统。

润扬长江大桥主缆采用刚性中央扣，以改善结构性能并减轻短吊杆弯折；用中央稳定板提高大桥的抗风稳定性；施工猫道不设抗风索；采用干空气除湿防护来提高主缆的耐久性。南锚碇基坑施工采用大型排桩冻结围护技术，北锚碇采用矩形地下连续墙支护结构。

Runyang Highway Bridge over the Yangtze River, having a total length of 35.66km and a deck width of 32.5m with six traffic lanes in dual direction, is located in Jiangsu Province connecting Yangzhou in the north bank and Zhenjiang in the south bank.

The main bridge crossing southern branch of the Yangtze River is a single span suspension bridge with a central span of 1490m. The bridge girder is a 38.7m wide and 3.0m deep steel box. The sag-to-span ratio of the main cables is 1/10. Each main cable consists of 184 parallel wire bundles, and each bundle includes 127 ϕ 5.3mm steel wires. The hangers are made with parallel wire bundles. The towers supported by bored piles are portal frame shape structures with a height of 210m. Both the northern and southern anchor blocks are gravity anchorages with prestressing anchorage systems.

The main features of the bridge are the rigid central clamps applied on the main cable to improve the structural performance and to reduce the bending moment of short hanger rods; the central stabilizer plates to improve the wind-resistant stability; the construction catwalks without wind-resistant cables; and the development of a cable dehumidification system to improve the durability of main cables. Its south anchorage foundation is constructed using the large freezing piles retaining technology. Its north anchorage is a rectangular continuous wall supporting structure.

刚性中央扣
Rigid central clamps

桥　　名：润扬长江公路大桥南汊桥
桥　　型：单跨吊钢箱梁悬索桥
主　　跨：1490m
桥　　址：江苏省镇江市和扬州市
完成日期：2005 年
设计单位：江苏省交通规划设计院有限公司
施工单位：中交第二公路工程局有限公司
　　　　　中交第二航务工程局有限公司
　　　　　中交第三航务工程局有限公司

Name: Runyang Highway Bridge over Southern Branch of the Yangtze River
Type: Single-suspended-span suspension bridge with steel box girder
Main span: 1490m
Location: Zhenjiang to Yangzhou, Jiangsu Province
Completion: 2005
Designer(s): Jiangsu Provincial Communications Planning and Design Institute Co., Ltd.
Contractor(s): CCCC Second Highway Engineering Co., Ltd.
　　　　　　　　　CCCC Second Harbor Engineering Co., Ltd.
　　　　　　　　　CCCC Third Harbor Engineering Co., Ltd.

北锚碇地下连续墙基础
North anchorage foundation with a rectangular continuous wall supporting structure

湘江三汊矶大桥
Sanchaji Bridge over the Xiangjiang River

湘江三汊矶大桥是长沙市市内跨越湘江的八座大桥之一，是北二环线上的一座大桥。全桥总长1577m，桥面宽29m，设双向六车道。

主桥为自锚式三跨吊钢箱梁悬索桥，跨径为70m+132m+328m+132m+70m。钢箱梁全宽35m，梁高3.6m。主缆跨径为132m+328m+132m，主跨垂跨比1/5，采用127ϕ5.1mm预制平行钢丝索股，每根主缆37股。吊索纵向间距9m，分柔性吊索和刚性吊杆两种，柔性吊索采用平行钢丝束。主塔采用花瓶形变截面钢筋混凝土结构，东、西主塔分别高104.453m和106.16m，采用钻孔灌注桩基础。

湘江三汊矶大桥采用五跨连续梁体系，有效地克服了主缆的上拔力，并减小了梁端转角；采用全焊钢锚箱进行主缆锚固，不需在锚固区加高梁高，便于主梁顶推施工；采用无应力长度控制吊索长度，安装吊索后再落梁的方法完成体系转换，减少了吊杆反复张拉的程序。

桥　　名：湘江三汊矶大桥
桥　　型：自锚式三跨吊钢箱梁悬索桥
主　　跨：328m
桥　　址：湖南省长沙市
完成日期：2006年
设计单位：长沙市规划设计院有限责任公司
　　　　　中南大学
施工单位：中铁大桥局集团第五工程有限公司

Name: Sanchaji Bridge over the Xiangjiang River
Type: Self-anchored three-suspended-span suspension bridge with steel box girder
Main span: 328m
Location: Changsha, Hunan Province
Completion: 2006
Designer(s): Changsha Planning & Design Institute Co., Ltd.
　　　　　　　 Central South University
Contractor(s): The 5th Engineering Co.,Ltd.,MBEC

Sanchaji Bridge over the Xiangjiang River, having a total length of 1577m and a deck width of 29m with six traffic lanes in dual direction, is located in Changsha, Hunan Province.

The main bridge is a self-anchored three-suspended-span suspension bridge with the spans of 132m+328m+132m. The bridge girder is a 35m wide and 3.6m deep steel box. The sag-to-span ratio of the main cables is 1/5. Each main cable consists of 37 parallel wire bundles, and each bundle includes 127ϕ5.1mm steel wires. The hangers placed along the bridge at each 9 meters include two types: the flexible hangers and the rigid hangers. The flexible hangers are prefabricated with parallel wire bundles. The towers supported by bored piles are vase-shaped structures with variable sections. The height of the towers is 104.453m in the east and 106.16m in the west, respectively.

The main features of the bridge are: (1) A five-span continuous beam system is used and thus most of the main cable pulling force can be self-balanced and the rotation angles at the two ends of the bridge can be reduced; (2) The fully welded steel anchorage box is adopted to fix the main cables, which can avoid the height increase treatment of the anchorage segment of the main girder and make the construction of the main girder more convenience using the incremental launching technique; (3) The unstressed length of hangers is computed as the main control parameter for the bridge construction and no repeated hanger tensioning works are required as structure system transformation is conducted once after all hangers are connected and tensioned.

佛山平胜大桥
Pingsheng Bridge in Foshan

佛山平胜大桥位于广东省佛山市，是佛山市快速环线上的一座大桥。全桥长3.2km，宽56m，设双向十车道与双向人行道。

主桥为独塔四索面自锚式单跨吊钢箱梁悬索桥，跨径为39.64m+5×40m+30m+350m+30m+29.6m。主梁为分离式双主梁，单幅宽26.1m，两幅净距3.8m，全宽56m。主跨为钢箱梁，边跨及锚跨采用预应力混凝土箱梁，梁高3.5m。主缆跨径为200m+350m，主跨垂跨比1/12.5，采用127φ5.1mm预制平行钢丝索股，主缆共4根，每根48股。吊索纵向间距12m，分柔性吊索和刚性吊杆两种，柔性吊索采用平行钢丝索股，刚性吊杆为材质40CrNiMoA的钢杆。索塔采用三柱门式结构，自承台以上高138.87m，采用钻孔灌注桩基础。

佛山平胜大桥施工中开发了钢箱梁顶推施工的自适应变形滑道系统；测得了串列双主缆的尾流驰振规律、最小安全距离以及串列双桥面涡激共振规律。

Pingsheng Bridge in Foshan, having a total length of 3.2km and a deck width of 56m with ten traffic lanes in dual direction and sidewalks in dual direction, is located in Foshan of Guangdong Province.

The main bridge is a self-anchored single-suspended-span suspension bridge with a central span of 350m, four main cable planes and one bridge tower. The main girder includes twin 26.1m-wide steel box girders separated by a 3.8m wide gap. The bridge girders of the side span and anchored span are 3.5m-deep prestressed concrete box girders. The sag-to-span ratio of the main cables is 1/12.5. Each main cable consists of 48 parallel wire bundles, and each bundle includes 127 ϕ 5.1mm steel wires. The hangers placed along the bridge at each 12m include two types: the flexible hangers and the rigid hangers. The flexible hangers are prefabricated with parallel wire bundles. The rigid hangers are 40CrNiMoA steel rods. The tower supported by bored piles is a portal frame shape structure with three columns. The tower height above the pile caps is 138.87m.

The main technical contributions of the bridge are: (1) The development of a slide system of the capacity to adapt deformation by itself during incremental launching of the bridge; (2) The observation and rule summarization of the wake galloping of double main cables placed in series, which is used to determine the minimum safety distance of main cables placed in series, and the observation and rule summarization of the vortex induced resonance of double main girders placed in series.

Name: Pingsheng Bridge in Foshan

Type: Self-anchored single-suspended-span suspension bridge with single tower, four cable planes and steel box girder

Main span: 350m

Location: Foshan, Guangdong Province

Completion: 2006

Designer(s): Hunan Provincial Communications Planning, Survey and Design Institute

Contractor(s): China Railway Major Bridge Engineering Group Co., Ltd.
Guangdong Provincial Foshan Highway Engineering Co., Ltd.

阳逻长江公路大桥
Yangluo Highway Bridge over the Yangtze River

主缆索股预应力锚固系统　Prestressing cable anchorage system

阳逻长江公路大桥位于武汉市东北部，是武汉绕城高速公路跨越长江的一座大桥。全桥长2.725km，桥面净宽33m，设双向六车道。

主桥为单跨吊钢箱梁悬索桥，主跨跨径1280m。钢箱梁宽38.5m，梁高3.0m。主缆跨径为250m+1280m+440m，主跨垂跨比1/10.5，采用127ϕ5.35mm预制平行钢丝索股，每根主缆154股，北边跨增加8股，吊索纵向间距16m，采用平行钢丝索股。索塔采用带有钢剪刀撑的混凝土框架结构，南、北塔分别高169.812m和163.312m，采用分离式承台的钻孔灌注桩基础。北锚碇采用深埋基础重力式锚碇，南锚碇采用深埋圆形扩大基础重力式锚碇。

阳逻长江公路大桥在国内首先采用带有钢剪刀撑的混凝土框架结构索塔；开发"即时监测无黏结可更换式"主缆索股预应力锚固系统，解决了悬索桥锚固系统的更换问题。

Yangluo Highway Bridge over the Yangtze River, having a total length of 2.725km and a deck width of 33m with six traffic lanes in dual direction, is located in Wuhan, Hubei Province.

The main bridge is a single-suspended-span suspension bridge with a central span of 1280m. The bridge girder is a 38.5m wide and 3.0m deep steel box. The sag-to-span ratio of the main cables is 1/10.5. Each main cable consists of 154 parallel wire bundles but increased by 8 bundles in the north side span, and each bundle includes 127ϕ5.35mm steel wires. The hangers are made with parallel wire bundles. The towers supported by bored piles are reinforced concrete portal frames with X-shaped steel bracings. The south tower is 169.812m high and the north tower is 163.312m high. The northern and southern anchor blocks are deep-buried gravity anchorages.

The main features of the bridge are: (1) The application of portal reinforced concrete frame towers with X-shaped steel bracings in China for the first time; (2) The development of an online-monitoring unbonded replaceable cable anchorage system.

桥　名：阳逻长江公路大桥
桥　型：单跨吊钢箱梁悬索桥
主　跨：1280m
桥　址：湖北省武汉市
完成日期：2007年
设计单位：湖北省交通规划设计院
　　　　　中交公路规划设计院有限公司
施工单位：中交第二航务工程局有限公司
　　　　　中铁大桥局集团有限公司

Name: Yangluo Highway Bridge over the Yangtze River
Type: Single-suspended-span suspension bridge with steel box girder
Main span: 1280m
Location: Wuhan, Hubei Province
Completion: 2007
Designer(s): Hubei Provincial Communications and Design Institute
　　　　　　　CCCC Highway Consultants Co., Ltd.
Contractor(s): CCCC Second Harbor Engineering Co., Ltd.
　　　　　　　　China Railway Major Bridge Engineering Group Co., Ltd.

镇胜公路北盘江大桥
Zhensheng Highway Bridge over the Beipan River

桥　　名：镇胜公路北盘江大桥
桥　　型：单跨吊钢桁梁悬索桥
主　　跨：636m
桥　　址：贵州省关岭县和晴隆县
完成日期：2008 年
设计单位：贵州省交通规划勘察设计研究院股份有限公司
　　　　　中铁大桥局集团有限公司
施工单位：贵州路桥集团有限公司

Name: Zhensheng Highway Bridge over the Beipan River
Type: Single-suspended-span suspension bridge with steel truss girder
Main span: 636m
Location: Guanling and Qinglong, Guizhou Province
Completion: 2008
Designer(s): Guizhou Transportation Planning Survey & Design Academe Co., Ltd.
　　　　　　　China Railway Major Bridge Engineering Group Co., Ltd.
Contractor(s): Guizhou Road & Bridge Group Co., Ltd.

镇胜公路北盘江大桥位于贵州省关岭县与晴隆县交界的北盘江大峡谷，是沪瑞国道主干线镇宁至胜境关高速公路上的一座大桥。全桥长1020m，设双向四车道。

主桥为单跨吊钢桁梁悬索桥，主跨跨径636m，钢桁梁高5.0m，桥面系采用正交异性钢桥面板。主缆跨径为192m+636m+192m，主跨垂跨比1/10.5，采用91φ5.1mm预制平行钢丝索股，每根主缆91股。吊索纵向间距7.0m，采用平行钢丝索股。索塔采用门式框架结构，为适应地形，两座索塔的四根塔柱柱底高程均不相同，塔高为120.5～159.5m，采用钻孔灌注桩基础。锚碇为隧道式锚碇。

镇胜公路北盘江大桥钢桁梁中间设稳定板，保证了结构抗风安全，并采用了全桥通长连续的钢桥面系；以不等高的塔柱柱底高程适应了地形；钢桁梁吊装中采用了上弦刚接的连接方案，并采用缆索吊机安装钢桁梁。

钢桁梁与钢桥面系　Steel truss beam and steel deck

Zhensheng Highway Bridge over the Beipan River, having a total length of 1020m and four traffic lanes in dual direction, is located in the border of Guanling County and Qinglong County, Guizhou Province.

The main bridge is a single span suspension bridge with a central span of 636m. The bridge girder is a 5.0m deep steel truss. The sag-to-span ratio of the main cables is 1/10.5. Each main cable consists of 91 parallel wire bundles, and each bundle includes 91 φ 5.1mm steel wires. The hangers placed along the bridge at each 12m are made with parallel wire bundles. The towers supported by bored piles are portal frame shape structures with different height from 120.5m to 159.5m. Both northern and southern anchor blocks are rock tunnel anchorages.

The main features of the bridge are that the central stabilizer plate is installed in the middle of steel truss beams for ensuring structural safety under wind and the top chords are connected rigidly during the erection of the steel truss beam.

广州珠江黄埔大桥南汉桥
Huangpu Bridge over Southern Branch of the Pearl River in Guangzhou

广州珠江黄埔大桥位于广东省广州市，为国道主干线广州绕城高速公路东段的一座大桥。全桥长7016.5m，跨珠江的南北两汉，设双向六车道。

南汉主桥为单跨吊钢箱梁悬索桥，主跨跨径1108m。钢箱梁宽41.69m，高3.5m。主缆跨径为290m+1108m+350m，主跨垂跨比1/10，采用127φ5.2mm预制平行钢丝索股，每根主缆147股，北边跨增加6股，南边跨增加2股。吊索纵向间距16m，采用钢丝绳索股。桥塔采用钢筋混凝土门式索塔，塔高190.476m，采用钻孔灌注桩基础。锚碇为重力式锚碇。

广州珠江黄埔大桥采用无抗风缆和下压装置的猫道体系；研发了大跨度悬索桥上部结构快速施工和高精度控制成套技术；研发了嵌岩式地下连续墙"抓、冲、铣"相结合的成槽工法；研制了62.5m大跨度移动模架体系。

Huangpu Bridge over the Pearl River in Guangzhou, having a total length of 7016.5m and six traffic lanes in dual direction, is located in Guangzhou of Guangdong Province crossing the northern branch and southern branch of the Pearl River.

The main bridge crossing the southern branch of the Pearl River is a single-suspended-span suspension bridge with a central span of 1108m. The bridge girder is a 41.69m wide and 3.5m deep steel box. The sag-to-span ratio of the main cables is 1/10. Each main cable consists of 147 parallel wire bundles and each bundle includes 127 φ 5.2mm steel wires. The hangers placed along the bridge at each 16m are made with wire ropes. The towers supported by bored piles are portal frame shape structures with a height of 190.476m. Both northern and southern anchor blocks are of gravity anchorages.

The main features of the bridge are: (1) The catwalk without wind-resistant cables is adopted in the construction of the bridge; (2) A complete set of technology is developed to accelerate and precisely monitor the construction of bridge superstructure; (3) A 62.5m-long movable scaffolding is developed for constructing the beam of the approach bridges.

桥　　名：广州珠江黄埔大桥南汊桥
桥　　型：单跨吊钢箱梁悬索桥
主　　跨：1108m
桥　　址：广东省广州市
完成日期：2008 年
设计单位：中交公路规划设计院有限公司
施工单位：广东省长大公路工程有限公司

Name: Huangpu Bridge over Southern Branch of the Pearl River in Guangzhou
Type: Single-suspended-span suspension bridge with steel box girder
Main span: 1108m
Location: Guangzhou, Guangdong Province
Completion: 2008
Designer(s): CCCC Highway Consultants Co., Ltd.
Contractor(s): Guangdong Provincial Changda Highway Engineering Co., Ltd.

杭州江东大桥
Jiangdong Bridge in Hangzhou

杭州江东大桥位于杭州市区的东北角，西起下沙，东接萧山。全桥长3.55km，桥宽37.5m，设双向八车道。

主桥为自锚式单跨吊钢箱梁悬索桥，东、西侧各一座，跨径为83m+260m+83m，两座主桥之间采用预应力混凝土连续刚构桥连接。主梁为分离式钢箱梁，横向净距5m，全宽47m，梁高3.5m。主缆由独柱塔支承，在中跨分开，通过锚于主梁两侧的吊索形成横向19°的空间索面，边跨主缆在竖直平面内锚于主梁中间。主跨垂跨比1/4.5，采用91ϕ5.3mm预制平行钢丝索股，每根主缆37股。吊索纵向间距9m，采用平行钢丝索股。主塔为混凝土独柱式塔，塔高约97m，采用钻孔灌注桩基础。

杭州江东大桥采用了空间缆索、独柱塔、宽桥面、分离式钢箱梁的新颖自锚式悬索桥设计；施工过程中解决了多段竖曲线钢箱梁的顶推工艺问题和空间主缆自锚式悬索桥缆索系统的安装技术问题；采用了适应空间索面的新型球铰式吊索体系和主鞍座。

Jiangdong Bridge in Hangzhou, having a total length of 3.55km and a deck width of 37.5m with six traffic lanes in dual direction, is located in Hangzhou, Zhejiang Province connecting Xiasha in the west and Xiaoshan in the east.

The main bridge is composed of two self-anchored single suspended-span suspension bridges with central spans of 260m connected with each other by a PC continuous bridge with integral piers. The main girder is a twin separated steel box girder, 47m wide and 3.5m deep. The width of the central slot is 5.0m. The sag-to-span ratio of the main cables is 1/4.5. Each main cable consists of 37 parallel wire bundles, and each bundle includes 91 ϕ 5.3mm steel wires. The hangers placed along the bridge at each 9m are made with parallel wire bundles. The towers supported by bored piles are reinforced concrete single-columns with a height of 97m.

The main features of the bridge are: (1) The development of a new self-anchored suspension bridge system consisting of the spatial cable, the single-column tower, the wide deck and the separated box girder; (2) The development of the incremental girder launching technique for the steel box girder bridge with different vertical curvatures and the cable system installment technique for self-anchored suspension bridges with spatial main cables; (3) The application of a new hanger system with spherical hinges which is appropriate for the anchorage of the spatial cable planes.

Name: Jiangdong Bridge in Hangzhou
Type: Self-anchored single-suspended-span suspension bridge with steel box girder
Main span: 260m
Location: Hangzhou, Zhejiang Province
Completion: 2008
Designer(s): Shanghai Municipal Engineering Design Institute (Group) Co., Ltd.
Contractor(s): CCCC Second Highway Engineering Co., Ltd.
Road and Bridge Southern China Engineering Co., Ltd.

恩施四渡河大桥
Enshi Bridge over the Sidu River

桥　　名：	恩施四渡河大桥
桥　　型：	单跨吊钢桁梁悬索桥
主　　跨：	900m
桥　　址：	湖北省恩施市
完成日期：	2009 年
设计单位：	中交第二公路勘察设计研究院有限公司
	湖北省交通规划设计院
施工单位：	路桥华南工程有限公司

Name: Enshi Bridge over the Sidu River
Type: Single-suspended-span suspension bridge with steel truss girder
Main span: 900m
Location: Enshi, Hubei Province
Completion: 2009
Designer(s): CCCC Second Highway Consultants Co., Ltd.
　　　　　　　Hubei Provincial Communications Planning and Design Institute
Contractor(s): Road and Bridge Southern China Engineering Co., Ltd.

刚性中央扣
Rigid central clamps

恩施四渡河大桥位于湖北巴东县，跨越四渡河，是沪蓉国道主干线湖北宜昌至恩施段的一座大桥。全桥长1365m，宽24.5m，设双向四车道。

主桥为单跨吊钢桁梁悬索桥，主跨跨径900m。钢桁梁高6.5m。宜昌侧直接与隧道相接，恩施侧边跨采用预应力混凝土连续箱梁。主缆跨径为114m+900m+208m，主跨垂跨比1/10，采用127ϕ5.1mm预制平行钢丝索股，每根主缆127股。吊索纵向间距12.8m，采用平行钢丝索股。桥塔采用钢筋混凝土门式框架结构，塔高分别为117.6m和122.2m，采用钻孔灌注桩基础。宜昌侧采用隧道式锚碇，恩施侧采用重力式锚碇。

恩施四渡河大桥桥面至谷底的高差达560m；桥面系采用工字钢梁与混凝土桥面板组合形式，提高了钢桁梁结构刚度，并改善了桥面的使用性能；设置刚性中央扣，改善了结构受力特性和抗风稳定性，减少了短吊索弯折。

Enshi Bridge over the Sidu River, having a total length of 1365m and a deck width of 24.5m with four traffic lanes in dual direction, is located in Badong, Hubei Province.

The main bridge is a single-suspended-span suspension bridge with a central span of 900m. The bridge girder is a 24.5m wide and 6.5m deep steel truss. The sag-to-span ratio of the main cables is 1/10. Each main cable consists of 127 parallel wire bundles, and each bundle includes 127ϕ5.1mm steel wires. The hangers placed along the bridge at each 12.8m are made with parallel wire bundles. The towers supported by bored piles are portal frame shape structures with different height of 117.6m and 122.2m. The anchor blocks in the Yichang side and in the Enshi side are a rock tunnel anchorage and a gravity anchorage, respectively.

The main features of the bridge are: (1) The deck is 560m high above the valley bottom; (2) The composite deck system consisting of I-shaped steel girders and R.C. slabs is adopted to increase the structural stiffness of steel truss beams and to improve the service performance of the deck; (3) The rigid central clamps are installed to improve structural performances and wind-resistant stability.

贵州坝陵河大桥
Balinghe Bridge in Guizhou

贵州坝陵河大桥位于关岭县镇胜高速公路上，全桥长2237m，桥面宽24.5m，设双向四车道。

主桥为单跨吊钢桁梁悬索桥，主跨跨径1088m。钢桁梁高10.0m。主缆跨径为268m+1088m+228m，主跨垂跨比1/10.3，采用91ϕ5.2mm预制平行钢丝索股，每根主缆208股，边跨增加8股。吊索纵向间距10.8m，采用钢丝绳，上端为骑跨索夹，下端为销铰式连接。索塔采用门式框架结构，东西塔分别高185.788m和201.316m，采用人工挖孔群桩基础。东锚碇采用重力式框架锚，西锚碇采用隧道式锚碇。

贵州坝陵河大桥是国内首座超千米的钢桁梁悬索桥；中跨缆、梁间设置柔性中央扣作为纵向约束系统；在喀斯特地区采用大型隧道锚，并在下检修道位置设置气动翼板来提高桥梁颤振稳定性。

Balinghe Bridge in Guizhou, having a total length of 2237m and a deck width of 24.5m with four traffic lanes in dual direction, is located in Guanling, Guizhou Province.

The main bridge is a single-suspended-span suspension bridge with a central span of 1088m. The bridge girder is a 24.5m wide and 10.0m deep steel truss. The sag-to-span ratio of the main cables is

1/10.3. Each main cable consists of 208 parallel wire bundles and each bundle includes 91 ϕ 5.2mm steel wires. The hangers placed along the bridge at each 10.8m are made with wire ropes. The towers supported by artificial group piles are portal frame shape structures with different height: 185.788m in the east and 201.316m in the west. The eastern and western anchor blocks are a gravity frame anchorage and a rock tunnel anchorage, respectively.

The main features of the bridge are: (1) The steel truss stiffening girder with the span over 1000m is applied in suspension bridges in China for the first time; (2) The flexible central clamp is installed on the cable at the mid-span to restrain the longitudinal movement of the bridge; (3) The large rock tunnel anchorage is adopted in Karst region; (4) The aerodynamic wings are installed to improve the structural flutter stability.

Name: Balinghe Bridge in Guizhou
Type: Single-suspended-span suspension bridge with steel truss girder
Main span: 1088m
Location: Zhenning and Guanling, Guizhou Province
Completion: 2009
Designer(s): CCCC Highway Consultants Co., Ltd.
Contractor(s): Guizhou Provincial Bridge Engineering Corporation
CCCC Second Harbor Engineering Co., Ltd.

西堠门大桥
Xihoumen Bridge

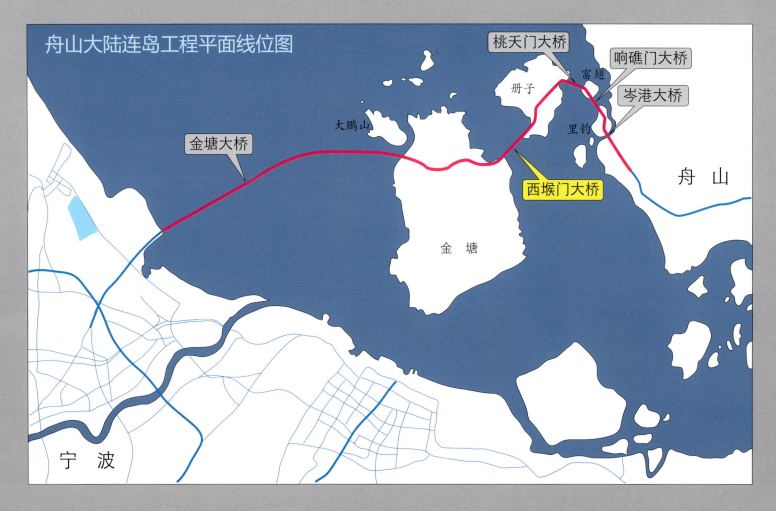

西堠门大桥位于浙江省舟山市,是长达50km的舟山大陆连岛工程中的4座跨海特大桥之一,连接舟山群岛的册子岛与金塘岛,全长2588m,桥面宽2×11.5m,设双向四车道。

主桥为两跨吊分体式连续钢箱梁悬索桥,跨径为578m+1650m。分体式钢箱梁横向净距6m,全宽37.4m,梁高3.5m。主缆跨径为578m+1650m+485m,主跨垂跨比1/10,采用127ϕ5.25mm预制平行钢丝索股,每根主缆169股,南边跨增加2股,北边跨增加6股。吊索纵向间距18m,采用钢丝绳索股。索塔采用钢筋混凝土门式框架结构,塔高211.286m,采用钻孔灌注桩基础。北锚碇采用扩大基础的重力式锚,南锚碇为重力式嵌岩锚。

西堠门大桥采用双箱分体式钢箱梁,以中央开槽技术解决了大跨径小宽跨比悬索桥颤振稳定问题;采用国产1770MPa主缆索股,减轻了主缆自重;运用水平成圈放索技术,解决了索股架设中的"呼啦圈"现象,节省索盘,减轻运输重量。

Xihoumen Bridge, having a total length of 2588m and deck widths of 2×11.5m with four traffic lanes in dual direction, is located in Zhoushan, Zhejiang Province, connecting Cezi Island and Jintang Island.

The main bridge is a two-suspended-span suspension bridge with a central span of 1650m and a side span of 578m. The bridge girder is a 37.4m wide and 3.5m deep twin separated box girder with a central slot. The width of the central slot is 6.0m. The sag-to-span ratio of the main cables is 1/10. Each main cable consists of 169 parallel wire bundles and each bundle includes 127 ϕ 5.25mm steel wires. The hangers placed along the bridge at each 18m are made with wire ropes. The towers supported by bored piles are reinforced concrete portal frame shape structures with a height of 211.286m. The northern and southern anchor blocks are both gravity anchorages.

The main features of the bridge are: (1) The twin separated box girder with a central slot is applied to improve the flutter stability of long-span suspension bridges with small width-to-span ratios; (2)The weight of main cables are reduced by the use of wire bundles of 1770MPa tensile strength made in China; (3)The new technique of horizontal unreeling cables is developed to solve the " hoop " problem during the cable erection, to save the quality of the cable, and to reduce the shipping weight.

桥　　名：西堠门大桥
桥　　型：两跨吊分体式连续钢箱梁悬索桥
主　　跨：1650m
桥　　址：浙江省舟山市
完成日期：2009 年
设计单位：中交公路规划设计院有限公司
施工单位：中交第二公路工程局有限公司
　　　　　四川路桥建设股份有限公司

Name: Xihoumen Bridge
Type: Two-suspended-span continuous suspension bridge with separated steel box girder
Main span: 1650m
Location: Zhoushan, Zhejiang Province
Completion: 2009
Designer(s): CCCC Highway Consultants Co., Ltd.
Contractor(s): CCCC Second Highway Engineering Co., Ltd.
　　　　　　　Sichuan Road & Bridge Construction Co., Ltd.

矮寨大桥
Aizhai Bridge

　　矮寨大桥为湖南省吉首至茶洞高速公路上的一座大桥，跨越德夯河河谷，桥面高程与谷底高程差达330m。桥面设双向四车道。

　　主桥为单跨吊钢桁梁悬索桥。钢桁梁高7.5m。桥面系采用纵向工字梁与混凝土桥面板的组合结构。主缆跨径为242m+1176m+116m，主跨垂跨比1/9.6，采用127ϕ5.25mm预制平行钢丝索股，每根主缆169股，吉首侧边跨增加6股，跨中设三组柔性中央扣。吊索纵向间距14.5m，采用钢丝绳索股。索塔采用门式框架结构，吉首和茶洞侧塔高分别为129.316m和61.924m，采用扩大基础。吉首侧采用重力式锚碇，茶洞侧采用隧道式锚碇。

　　矮寨大桥结合桥址地形和地质条件，采用塔梁分离式悬索桥结构，减少了山体开挖；在主缆无吊索区设竖向碳纤维锚索解决了无索区过长的刚度问题；针对山区加劲梁运输和架设难的问题，采用了柔性轨索滑移法架设加劲梁的新工艺。

Aizhai Bridge over the valley of Dehang River, having a deck 330m above the valley bottom, is located on the highway from Jishou City to Chadong City, Hunan Province. It has four traffic lanes in dual direction.

The main bridge is a single-suspended-span suspension bridge with a central span of 1176m. The bridge girder is a 7.5m deep steel truss. The sag-to-span ratio of the main cables is 1/9.6. Each main cable consists of 169 parallel wire bundles and each bundle includes $127\phi 5.25$mm steel wires. The hangers placed along the bridge at each 14.5m are made with wire ropes. The towers supported by the spread foundation are portal frame shape structures with different height of 129.316m for the tower in the Jishou side and 61.924m for the tower in the Chadong side. The anchor blocks in the Jishou side and in the Chadong side are a gravity anchorage and a rock tunnel anchorage, respectively.

The main features of the bridge are: (1) The structure system of separated tower and main girder is adopted to reduce the work load on mountain excavation; (2) The application of CFRP anchor cables installed in the region without hangers increases the local structural stiffness; (3)The development of a new technique called flexible cable sliding method to solve the problem of transporting and launching the girders in a mountain area.

桥　名：矮寨大桥
桥　型：单跨吊钢桁梁悬索桥
主　跨：1176m
桥　址：湖南省吉首市
完成日期：2012年
设计单位：湖南省交通规划勘察设计院
施工单位：湖南路桥建设集团公司

Name: Aizhai Bridge
Type: Single-suspended-span suspension bridge with steel truss girder
Main span: 1176m
Location: Jishou, Hunan Province
Completion: 2012
Designer(s): Hunan Provincial Communications Planning, Survey & Design Institute
Contractor(s): Hunan Road & Bridge Construction Group Corporation

柳州双拥大桥
Shuangyong Bridge in Liuzhou

柳州双拥大桥位于广西省柳州市。全桥长1937m，设双向六车道。

主桥为单跨吊单主缆三跨连续钢箱梁悬索桥，跨径为40m+430m+40m。钢箱梁宽38m，梁高3.5m。主缆垂跨比1/9，采用127φ5.2mm预制平行钢丝索股，每根主缆91股。吊索纵向间距10m，采用平行钢丝索股，近塔侧5对吊索在横桥向为人字形布置，其余为竖直布置。主塔为A形钢塔，塔高104.811m，塔柱截面为变截面三角形，钻孔灌注桩基础，锚碇为重力式锚碇。

柳州双拥大桥为国内首座单主缆悬索桥，通过设置近塔侧的人字形吊索、边跨连续梁段、拉压支座等多种方式解决抗扭转问题；采用散索套实现主缆散开，减小了锚碇的埋置深度；采用顶推技术解决了缆载吊机无法在单主缆上吊升钢箱梁的施工难题。

Shuangyong Bridge in Liuzhou, having a total length of 1937m and a deck of six traffic lanes in dual direction, is located in Liuzhou, Guangxi Province.

The main bridge is a single-suspended-span suspension bridge with a central span of 430m. The bridge girder is a 38m wide and 3.5m deep three-span continuous steel box. The sag-to-span ratio of the main cables is 1/9. The main cable consists of 91 parallel wire bundles and each bundle includes 127 ϕ 5.2mm steel wires. The hangers placed along the bridge at each 10m are made with parallel wire bundles. The towers supported by bored piles are A-shaped steel structures with a height of 104.811m. Both the northern and southern anchor blocks are gravity anchorages.

The main features of the bridge are: (1) The system with a single main cable is built up in China for the first time; (2) The measures of herringbone hangers close to the tower, continuous beam segments of side spans, and tension-compression bearings improve the torsion resistance capacity; (3) The depth of burial for anchorages is reduced by the use of splay saddles; (4) The problem of erecting girder on the single main cable is solved by using the incremental launching technique.

重力式锚碇　Gravity anchorage

Name: Shuangyong Bridge in Liuzhou
Type: Earth-anchored single-suspended-span suspension bridge with single-cable and three-span continuous steel box girder
Main span: 430m
Location: Liuzhou, Guangxi Province
Completion: 2012
Designer(s): Sichuan Provincial Transport Department Highway Planning, Survey, Design and Research Institute
Contractor(s): Shanghai Civil Engineering Co., Ltd. of CREC
　　　　　　　　China Tiesiju Civil Engineering Group Co., Ltd.

泰州长江大桥
Taizhou Bridge over the Yangtze River

浮式沉井基础
Floating caisson

　　泰州长江大桥位于江苏省长江中段，北接泰州市，南连镇江市和常州市，全桥长62.088km，跨越长江与夹江。桥面宽33.0m，设双向六车道。

　　主桥为三塔两跨吊连续钢箱梁悬索桥，主跨跨径2×1080m。钢箱梁宽39.1m，梁高3.5m。主缆跨径为390m+2×1080m+390m，主跨垂跨比1/9，采用91φ5.2mm预制平行钢丝索股，每根主缆169股。吊索纵向间距16m，采用平行钢丝索股。边塔采用钢筋混凝土门式框架桥塔，塔高171.7m，采用钻孔灌注桩基础。中塔采用钢结构，横桥向为门式框架结构，纵桥向呈人字形，塔高191.5m，采用沉井基础。锚碇为沉井基础重力式锚碇。

　　泰州长江大桥是首座大跨度三塔两跨吊悬索桥体系，通过中塔采用刚度适中的人字形钢桥塔等措施，解决了中塔塔顶主缆与鞍座的抗滑移问题，又兼顾了结构刚度；中塔基础采用浮式沉井基础，确保了工程质量，简化了施工，节约了材料。

Taizhou Bridge over the Yangtze River, having a total length of 62.088km and a deck width of 33.0m with six traffic lanes in dual direction, is located in Jiangsu Province crossing the Yangtze River and the Jiajiang River respectively.

The main bridge is a three-tower two-suspended-span suspension bridge with central spans of 2×1080m. The bridge girder is a 39.1m wide and 3.5m deep two-span continuous steel box. The sag-to-span ratio of the main cables is 1/9. Each main cable consists of 169 parallel wire bundles, and each bundle includes 91 ϕ 5.2mm steel wires. The hangers placed along the bridge at each 16m are made with parallel wire bundles. The side towers supported by bored piles are portal frame shape reinforced concrete structures with the height of 171.7m. The mid-tower supported by a floating caisson is a steel structure with a portal frame in the lateral direction and with a herringbone shape in the longitudinal direction. Both the northern and southern anchor blocks are gravity anchorages with caissons.

The main features of the bridge are: (1) A new system with three towers and two main spans is applied in suspension bridges for the first time; (2) An inversed Y-shaped steel structure is adopted in the mid-tower of the bridge to solve the anti-slipping problem between the main cable and the cable saddle at the top of the mid-tower; (3) The floating caisson is adopted as the foundation of the mid-tower to ensure the engineering quality, simplify the construction procedure and save materials.

桥　　名：泰州长江大桥	**Name:** Taizhou Bridge over the Yangtze River
桥　　型：三塔两跨吊连续钢箱梁悬索桥	**Type:** Two-suspended-span suspension bridge with three towers and continuous steel box girder
主　　跨：2×1080m	**Main span:** 2×1080m
桥　　址：江苏省泰州市	**Location:** Taizhou, Jiangsu Province
完成日期：2012年	**Completion:** 2012
设计单位：江苏省交通规划设计院股份有限公司	**Designer(s):** Jiangsu Provincial Communications Planning and Design Institute Co., Ltd.
中铁大桥勘测设计院有限公司	China Railway Major Bridge Reconnaissance & Design Institute Co., Ltd.
同济大学建筑设计研究院（集团）有限公司	Tongji Architectural Design (Group) Co., Ltd.
施工单位：中交第二公路工程局有限公司	**Contractor(s):** CCCC Second Highway Engineering Co., Ltd.
中交第二航务工程局有限公司	CCCC Second Harbor Engineering Co., Ltd.
中铁大桥局集团有限公司	China Railway Major Bridge Engineering Group Co., Ltd.

南京长江第四大桥
The Fourth Nanjing Bridge over the Yangtze River

　　南京长江第四大桥是南京二环线上的一座大桥，全桥长5.448km，设双向六车道。
　　主桥为三跨吊连续钢箱梁悬索桥，跨径布置为410.2m+1418m+363.4m。主梁为三跨连续钢箱梁，全宽38.8m，梁高3.5m。主缆跨径为576.2m+1418m+481.8m，主跨垂跨比1/9，采用127ϕ5.35mm预制平行钢丝索股，每根主缆135股，北边跨增加6股，南边跨增加8股。吊索纵向间距15.6m，采用平行钢丝索股。桥塔采用混凝土门式框架结构，塔高227.2m，采用钻孔灌注桩基础。锚碇为重力式锚碇，北锚采用沉井基础，南锚采用井筒式地连墙支护明挖深基础。
　　南京长江第四大桥过渡墩处设置主缆限位装置约束其竖向位移，采用分布传力式主缆锚固系统，引入钢筋混凝土榫剪力键将巨大的缆力分步传递到锚碇混凝土中，有效减小了锚固系统各组件的应力集中；南锚碇基础采用"∞"形井筒式地下连续墙，降低了工程造价。

"∞"形井筒式地下连续墙　　"∞" type diaphragm wall

The Fourth Nanjing Bridge over the Yangtze River, having a total length of 5.448km and a deck of six traffic lanes in dual direction, is located in Nanjing, Jiangsu Province.

The main bridge is a three-suspended-span suspension bridge with a central span of 1418m. The bridge girder is a 38.8m wide and 3.5m deep three-span continuous steel box. The sag-to-span ratio of the main cables is 1/9. Each main cable consists of 135 parallel wire bundles and each bundle includes 127 ϕ 5.35mm steel wires. The hangers placed along the bridge at each 15.6m are made with parallel wire bundles. The towers supported by bored piles are portal frame shape structures with a height of 227.2m. The northern and southern anchor blocks are gravity anchorages with caissons and open-excavated diaphragm walls, respectively.

The main features of the bridge are: (1) The application of a new device restrains the cable movement in the vertical direction at the transition piers; (2) A new distributed cable anchor system is adopted to avoid the stress concentration of all components in the anchorage system; (3) A new "∞" type diaphragm wall is adopted for the foundation of the south anchorage to reduce its construction cost.

桥　　名：南京长江第四大桥	**Name:** The Fourth Nanjing Bridge over the Yangtze River
桥　　型：三跨吊连续钢箱梁悬索桥	**Type:** Three-suspended-span suspension bridge with continuous steel box girder
主　　跨：1418m	**Main span:** 1418m
桥　　址：江苏省南京市	**Location:** Nanjing, Jiangsu Province
完成日期：2012年	**Completion:** 2012
设计单位：中交公路规划设计院有限公司	**Designer(s):** CCCC Highway Consultants Co., Ltd.
施工单位：中交第二公路工程局有限公司	**Contractor(s):** CCCC Second Highway Engineering Co., Ltd.
中交第二航务工程局有限公司	CCCC Second Harbor Engineering Co., Ltd.
中铁大桥局集团有限公司	China Railway Major Bridge Engineering Group Co., Ltd.

（部分图片提供者：何超然）

马鞍山长江公路大桥
Ma'anshan Highway Bridge over the Yangtze River

马鞍山长江大桥位于马鞍山长江段江心洲，全桥长 11.209km，桥面宽 33.0m，设双向六车道。

主桥为三塔两跨吊连续钢箱梁悬索桥，主跨跨径 2×1080m。钢箱梁宽 38.5m，梁高 3.5m，中塔塔梁固结，梁高过渡至 5.0m。主缆跨径为 360m+1080m+1080m+360m，主跨垂跨比 1/9，采用 91ϕ5.2mm 预制平行钢丝索股，每根主缆 154 股。吊索纵向间距 16m，采用平行钢丝索股。中塔为钢－混混合的门式框架结构，上塔柱为钢结构，高 127.8m；下塔柱为预应力混凝土结构，高 37.5m。边塔为钢筋混凝土门式框架结构，高 165.3m。中、边塔均采用钻孔灌注桩基础。锚碇为沉井基础重力式锚碇。

马鞍山长江大桥中塔采用钢与混凝土混合结构和塔梁固结体系，有效解决了三塔悬索桥的主缆与鞍座间的抗滑移，并兼顾主梁的刚度问题。

Ma'anshan Highway Bridge over the Yangtze River, having a total length of 11.209km and a deck width of 33.0m with six traffic lanes in dual direction, is located in Ma'anshan, Anhui Province.

The main bridge is a three-tower two-suspended-span suspension bridge with two central spans of 1080m and two side spans of 360m. The bridge girder is a 38.5m wide and 3.5m deep two-span continuous steel box. The depth of the stiffening girder is increased to 5.0m approaching the mid-tower and fixed with it. The sag-to-span ratio of the main cables is 1/9. Each main cable consists of 154 parallel wire bundles, and each bundle includes 91 ϕ 5.2mm steel wires. The hangers placed along the bridge at each 16m are made with parallel wire bundles. The towers supported by bored piles in side spans are portal frame shape reinforced concrete structures with a height of 165.3m. And the mid-tower also supported by bored piles is a portal frame structure composed of a 127.8m high steel member above the deck and a 37.5m high prestressed concrete member below the deck. Both the northern and southern anchor blocks are gravity anchorages with caissons.

The main feature of the bridge is the development of a new system to fix the girder with the mid-tower composed of a steel member and a concrete member and the new system not only solves the anti-slipping problem between the main cable and the cable saddle effectively, but also ensures the rigidity of the girder.

Name: Ma'anshan Highway Bridge over the Yangtze River
Type: Two-suspended-span suspension bridge with three towers and continuous steel box girder
Main span: 2×1080m
Location: Ma'anshan, Anhui Province
Completion: 2013
Designer(s): Anhui Transport Consulting & Design Institute Co., Ltd.
　　　　　　China Railway Major Bridge Reconnaissance & Design Institute Co., Ltd.
Contractor(s): China Railway Major Bridge Engineering Group Co., Ltd.
　　　　　　　CCCC Second Highway Engineering Co., Ltd.
　　　　　　　CCCC Second Harbor Engineering Co., Ltd.

第三篇　斜拉桥
Chapter 3　Cable-stayed Bridges

引言

由德国 F.Dischinger 教授设计的主跨 182m 的瑞典 Strömsund 桥被公认为现代斜拉桥在二战后复兴的第一桥。从 20 世纪 50 年代到 60 年代，现代斜拉桥首先在德国推广，建成了许多莱茵河桥，1969 年建成的 Knie 独塔斜拉桥的主跨已达到 319m，因此可以认为双塔斜拉桥的跨越能力在 60 年代末已突破了 600m。

自 20 世纪 70 年代起，斜拉桥开始向世界各国传播。1975 年，法国的 St.Nazaire 桥已突破了 400m，著名的法国混凝土斜拉桥——主跨 320m 的 Brotonne 桥也于 1977 年建成。当时正在文革动乱中的中国工程师在十分困难的条件下建成了几座跨度不足百米的试验桥，为 80 年代改革开放以后的斜拉桥建设高潮作好了准备。

1988 年，上海决定自主建设主跨超过 400m 的南浦大桥，并于 1991 年胜利建成通车。此后，上海杨浦大桥 (602m，1993 年)、汕头礐石大桥 (518m，1999 年)、武汉白沙洲大桥 (618m，2000 年) 和青州闽江大桥 (605m，2003 年) 又陆续建成，使中国斜拉桥步入世界先进行列，在国际桥梁界赢得一席之地。

进入 21 世纪以来，中国的斜拉桥又迎来了新一轮的建设高潮，法国诺曼底大桥 (856m，1995 年) 和日本多多罗大桥 (890m，1999 年) 的建成让我们看到了差距，决心继续努力赶超世界先进水平。苏通长江大桥建设是一次重要的契机，在香港昂船洲大桥向千米级斜拉桥冲刺的鼓舞下，中国桥梁界选择了破纪录的 1088m 跨度斜拉桥方案，再加上为京粤高铁所建造的双层公铁两用钢桁梁斜拉桥——武汉天兴洲长江大桥，三座斜拉桥都在 2008 年建成，取得了重大的技术进步。

斜拉桥已成为当代大跨度桥梁的主流桥型，它在刚度、抗风性能、施工简便、拉索可更换、无锚碇等方面的优越性，已迫使悬索桥向更大跨度发展。斜拉桥在 200~1200m 的跨度范围都具有竞争力，而且可灵活采用独塔、双塔和多塔的布置，跨越从 300m 江面直至十公里宽的海峡。斜拉桥如采用双层桁架梁桥面可适用于公铁两用桥，又便于布置养护专用通道和应急逃生通道，十分有利于跨海长桥的建设，对隧道方案也具有竞争力。

本画册中入选的斜拉桥有 26 座，是最多的桥型，这充分反映出斜拉桥的竞争力。我们相信，由于斜拉桥的多样性和丰富的创新空间以及相对于悬索桥的突出优点，它一定能在新世纪内成为世界桥梁工程界最喜爱的主流桥型而大放光彩。

Introduction

The Strömsund Bridge in Sweden, designed after World War II by Prof. Franz Dischinger from Germany, is one of the first significant cable-stayed bridges. Several notable early cable-stayed bridges were built to span the Rhine River in Germany during 1950s and 1960s. The 319m main span of the single-tower Knie Bridge, built in 1969 in Germany, convinced engineers that cable-stayed bridges with twin towers could be built with spans in excess of 600m.

Since the 1970s, cable-stayed bridges have been built in all parts of the world. In France, the St. Nazaire Bridge with a main span more than 400m was completed in 1975, and the Brotonne Bridge, a concrete cable-stayed bridge with a main span of 320m was completed in 1977. During this time, Chinese engineers, suffering from the Cultural Revolution, managed to construct several cable-stayed bridges with spans less than 100m under extremely difficult conditions. Those experiences were very important preparation for the coming upsurge of cable-stayed bridge construction in 1980s after China instituted its reform and opening-up policy.

In 1988, the city of Shanghai decided to build the Nanpu Bridge, a cable-stayed bridge over the Huangpu River with a main span in excess of 400m. This bridge, which relied entirely on domestic bridge construction technology, was successfully put into operation in 1991. After that, many more long span cable-stayed bridges, e.g., the Yangpu Bridge in Shanghai (main span 602m, completed in 1993), the Queshi Bridge in Shantou (main span 518m, completed in 1999), the Baishazhou Bridge in Wuhan (main span 618m, completed in 2000), and the Minjiang Bridge in Qingzhou (main span 605m, completed in 2003), were built. These structures established China's reputation for cable-stayed bridges on the world stage.

At the beginning of the 21th century, China underwent its second cable-stayed bridge construction boom. The success of the Normandy Bridge in France (main span 856m, completed in 1995) and the Tatara Bridge in Japan (main span 890m, completed in 1999) demonstrated the lag in technology between China and the developed countries, and encouraged Chinese engineers to catch up with state-of-art techniques. The construction of the Sutong Bridge was an important opportunity to extend the span length of cable-stayed bridges to over one thousand meters. Encouraged by the Stonecutters Bridge, a kilometer-span-class cable-stayed bridge under construction in Hong Kong, Chinese bridge engineers developed the scheme of the Sutong Bridge to incorporate a record-breaking main span of 1088m. Another important bridge is the Tianxingzhou Bridge in Wuhan, which is a double-deck cable-stayed bridge with steel truss girder carrying both highway and high-speed railway along the Beijing-Guangzhou line. These three bridges, all opened to traffic in 2008, bear witness to the significant progress of cable-stayed bridge technology in China.

The cable-stayed bridge has become the preferred type for long span bridges due to its many advantages including stiffness, good behaviour under wind load, ease of construction, ability to replace stayed cables, and lack of earth anchorages. Because it is competitive for spans between 200m and 1200m, suspension bridges are generally suitable only for spans longer than this range. Cable-stayed bridges can be designed with single tower, twin tower, and even multi-tower arrangements to span rivers wider than 300m or to cross over straits even wider than 10km if required. Double-deck truss girder cable-stayed bridges can be used for combined highway and railway bridges, and are also convenient for maintenance and rescue, which makes them a suitable option for sea-crossing projects that include bridges as well as tunnels.

A total of 26 cable-stayed bridges are included in this book. The authors believe that cable-stayed bridges will have a bright future as a preferred bridge type in the new century, owing to their diversity of structural form, opportunities for innovation, and other outstanding advantages over suspension bridges.

舟山桃夭门大桥
Taoyaomen Bridge in Zhoushan

舟山桃夭门大桥是舟山大陆连岛工程的第三座跨海大桥。大桥为四车道高速公路特大桥，全宽27.6m。主桥为双塔双索面半飘浮体系混合梁斜拉桥，主桥跨径布置为：48m+48m+50m+580m+50m+48m+48m，是我国公路建桥史上首次在海洋环境中修建的大跨径斜拉桥。

舟山桃夭门大桥根据两岸海岛地形合理布跨，利用钢和混凝土两种主梁形式，实现边中跨之比为0.25，钢混接头设置在主跨距离索塔1.67m处；斜拉索在钢箱梁上的锚固采用销铰锚固技术为国内首创；斜拉索热挤一次成型双螺旋线抗风雨振技术实践证明能够有效抑制风雨振；风嘴底板采用可开启的硬聚氯乙烯塑料板，便于检修维护。

Taoyaomen Bridge in Zhoushan is one of the sea-crossing major bridges of Zhoushan Mainland-Island Linking Project. The deck is 27.6m wide and is equally assigned for four traffic lanes. The bridge has two main pylons with double cable planes, and the semi-floating system is adopted. Taoyaomen Bridge is the first large-span highway cable-stayed bridge built in marine environment of China.

Considering the terrain of the islands connected by Taoyaomen Bridge, a span arrangement of 48m+48m+50m+580m+50m+48m+48m is adopted and the ratio of side span to middle span is 0.25. Both steel and concrete girders are adopted to make the span arrangement reasonable and practical. The joint of two kinds of girders is 1.67m away from the main pylon in the main span. The cables are anchored in the steel girder by using pin-hinge connection anchorage technology, which is adopted for first time in China. It was proved that the wind-rain induced vibration of cables was effectively suppressed by aerodynamic measures of double-helical lines on cable PE surface, which was produced by adopting one-step hot extrusion forming technology. Removable UPVC plates were adopted as the fairing bottom plates for improving the workabilities of inspection and maintenance.

 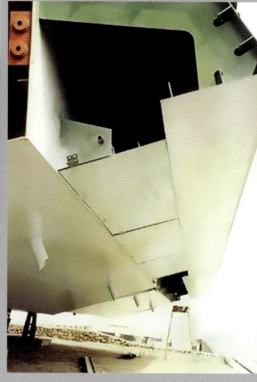

销铰锚固构造
Pin-hinge connection between the cable and the girder

安装完毕的风嘴塑料板
Installed plastic plate as the fairing bottom plate

桥　　名：舟山桃夭门大桥
桥　　型：双塔混合梁斜拉桥
主　　跨：580m
桥　　址：浙江省舟山市
完成日期：2003年
设计单位：中交公路规划设计院有限公司
施工单位：上海建工（集团）总公司
　　　　　中交第二航务工程局有限公司

Name: Taoyaomen Bridge in Zhoushan
Type: Double-tower steel and concrete hybrid girder cable-stayed bridge
Main span: 580m
Location: Zhoushan, Zhejiang Province
Completion: 2003
Designer(s): CCCC Highway Consultants Co., Ltd.
Contractor(s): Shanghai Construction Group Co., Ltd.
　　　　　　　CCCC Second Harbor Engineering Co., Ltd.

安庆长江大桥
Anqing Bridge over the Yangtze River

安庆长江大桥位于长江安庆河段,是安徽省第三条过江通道,也是安徽省第一座跨越长江的高速公路桥梁。主桥为 50m+215m+510m+215m+50m=1040m 五跨双塔双索面钢箱梁斜拉桥。

主梁为扁平流线型闭口钢箱梁,高 3m,宽 30m,采用正交异性钢桥面板。索塔基础为双壁钢围堰大直径钻孔桩复合基础,承台直径 29m,高 6m,下设 18 根 3m 直径的钻孔灌注桩。主桥采用承受疲劳应力幅 250MPa 的新型钢绞线拉索系统,外护套采用带螺旋线的 HDPE 圆管。大桥钢桥面铺装技术以科研为先导,在总结先期经验教训的基础上,科学地提出 3cm 厚浇筑式沥青混凝土下面层加 4.5cm 厚 SMA10 上面层铺装方案及整套技术,多年来使用效果良好。

Anqing Bridge over the Yangtze River, located at Anqing Reach of the Yangtze River, is the third river-crossing passageway and the first highway bridge crossing the Yangtze River in Anhui Province. The main bridge consists of five spans with double towers and double cable planes. The span arrangement is 50m+215m+510m+215m+50 m.

The flat streamlined steel-box girder, 3m in height and 30m in width, with orthotropic steel deck was adopted. The composite foundations with double-wall steel cofferdam and large diameter bored piles was adopted for the main pylons. The pile cap was cylindrical with a diameter of 29m and a length of 6m. A new steel strand cable system, which was capable of tolerating fatigue stress amplitude of 250MPa, was introduced in the main span. For the stay cables, there were helical lines on the surface of HDPE shields. The steel deck pavement adopted a new scheme, which consists of a 3cm thick sub cast-in-site asphalt concrete layer and a 4.5cm upper SMA10 layer. The new scheme has been proved to be greatly serviceable.

桥　　名：安庆长江大桥
桥　　型：双塔钢箱梁斜拉桥
主　　跨：510m
桥　　址：安徽省安庆市
完成日期：2004 年
设计单位：安徽省交通规划设计研究院有限公司
施工单位：中交第二航务工程局有限公司
　　　　　湖南路桥建设集团有限公司

Name: Anqing Bridge over the Yangtze River
Type: Double-tower steel girder cable-stayed bridge
Main span: 510m
Location: Anqing, Anhui Province
Completion: 2004
Designer(s): Anhui Communication Design Institute Co., Ltd.
Contractor(s): CCCC Second Harbor Engineering Co., Ltd.
　　　　　　　　　Hunan Highway and Bridge Construction Group Co., Ltd.

南京长江第三大桥
The Third Nanjing Bridge over the Yangtze River

南京长江第三大桥是上海至成都国道于南京跨越长江的快速过江通道。大桥及连接线全长约15.6km,其中跨江大桥长4744m,南引桥长680m,北引桥长2780m。全线采用双向六车道高速公路标准,跨江主桥为双塔双索面五跨连续钢箱梁斜拉桥,跨径布置为63m+257m+648m+257m+63m=1288m。

南京长江第三大桥建设的两大重点和难点在于主桥南主墩处水深流急,常水位下水深45m,水流速度2.9m/s,施工难度特别大,为我国建桥史上遇到的水深最深、水文条件复杂的深水基础,充分利用钢套箱和钢护筒有机结合形成稳定的刚构平台进行深水基础施工,将施工临时结构与永久结构合二为一,形成先浮运钢套箱、后插打钢护筒的深水基础施工创新技术;索塔为人字形钢塔,下横梁以下部分为混凝土,以上部分为钢,属国内首次采用。上下塔柱连接处钢混结合段采用PBL剪力键作为传递荷载的主要构件,即在钢塔柱板件上开孔,与穿过的钢筋和混凝土形成PBL剪力键的构造设计。综合弧线形钢塔设计施工形成了我国钢塔设计、制造及架设工艺等新技术。

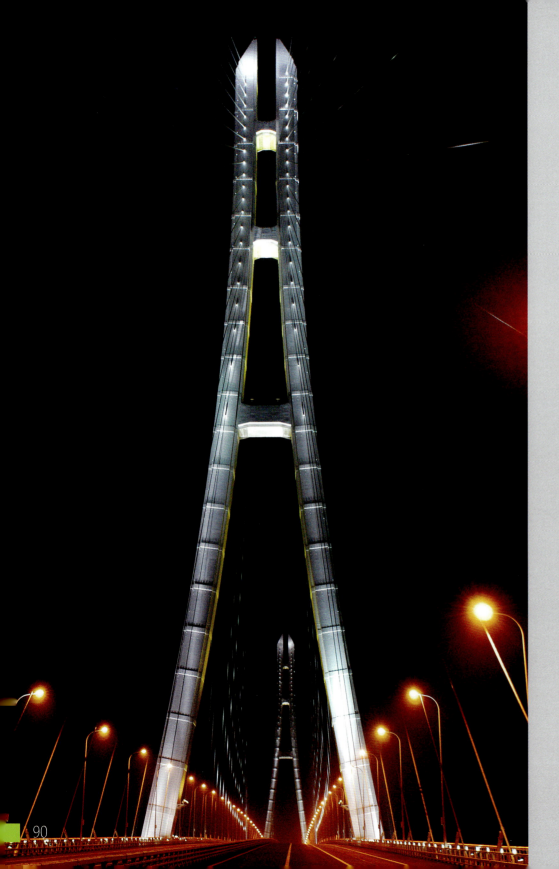

The Third Nanjing Bridge over the Yangtze River is located in Nanjing, the total length of the bridge including approaches is 15.6km. The main bridge, the southern and the northern approaching bridges are 4744m, 680m and 2780m in length, respectively. The main bridge consists of five spans with two main towers and double cable planes. The span arrangement is 63m+257m+648m+257m+63m.

There were two primary technical difficulties in the construction of this bridge. Firstly, the construction of the foundation of the southern main pylon was extremely difficult. It was the deepest foundation with the most complicated hydrological conditions in the bridge construction history of China. To overcome this problem, a creative approach combining the construction temporary structures and permanent structures was proposed. The approach provided with an innovative construction sequence that floating the steel boxed cofferdam into position first and then piling the steel casing. Secondly, the main pylon was designed in a reversed Y-shaped, which consisted of two segments. The upper part was steel and the lower one was concrete, which was also adopted for the first time in China. The connection between the two segments adopted PBL shear connector as the main mechanical components. Along with the design and construction of the curved steel pylon, an integrated technology innovation in the design, construction and erection technique of steel bridge pylon developed.

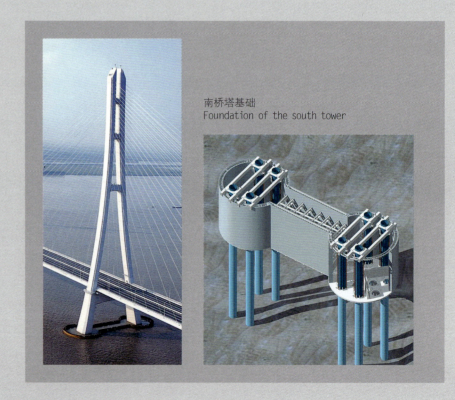

南桥塔基础
Foundation of the south tower

桥　　名：南京长江第三大桥
桥　　型：双塔钢箱梁斜拉桥
主　　跨：648m
桥　　址：江苏省南京市
完成日期：2005 年
设计单位：中交公路规划设计院有限公司
施工单位：湖南路桥建设集团公司
　　　　　中交第二航务工程局有限公司

Name: The Third Nanjing Bridge over the Yangtze River
Type: Double-tower steel box girder cable-stayed bridge
Main span: 648m
Location: Nanjing, Jiangsu Province
Completion: 2005
Designer(s): CCCC Highway Consultants Co., Ltd.
Contractor(s): Hunan Highway and Bridge Construction Group Co., Ltd.
　　　　　　　　CCCC Second Harbor Engineering Co., Ltd.

奉节长江大桥
Fengjie Bridge over the Yangtze River

奉节长江大桥位于重庆市奉节县，主桥采用双塔双索面预应力混凝土斜拉桥，跨度布置为30.4m+202.6m+460m+174.7m+25.3m。塔梁间采用纵向弹性半飘浮体系；主塔采用A形空间混凝土结构，承台以上南、北塔高分别为206m、211.606m；主梁边跨及部分次边跨因压重需要采用箱形梁，其余均采用矩形边主梁，桥轴线处梁高2.5m，梁宽20.5m，梁上标准索距7.85m；每塔布置28对，全桥共计224根斜拉索。

奉节长江大桥地处三峡峡口河段，大桥的设计方案稳妥解决了大跨、高塔及峡谷风效应等引起的技术问题，建成后的奉节长江大桥推动了奉节及三峡库区社会、经济进步。

The main bridge of Fengjie Bridge over the Yangtze River in Chongqing consists of five spans with two main pylons and double cable planes. The span arrangement is 30.4m+202.6m+460m+174.7m+25.3m. A longitudinal elastic floating system is adopted for conneting the main pylons and the girder. The concrete main pylons, which own a height of 206m in the south and 211.606m in the north respectively, were designed as A-shaped dimension. The girders for the long side spans and part of the short side spans adopted box section while the other parts adopted rectangle side beams. The girder owns a height of 2.5m in the axle centerline direction and a width of 20.5m. There are 224 stayed cables in total, and the standard interval of these cables is 7.85m.

This bridge is located in a narrow reach of the Three Gorges. The design scheme of the bridge solved the technical issues caused by large span, tall tower and gorge wind effects. The completion of the bridge is of tremendous help to the economic and social development of Fengjie County and the whole reservoir area of the Three Gorges.

Name: Fengjie Bridge over the Yangtze River
Type: Double-tower PC girder cable-stayed bridge
Main span: 460m
Location: Fengjie County, Chongqing City
Completion: 2006
Designer(s): China Railway Major Bridge Reconnaissance & Design Institute Co., Ltd.
Contractor(s): CCCC Second Harbor Engineering Co., Ltd.

香港昂船洲大桥
Stonecutters Bridge in Hong Kong

昂船洲大桥跨越蓝巴勒海峡，连接青衣与昂船洲两地，是8号干线疏缓工程青衣至长沙湾段中的主要工程。大桥采用六车道高速公路标准，设计车速100km/h，桥面宽度53.3m，通航净高73.5m，净宽900m。

主桥为双塔双索面混合梁斜拉桥，跨径布置为69.25m+2×70m+79.75m+1018m+79.75m+2×70m+69.25m。桥塔基础采用钻孔桩，承台尺寸为47.4m×36.4m×8m。主跨及伸延至边跨49.75m的主梁为流线型分离式钢箱梁，其余边跨部分为双箱预应力混凝土梁。桥塔为独柱式，圆锥形截面，塔高298m，从塔底至塔高175m段为混凝土结构，175～293m段为钢—混凝土组合结构，外层表面采用不锈钢材料；再向上5m至塔顶为外装玻璃的通透钢结构，用作建筑照明标志。斜拉索为半扇形布置，主跨梁上索距18m，边跨梁上索距10m，索梁锚固采用钢锚箱的形式。

昂船洲大桥体现了世界先进的设计理念与建筑美学的和谐统一。桥塔是造型方面的突出特点，上半部混凝土塔壁采用不锈钢包裹，既解决了耐久性问题，同时保持了金属质感，结合独特的照明设计，使全桥更富现代感。在桥塔与主梁之间加装垂直支座承托和纵向液压缓冲器，形成了独特的超大跨径斜拉桥结构体系。边跨施工中采用少支架施工、利用桥塔一次性提升4000t钢主梁节段等创新技术。

Stonecutters Bridge in Hong Kong is the major project in Tsing-Cheung Sha Wan section of the Route 8 Expressway, connecting Tsing Yi and Stonecutters Island. The bridge was designed for six traffic lanes and the design vehicle speed is 100km/h. The width of the bridge is 53.3m. The height and width of the navigation clearance are 73.5m and 900m, respectively.

The main bridge adopts the structural form of two pylons and double cable planes. The span arrangement is 69.25m+2×70m+79.75m+1018m+79.75m+2×70m+69.25m. Bored piles were adopted for the foundation of the main pylons. The dimension of the pile cap is 47.4m×36.4m×8m. A streamlined separated steel box girder and a prestressed concrete twin box girder were adopted for the main spans and back spans, respectively. The height of the single column main pylon is 298m, and the bottom 175m is concrete, the top 5m is employed as structure illuminated sign and the rest part is steel-concrete composite structure with stainless steel skin. The stayed cables are arranged in semi fan shape. The distances between two adjacent cables are 18m in the main span and 10m in the side spans.

The design of Stonecutters Bridge represened the harmonic union of both the world leading design concept and architectural aesthetics. A typical example is the design of the main pylons. The modern flavor of the pylon is expressed perfectly by the combination of the unique illumination design on the top and the middle part with metal texture brought by the stainless steel skin which additionally provides a durable skin. The vertical support bearing and longitudinal hydraulic buffer installed between the main pylon and girder create a special structure form of mega cable-stayed bridge. In the construction of the side span, innovative technologies such as lifting 4000t steel deckaround the pylons by strand jacks supported on temporary cable-supported structures have been used and proved to be of tremendous practical value.

① 桥塔与主梁之间的纵向液压缓冲器
Longitudinal buffer between the pylon and the girder

② 不锈钢塔壁及其内设的剪力钉、索套管
Stainless steel skin of the concrete pylon, with steel cable sheaths and shear studs inside

桥　　名：香港昂船洲大桥
桥　　型：双塔混合梁斜拉桥
主　　跨：1018m
桥　　址：香港特别行政区
完成日期：2008 年
设计单位：奥雅纳工程顾问公司（香港）
施工单位：Maeda-Hitachi-Yokogawa-Hsin Chong JV

Name: Stonecutters Bridge in Hong Kong
Type: Double-tower steel concrete hybrid girder cable-stayed bridge
Main Span: 1018m
Location: Hong Kong SAR
Completion: 2008
Designer(s): Ove Arup & Partners Hong Kong Ltd.
Contractor(s): Maeda-Hitachi-Yokogawa-Hsin Chong JV

本桥资料及图片由奥雅纳工程顾问公司（香港）提供
The illustrations of Stonecutters Bridge were provided by Ove Arup & Partners Hong Kong Ltd.

苏通长江大桥
Sutong Bridge over the Yangtze River

苏通长江大桥位于江苏省东南部长江口南通河段，连接苏州、南通两市，上游距江阴大桥约82km，下游离长江入海口约108km。大桥全长8.146km，由主桥、辅桥和引桥组成，全线采用双向六车道高速公路标准。

主桥跨径布置为100m+100m+300m+1088m+300m+100m+100m=2088m，桥面宽度为36.5m（不含风嘴），是我国自主设计和建造的世界最大跨径斜拉桥。

苏通大桥的主桥结构体系为纵向具有额定行程限位功能的黏滞阻尼约束、横向为主从约束，有效减小了极限风和地震作用下的结构响应，提高了结构防灾能力。主墩冲刷防护设计采用护底防冲方案，平面分为核心区、永久防护区和护坦区，防护结构采用反滤层和护面层结合的形式，反滤层由袋装砂和级配碎石构成，护面层采用块石。索塔锚固采用钢锚箱布置在混凝土塔壁内侧的组合锚固体系，即钢锚箱和混凝土塔壁组成的组合结构。采用基于非线性理论的全过程自适应"精确几何控制法"，将施工控制阶段进一步拓展至制造及安装的全过程，从制造"源头"控制结构尺寸误差和掌握结构参数的误差分布规律，为现场安装误差调整提供了可靠数据。

Sutong Bridge over the Yangtze River is located at Nantong reach of the Yangtze River in southeast Jiangsu Province, connecting Suzhou and Nantong. It is 82km far from Jiangyin Bridge over the Yangtze River in the upstream and 108km far from Yangtze Estuary in the downstream. The total length of the bridge project is 8.146km, consisting of the main bridge, auxiliary bridges and approach bridges. The main bridge is designed for six traffic lanes in dual direction.

The span arrangement is 100m+100m+300m+1088m+300m+100m+100m. The width of the main bridge is 36.5m. The 1088m is the largest span in cable-stayed bridges worldwide.

The bridge was designed and constructed independently by China. As a improved structural form, the main bridge adopted viscous damping constraints with rating leading limit function in longitude and fixed system in transverse to reduce the daynamic responses by wind and earthquake. The bottom protection scheme was adopted for scour protection of the main tower foundations. The protection area was divided into three area, namely core area, permanent protection area and apron area. The protection structure was the combination of filter and protective layer. Pylon anchorage adopted composite system of steel anchor boxes planted in the internal side of the concrete pylon. The construction adopted whole-process adaptive "precise geometric control approach" based on nonlinear theory, expanding the construction process to both the manufacture and installation course. This approach provides the on-site installations with reliable cognition by controlling component dimension errors and understanding the distribution laws of the errors from the start.

索塔与主梁之间的黏滞阻尼器
The viscous damping between the tower and the girder

桥　　名：	苏通长江大桥
桥　　型：	双塔钢箱梁斜拉桥
主　　跨：	1088m
桥　　址：	江苏省苏州市和南通市
完成日期：	2008年
设计单位：	中交公路规划设计院有限公司
	江苏省交通规划设计院有限公司
	同济大学建筑设计院（集团）有限公司
施工单位：	中交第二航务工程局有限公司
	中交第二公路工程有限公司

Name: Sutong Bridge over the Yangtze River
Type: Double-tower steel box girder cable-stayed bridge
Main span: 1088m
Location: Suzhou and Nantong, Jiangsu Province
Completion: 2008
Designer(s): CCCC Highway Consultants Co., Ltd.
　　　　　　　Jiangsu Communication Design Institute Co., Ltd.
　　　　　　　Tongji Architecture Design Co., Ltd.
Contractor(s): CCCC Second Harbor Engineering Co., Ltd.
　　　　　　　　CCCC Second Highway Engineering Co., Ltd.

康家沱长江大桥
Kangjiatuo Bridge over the Yangtze River

桥　　名：康家沱长江大桥
桥　　型：双塔预应力混凝土斜拉桥
主　　跨：460m
桥　　址：重庆市忠县
完成日期：2008年
设计单位：重庆交通科研设计院
施工单位：中交第二航务工程局有限公司

Name: Kangjiatuo Bridge over the Yangtze River
Type: Double-tower PC grider cable-stayed bridge
Main Span: 460m
Location: Zhong County, Chongqing City
Completion: 2008
Designer(s): Chongqing Communications Research and Design Institute
Contractor(s): CCCC Second Harbor Engineering Co., Ltd.

康家沱长江大桥位于重庆忠县县城上游约 8km，是沪蓉国道支线石忠高速公路跨越长江的大桥。设计采用四车道高速公路标准，桥面标准宽度 24.5m。

主桥为双塔双索面预应力混凝土斜拉桥，跨径布置为 205m+460m+205m。主塔基础采用钻孔灌注桩，承台直径 33m，厚 6m。主梁为整体开口梁板式断面，梁高 2.965m，标准截面纵向每隔 8m 设横隔板。索塔为墩塔固结的钢筋混凝土和部分施加预应力结构，塔墩高 47.5m，塔柱高 200m，总高 247.5m。塔柱为分离式 H 形箱形断面，设两道预应力混凝土箱形横梁。

受通航要求限制，本桥边中跨比偏大，设计采用了逐渐加宽边跨肋板、加密中跨跨中部分斜拉索索距等方法优化体系性能。混凝土主梁施工过程中的最大双悬臂状态达到 194m，控制难度大。

Kangjiatuo Bridge over the Yangtze River is 8km away from the main city of Zhong County, Chongqing in the upstream of the Yangtze River and serves as the river crossing bridge for the branch of Shanghai-Chengdu National Highway. The bridge is designed for four traffic lanes. The standard width of the bridge is 24.5m.

Kangjiatuo Bridge over the Yangtze River consists of three spans with two pylons and double cable planes. The span arrangement is 205m+460m+205m. Bored piles are adopted for the foundation of the main pylons. The pile cap is cylindrical with a diameter of 33m and depth of 6m. The main girder adopts integral open beam-slab section with a height of 2.965m. In the standard segments, diaphragms are set in every 8m. The pylons, fixed with the foundations, are the composite structures of reinforced concrete and partially pre-stressed concrete. The total height of each pylon is 247.5m, consists of a 47.5m pier and a 200m main pylon above. The section of the pylon adopts H-shaped separated box.

The ratio of side span to main span is comparatively large because of navigation constraints. Optimization design measures have been considered, such as the gradually broadening rib in the side span and shortening the interval of stayed cables in the middle span. During the construction process, the maximum cantilever length was as long as 194m, posing an extreme challenging problem for the construction.

上海闵浦大桥
Minpu Bridge in Shanghai

上海闵浦大桥为双层公路桥梁，上层桥面为八车道高速公路，下层桥面为六车道的地方道路。主桥跨径布置为 4×63m+708m+4×63m，是目前世界上跨度最大、桥面最宽、车道数最多的双层公路斜拉桥。中跨主梁采用全焊板桁结合整体节点钢桁梁，N形桁式，桁高 9m，主桁宽 27m，节间长度 15.1m。横断面为倒梯形，上、下层结构宽分别为 44m 和 28m。边跨主梁采用双层复合桁架体系，由钢竖腹杆、钢斜腹杆、钢斜撑杆及以钢弦杆为劲性骨架的预应力混凝土桥面结构（包括弦杆、横梁及桥面板）组成，节间长度为 10.5m。

拉索为扇形双索面，采用平行钢丝斜拉索体系，全桥共 192 根，最大拉索型号为 439φ7。主塔采用H形塔，高 210m，五边形空心断面，顺桥向为 8m，横桥向为 7m。主塔基础采用直径 0.9m 的钢管桩，浦东侧主塔桩长 51.1~53.1m，共 385 根，浦西主塔桩长约 66.85m，共 345 根。

主塔塔柱采用翻模法施工，主梁施工采用先施工边跨再施工中跨的方法。边跨施工方法为钢桁梁整孔垂直提升后纵向滑移就位，再现浇上下层桥面结构混凝土。中跨钢桁梁采用大节段由钢结构加工厂浮运至桥位，用桥面吊机垂直提升安装就位。单个节段长 15.1m，吊装质量约为 450t。

Minpu Bridge is a double-deck highway bridge with eight traffic lanes on the upper deck for highway traffic and six traffic lanes on the lower deck for local traffic. As a double-deck cable-stayed bridge, Minpu Bridge currently holds the records of the longest span length, the maximum deck width and the most lanes in the world. The bridge is composed of nine spans in total, i.e., 4×63m+708m+4×63m. The bridge main span, in length of 708 m, has fully-welded steel plate truss composite girders with integral joints of N-truss with 9m in height, 27m in width and 15.1m in length of each segment. The transverse section is inverse trapezium cross-section with 44m in width at upper level and 28m in width at lower level. The side spans of the bridge have double-deck composite truss girders, which are composed of vertical steel web members, diagonal web members, diagonal brace members and prestressed concrete deck (chords, diaphragms and deck) with rigid skeleton of steel chord members. Each segment is 10.5m long.

The bridge has fan-shaped double cable planes with 192 cables (maximum 439 ϕ 7), which employs parallel wire cable system. The bridge has two 210m H-shaped towers with pentagon hollow section that measures 8m in longitudinal length and 7m in transverse width. 0.9m-diameter steel pipe piles are used for the tower foundations. The east tower has 385 piles from 51.1m to 53.1m in length and the west tower has 345 piles with about 66.85m in length.

The main towers were constructed with turnover form method. The side spans were constructed firstly that steel truss girders was erected by slippage after lifted, and the double concrete deck was then casted. The main span was constructed secondly. The segments of steel truss girders were transported to the bridge site from the fabrication, and were installed by loop wheel machine. Each segment was 15.1m long with the weight of 450t.

桥　　名：上海闵浦大桥
桥　　型：双塔钢桁梁斜拉桥
主　　跨：708m
桥　　址：上海市
完成日期：2009 年
设计单位：上海市政工程设计研究总院（集团）有限公司
施工单位：上海市基础工程有限公司

Name: Minpu Bridge in Shanghai
Type: Double tower steel truss girder cable-stayed bridge
Main span: 708m
Location: Shanghai
Completion: 2009
Designer(s): Shanghai Municipal Engineering Design Institute
Contractor(s): Shanghai Foundation Engineering Co., Ltd.

观音岩长江大桥
Guanyinyan Bridge over the Yangtze River

观音岩长江大桥在重庆市江津区观音岩附近跨越长江，是重庆绕城公路南段的重要工程。大桥按六车道高速公路标准设计，桥梁宽度为34.5m。

主桥为双塔双索面结合梁斜拉桥，跨径布置为35.5m+186m+436m+186m+35.5m。桥塔基础采用嵌岩钻孔桩。主梁采用结合梁，钢主梁截面为双工字形截面，混凝土桥面板采用C60高强混凝土，边跨82m和中跨164m范围内的混凝土桥面板中设置纵向预应力。索塔为混凝土A形塔，索梁之间采用锚拉板连接形式。全桥纵向不设固定支座，在索塔下横梁与梁体间设置油压阻尼器，横向采用限位支座。

主梁混凝土桥面板沿桥横向变厚度，减轻了桥面重量，同时增加了桥面板的有效宽度，增加了桥梁横向的抗剪能力。钢料全部国产，尤其是大规模地使用了厚度为80mm的国产厚板。

Guanyinyan Bridge over the Yangtze River is located in Jiangjin District, Chongqing City. It is an important bridge on south Chongqing ring road. The bridge is designed according to the standard of six traffic lanes highway road with a 34.5m width.

The main bridge is a double–tower cable-stayed bridge with double planes and composite girders, which is composed of five spans, i.e., 35.5m+186m+436m+186m+35.5m. The main girders have double-I sections with C60 high performance concrete deck. The concrete deck has longitudinal prestressed tendons in the range of 82m of the side spans and 164m of the main span. The towers are A-shaped and connected to girders with tensile anchorage plates. There is no fixed supports along the bridge, but there are restrict-sliding supports transversely and dampers between tower diaphragms and girders in longitudinal.

The concrete deck is designed with varying thickness along transverse direction, for reducing deck weight, increasing effective width of the deck and transverse shear capacity. 80mm steel plates are widely used and all steel material is made in China.

桥　　名：观音岩长江大桥
桥　　型：双塔结合梁斜拉桥
主　　跨：436m
桥　　址：重庆市
完成日期：2009 年
设计单位：中铁大桥勘测设计院有限公司
　　　　　四川省交通运输厅公路规划勘察设计研究院
施工单位：重庆高速公路集团有限公司

Name: Guanyinyan Bridge over the Yangtze River
Type: Double-tower steel and concrete composite girder cable-stayed bridge
Main span: 436m
Location: Chongqing
Completion: 2009
Designer(s): China Railway Major Bridge Reconnaissance & Design Institute Co.,Ltd.
　　　　　　Sichuan Provincial Transport Department Highway Planning, Survey, Design and Research Institute
Contractor(s): Chongqing Expressway Group Co.,Ltd.

天兴洲长江大桥
Tianxingzhou Bridge over the Yangtze River

　　天兴洲长江大桥是国家干线铁路、京广高速铁路、武汉三环快速路的共用过江通道，是中国首座跨越长江的高速铁路桥梁。大桥上层公路部分按城市快速路标准设计，双向六车道，桥面宽27m，下层铁路部分按照双线客运专线和双线Ⅰ级干线共四线设计；旅客列车设计行车速度：200km/h以上，按250km/h作动力仿真设计；设计荷载为客运专线采用"ZK活载"，Ⅰ级铁路采用"中－活载"。主桥是世界首座按照四线铁路、六线公路标准建设的公铁两用斜拉桥，跨径布置为98m+196m+504m+196m+98m。

　　斜拉桥采用半飘浮体系，主梁采用板桁结合钢桁梁，三片主桁，N形桁架，外侧桁中心宽度30m，桁高15.2m，节间长度14m。斜拉索采用三索面分别锚于三片主桁的上弦。上层公路桥面在梁端168m范围内采用混凝土板，其余范围为钢正交异性板，钢桁梁与桥面板结合共同受力。主塔结构设计为倒Y形钢筋混凝土结构，塔高（从塔座顶面算起）为190m。斜拉索采用镀锌高强平行钢丝束，最长索271m，单根索力最大约12500kN，主塔墩基础均采用φ3.4m大直径钻孔灌注桩。钢梁架设除墩顶采用散拼的方式外，其余全部采用整节段架设，一个节间最大吊重为700t。

　　本桥具有跨度大、活载重、列车速度高等特点，采用了三索面三主桁斜拉桥新结构体系，钢桥面板、混凝土桥面板与主桁结合的组合结构，以及黏滞阻尼器与磁流变阻尼器约束体系等一系列新技术。

Tianxingzhou Bridge, serving as the common river-crossing passageway of National Railway Network, Beijing-Guangzhou High-speed Railway and Expressway of Wuhan Urban Third Ring, is the first bridge for high-speed railway over the Yangtze River in China. It is the first highway-railway bridge constructed in the standard of four railway lanes and six highway lanes in the world. The main bridge consists of five spans with two main pylons, three cable planes and three main truss girders, which is an innovative structure form. The span arrangement is 98m+196m+504m+196m+98m. As a railway bridge, the design train speed is as high as 200km/h for standard design and 250km/h for the dynamic simulation design.

Semi-floating system was adopted for connecting the main pylon and girder. The main plate-truss composite girder consists of three main N-shaped trusses. The transverse dimension of the truss is 30m in the width and 15.2m in the height. The stayed cables in the three planes were anchored at the top chord of the three main trusses respectively. The highway deck was a combination of concrete slabs and steel orthotropic plates, so the load effect was shared by both steel trusses and the deck. The main reinforced concrete pylons were designed in reversed Y shape and is 190m tall. Zinc coated high strength steel wire bunches were adopted as stayed cables. The length of the longest cable is 271m and the maximum cable force is about 12500kN. The bored piles with a diameter of 3.4m were employed for the foundation of main pylons. The steel girders over the piers were assembled and the other parts were erected integrally.

To overcome the technical problems brought up by long span, heavy loads and high speed of trains, the new technologies such as composite structure combing steel and concrete deck and main trusses, viscous and MR dampers were introduced.

桥　名：天兴洲长江大桥	
桥　型：双塔钢桁梁斜拉桥	
主　跨：504m	
桥　址：湖北省武汉市	
完成日期：2009年	
设计单位：中铁大桥勘测设计院集团有限公司	
施工单位：中铁大桥局股份有限公司	
中铁十二局集团有限公司	
中交第二航务工程局有限公司	

Name: Tianxingzhou Bridge over the Yangtze River
Type: Double-tower steel truss girder cable-stayed bridge
Main span: 504m
Location: Wuhan, Hubei Province
Completion: 2009
Designer(s): China Railway Major Bridge Reconnaissance & Design Institute Co., Ltd.
Contractor(s): China Major Bridge Engineering Co., Ltd.
　　　　　　　　China Railway 12th Bureau Group Co., Ltd.
　　　　　　　　CCCC Second Harbor Engineering Co., Ltd.

上海长江大桥
Shanghai Bridge over the Yangtze River

　　上海长江大桥位于长江入海口，主航道桥为主跨730m的双塔双索面斜拉桥，单侧引桥长度700m，主桥跨径布置为92m+258m+730m+258m+92m=1430m，全宽分成两幅，单幅宽度17.15m，双向六车道高速公路并预留双线轻轨。

　　主桥塔梁间采用自主开发的黏滞阻尼器加刚性限位约束，以减小梁端位移，提高了轨道交通行车安全性。主梁采用分离式钢箱梁，全宽51.5m，梁高4m，标准节段长度为15m，分离钢箱梁之间由间距15m的钢横梁连接。索梁连接锚固采用锚箱式结构。箱梁顶板板厚16mm，纵向采用U形加劲，在轨道线下设两条倒T形加劲构造。钢箱梁采用Q345qD。斜拉索梁上索距15.0m，采用扭绞型平行钢丝斜拉索，最大索力超过10000kN，由409根标准强度1670MPa的φ7镀锌钢丝构成。主塔采用人字形钢筋混凝土结构，锚固采用钢锚箱，全高216.3m，采用C50高性能混凝土。主塔基础设60根φ3m（上段）~2.5m（下段）变截面钻孔灌注桩，桩长105m。主塔墩承台大型钢围堰采用整体制作、浮运吊装施工。

　　引桥采用钢—混凝土结合连续箱梁结构，每联分跨为90m+5×105m+85m。单幅结合箱梁由槽形钢梁与混凝土桥面板通过焊钉结合成整体，支点附近采用钢与混凝土组合底板；桥面板内配有横向预应力束。

　　每联结合梁纵向划分为7个整跨梁段，桥面板分块预制，钢梁单元工厂制造预制场组拼，施工采用先顶升中支点，后完成墩顶段桥面板结合，再降落支点的方案，使墩顶负弯矩段桥面板处于预压状态。

Shanghai Bridge over the Yangtze River is located at the estuary of the Yangtze River. The bridge consists of a 730m main span double-tower cable-stayed bridge with double cable planes and two 700m approaching bridges on both sides. Span arrangement of the main bridge is 92m+258m+730m+258m+92m. The width of the bridge is 34.3m and is divided into two equal parts. The bridge has six traffic lanes in dual direction with reserved light railways on two sides.

Constrains between the towers and girders are restrained by viscous dampers and rigid restraints to decrease girder displacements and improve safety. Separated steel box girders, with 51.5m width, 4m height and 15m length, are adopted and connected with steel diaphragms. The main girders are connected to towers with box-shaped anchorage. The thickness of top plate of box girder is 16mm and is longitudinally braced inside with U ribs. Two strips of T-ribs are used to brace under the light rail lanes. Q345qD is used for box girders. The regular distance between cables on girders is 15.0m. Twisted parallel strand stayed cables, composed of 409 ϕ 7 galvanized steel wires with standard strength 1670MPa and the maximum force of larger than 10000kN, were employed in the bridge. The main towers are herringbone-shaped concrete structure with 216.3m in height and C50 concrete applied. Steel anchor boxes are used in the anchorage zones. Each towers foundation has 60 bored piles with the diameters from 2.5m to 3m and 105m lengths. The steel cofferdam of the tower piers was constructed by floating cranes after integral fabrication.

The span arrangement of the approach bridge is 90m+5×105m+85m. The welded studs are used to connect the U-shaped steel girder with concrete deck. Steel-concrete composite bottom slabs are adopted in the vicinity of supports. Transverse prestressing tendons are arranged in the deck slabs.

The steel girders are prefabricated in full length of the span and the deck slabs are pre-cast in segments. During construction the steel girders are erected and connected first. Then the middle supports are jacked up and the pre-cast concrete slabs on piers are installed and connected to the girder. The middle supports are then lowered down to create compression in concrete slabs on piers.

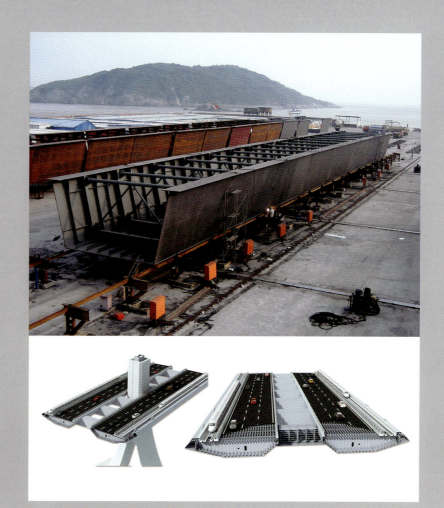

桥　　名：上海长江大桥
桥　　型：双塔钢箱梁斜拉桥
主　　跨：730m
桥　　址：上海市
完成日期：2009 年
设计单位：上海市政工程设计研究总院（集团）有限公司
施工单位：中交第二航务工程局有限公司

Name: Shanghai Bridge over the Yangtze River
Type: Double-tower steel box girder cable-stayed bridge
Main span: 730m
Location: Shanghai
Completion: 2009
Designer(s): Shanghai Municipal Engineering Design Institute (Group) Co., Ltd.
Contractor(s): CCCC Second Harbor Engineering Co., Ltd.

鄂东长江大桥
Edong Bridge over the Yangtze River

桥　　名：鄂东长江大桥
桥　　型：双塔混合梁斜拉桥
主　　跨：926m
桥　　址：湖北省黄石市
完成日期：2010 年
设计单位：中交公路规划设计院有限公司
　　　　　湖北省交通规划设计院
施工单位：中交第二公路工程局有限公司
　　　　　中交第二航务工程局有限公司

Name: Edong Bridge over the Yangtze River
Type: Double-towers steel and concrete hybrid girder cable-stayed bridge
Main span: 926m
Location: Huangshi, Hubei Province
Completion: 2010
Designer(s): CCCC Highway Consultants Co., Ltd.
　　　　　　　　Hubei Communications Planning & Design Institute
Contractor(s): CCCC Second Highway Engineering Co., Ltd.
　　　　　　　　　CCCC Second Harbor Engineering Co., Ltd.

鄂东长江公路大桥位于长江中、下游黄石市与黄冈市交界区域,是沪蓉高速公路湖北省东段和国家高速公路网大庆至广州高速公路在湖北东部跨越长江的共用过江通道。

鄂东长江公路大桥主桥为3×67.5m+72.5m+926m+72.5m+3×67.5m九跨连续半飘浮体系的双塔双索面混合梁斜拉桥,全长1476m。索塔采用凤翎外形,索塔基础采用直径2.8~2.5m变截面钻孔灌注桩。主梁为主跨钢箱梁与边跨预应力混凝土箱梁组成的混合梁,分离式双箱单室结构(PK断面)包括风嘴箱梁全宽38m,梁高3.8m。钢混结合段位于主跨侧,距索塔中心12.5m。

主梁钢混结合段创新地采用了后承压板+钢格室+PBL键部分连接填充混凝土的方式,在结合段钢箱梁端部设置了填充混凝土的钢格室结构,在钢格室腹板上设置开孔剪力键,孔洞中混凝土处于三面受力状态,提高了剪力键的强度和抗滑移性能。

钢混结合段1:2加载试验段
Testing segment of steel and concrete connection with the scal of 1:2

钢混结合段钢格室细部构造
Detail of the connecting segment between the concrete part and the steel part

Edong Bridge over the Yangtze River is located at the junction area between Huangshi City and Huanggang City in the middle and downstream reaches of the Yangtze River.

The main bridge is a double-tower cable-stayed bridge with double cable planes and hybrid girders, and it is a half floating system composed of nine spans, i.e., 3×67.5m+72.5m+926m+72.5m+3×67.5m. The towers have a special shape called "tail feather of phoenix" shape, and the foundations employ bored piles with varying diameters from 2.5m to 2.8m. The girder of the main span is steel box section and the girder of side spans is prestressed concrete box. All sections are separated double boxes with single cell and is 38m in width and 3.8m in height. The connecting segments of the steel boxes girders and the concrete girders are located near the main span, which is 12.5m away from the towers.

The connecting segments innovatively employ steel grids and PBL bolts with concrete fillet. In the steel box girders of the segment, steel grids filled with concrete were designed, and the axial forces, shear and moments are transferred by the bearing plates and the friction between PBL bolts and concrete.

荆岳长江大桥
Jingyue Bridge over the Yangtze River

荆岳长江大桥位于湖北、湖南两省交界处，大桥采用双向六车道高速公路标准建设，主桥桥面宽度38.5m。

主桥为100m+298m+816m+80m+2×75m的双塔单侧混合梁斜拉桥，采用半飘浮结构体系，在索塔、辅助墩、过渡墩处设置竖向活动支座，每个索塔处设4组纵向黏滞阻尼器。桥塔为H形混凝土桥塔。北边跨和中跨主梁采用扁平钢箱梁，在结合段中采用了前、后承压板的构造方式，主梁结合部与混凝土梁过渡段通过预制拼装进行结合，两者间通过剪力块传递剪力作用。南边跨采用了与中跨钢箱梁外形统一的预应力混凝土箱梁；北塔区和北边跨辅助墩、过渡墩墩顶压重区梁段采用整体式单箱三室断面。南北塔塔高不同，分别为224.5m和265.5m。

Jingyue Bridge over the Yangtze River is located at the junction area of Hubei Province and Hunan Province. It is designed according to the specification of six traffic lanes in dual direction highway with a 38.5m width.

The main bridge is a double-tower cable-stayed bridge with one side concrete steel hybrid spans. It consists of 6 spans, i.e., 100m+298m+816m+80m+75m+75m. The structure is a half floating system, with vertical supports at the towers, auxiliary piers, transition piers. There are 4 sets of viscous dampers at each tower to connect the girder. The main towers are H-shaped concrete structure with the height of 224.5m in north and 265.5m in south, respectively. The north side spans and the main span have flat steel box girders, while the south side spans have prestressed concrete box girders. Front and back bearing plates are used in the prefabricated joint segments, and shear forces are transferred by the shear blocks. The north tower, the north side auxiliary pier, and the transition piers have integral single box with three cells.

桥　　名：荆岳长江大桥
桥　　型：双塔混合梁斜拉桥
主　　跨：816m
桥　　址：湖北省荆州市
完成日期：2010年
设计单位：湖北省交通规划设计院
施工单位：四川公路桥梁建设集团有限公司

Name: Jingyue Bridge over the Yangtze River
Type: Double-tower hybrid girder cable-stayed bridge
Main Span: 816m
Location: Jingzhou, Hubei Province
Completion: 2010
Designer(s): Hubei Provincial Communication Planning and Design Institute
Contractor(s): Sichuan Road and Bridge Construction Group Co., Ltd.

宜宾长江大桥
Yibin Bridge over the Yangtze River

宜宾长江大桥也称菜园沱长江大桥，坐落于岷江、金沙江两江汇合口下游。大桥双向四车道，设计车速60km/h，桥面全宽22.5m。

主桥为半飘浮体系双塔双索面预应力混凝土斜拉桥，跨径布置为184m+460m+184m，基础采用钻孔灌注桩，矩形承台。索塔塔形为H形，南岸索塔高159.93m，北岸索塔高172.52m，设两道箱形横系梁。主梁采用分离式双箱断面，边跨密索段和索塔处零号段采用闭口箱形断面，单箱三室，全桥共152对斜拉索，平行索面布置。

采取大吨位拉压支座和边跨压重并举的措施，解决边、中跨比较小带来的困难。针对桥址区空气污染较重的问题，斜拉索采用了具有四重防护的环氧喷涂钢绞线。

桥　　名：	宜宾长江大桥
桥　　型：	双塔预应力混凝土斜拉桥
主　　跨：	460m
桥　　址：	四川省宜宾市
完成日期：	2010年
设计单位：	湖北省交通规划设计院
施工单位：	四川公路桥梁建设集团有限公司

Name: Yibin Bridge over the Yangtze River
Type: Double-tower PC girder cable-stayed bridge
Main Span: 460m
Location: Yibin, Sichuan Province
Completion: 2010
Designer(s): Hubei Provincial Communication Planning and Design Institute
Contractor(s): Sichuan Road and Bridge Construction Group Co.,Ltd.

Yibin Bridge over the Yangtze River, also called Caiyuantuo Bridge, is located at the lower reach of the Min River and the Jinsha River. It has four traffic lanes in dual direction with a 22.5m width and the design vehicle speed is 60km/h.

The main bridge is a double-tower prestressed concrete cable-stayed bridge with double cable planes, adopting a half floating system and arragnged as three spans of 184m+460m+184m. The foundations are rectangular footings with bored piles. The towers are H-shaped with the height of 159.93m in south and 172.52m in north, respectively. Two diaphragms with box sections are installed between tower legs. The main girder is generally in separate double boxes sections, while a single box section with three cells is adopted for the segment at the tower position and the segments with gathered cables in side spans. There are 152 sets of parallel cables in total.

Since the ratio of side span to main span is small, large tension compression bearings and side span weighting are used to resist the self-weight of the main span. The epoxy coated steel strands with four-layer protections are used to prevent the cables from air pollution.

上海闵浦二桥
The Second Minpu Bridge in Shanghai

桥　　名：上海闵浦二桥
桥　　型：独塔钢桁梁斜拉桥
主　　跨：251.4m
桥　　址：上海市
完成日期：2010年
设计单位：上海市城市建设设计研究院
　　　　　上海市隧道工程轨道交通设计研究院
施工单位：中铁大桥局股份有限公司
　　　　　中交第三航务工程局有限公司

Name: The Second Minpu Bridge in Shanghai
Type: Single-tower steel truss girder cable-stayed bridge
Main span: 251.4 m
Location: Shanghai
Completion: 2010
Designers(s): Shanghai Urban Construction Design and Research Institute,
　　　　　　　　Shanghai Tunnel Engineering & Rail Transit Design and Research Institute
Contractor(s): China Major Bridge Engineering Co., Ltd.
　　　　　　　　CCCC Third Harbor Engineering Co., Ltd.

上海闵浦二桥线路北起上海市沪闵路的东川路以北，沿沪闵路走向至西渡渡口跨越黄浦江，向南沿沪杭公路跨过西闸路后至规划大同路以南，桥位距下游的奉浦大桥1.7km。

大桥为公轨两用双层特大桥，上层桥面为二级公路，双向四车道，桥面宽度18m；下层桥面为双线轻轨（上海轨道交通5号线延伸段），标准线间距3.3m。

主桥为独塔双索面连续钢板桁结合梁斜拉桥，跨径为38.25m+147m+251.4m。主墩基础采用125根φ900钢管桩，索塔为H形钢筋混凝土结构，高148m。

主梁为钢板桁组合梁形式，主跨及锚跨（索塔与辅助墩之间）为三角形桁架，锚跨尾段（辅助墩与过渡墩之间）为N形桁架。桁高9.6m，主桁间距19.4m，标准节间长14.7m，桁梁弦杆和腹杆为箱形截面。上、下层桥面为钢正交异性板与纵、横梁组合形式。

The Second Minpu Bridge in Shanghai starts from north Dongchuan road of Shanghai Humin road and crosses Huangpu River along Humin road from west to east ferry, then goes to south Dadong road across Xizha road along south Shanghai-Hangzhou Highway. The bridge is located at 1.7m upstream away from Fengpu Bridge.

The bridge is a double-deck bridge for both highway and railway. The upper lever deck has four traffic lanes in dual direction as Class II motorway with a width of 18m, and the lower level deck has double rails (extension route of Subway Line 5) with 3.3m spacing.

The main bridge is a double cable planes cable-stayed bridge with a single tower and continuous steel plate-truss composite girders, arranged in three spans, i.e., 38.25m+147m+251.4m. There are 125 φ900 steel piles in the main foundation. The tower is H-shaped concrete structure with 148m in height.

The main girders have steel plate truss composite sections with triangular trusses at main span and anchorage spans, and N-shaped trusses at the end of anchorage spans. The trusses have 9.6m height with 19.4m space. Each segment is 14.7m long. Both chord members and web members employ box sections. Both of upper and lower decks are orthotropic steel plates connected to main girders and diaphragms.

郑州黄河公铁两用桥
Zhengzhou Highway and Railway Bridge over the Yellow River

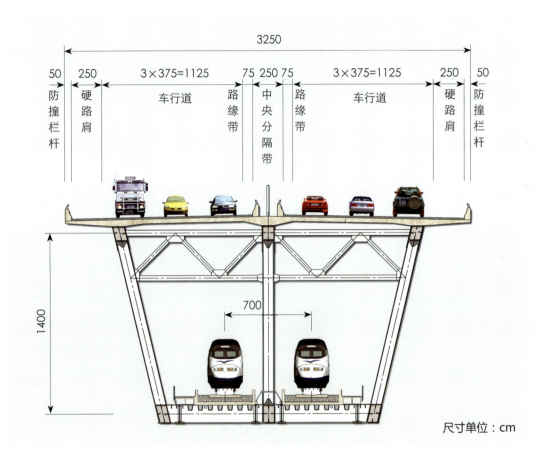

  郑州黄河公铁两用桥是铁路客运专线与一级公路共用桥梁。铁路为双线客运专线，速度目标值为线下部分350km/h，铁路设计活载为ZK活载；公路为一级公路，双向六车道，设计速度100km/h，设计荷载为公路－Ⅰ级的1.3倍。主桥采用六塔连续钢桁结合梁斜拉桥，跨度布置为120m+5×168m+120m，主桁采用三角形桁式，桁高14m，节间距12m。横向布置为三片桁，中桁垂直，边桁倾斜，首次采用两片边主桁倾斜的三片主桁结构。下弦桁间距8.5m，上弦桁间距12m。中主桁布置桥塔，桥塔采用钢箱结构，主塔立面布置为人字形，塔高37m。每个主塔布置有5对斜拉索。主桥上部结构采用多点顶推法施工。

Zhengzhou Highway and Railway Bridge over the Yellow River is a railway/highway bridge. The railway has two rail lines for passenger trains with the design speed of 350km/h and design live load of ZK. The highway has six traffic lanes in dual direction with the design speed of 100km/h and 1.3 times of Class I design live load. The main bridge is a six-tower cable-stayed bridge with continuous steel truss composite girders, which is composed of span length: 120m+5×168m+120m. The triangular trusses were used with 14m height and 12m spacing. In the transverse direction, there are three planes of trusses with vertical middle members and inclined side members. It is the first time to use two inclined main members of three-member trusses in China. The spacing between lower members is 8.5m and that for upper members is 12m. The towers are in herringbone shape with 37m in height and its section is steel box. There are 5 sets of cables for each tower. The superstructure was constructed with multipoint incremental launching method.

桥　　名：郑州黄河公铁两用桥
桥　　型：六塔钢桁结合梁斜拉桥
主　　跨：5×168m
桥　　址：河南省郑州市
完成日期：2010年
设计单位：中铁大桥勘测设计院有限公司
施工单位：中铁大桥局股份有限公司
　　　　　中铁七局集团有限公司
　　　　　中交第一公路工程局有限公司

Name: Zhengzhou Highway and Railway Bridge over the Yellow River
Type: Six-tower steel truss and concrete composite girder cable-stayed bridge
Main span: 5×168m
Location: Zhengzhou, Henan Province
Completion: 2010
Designer(s): China Railway Major Bridge Reconnaissance & Design Institute Co., Ltd.
Contractor(s): China Major Bridge Engineering Co, Ltd.
　　　　　　　　China Railway Seventh Group Co., Ltd.
　　　　　　　　CCCC First Highway Engineering Co., Ltd.

武汉二七长江大桥
Erqi Bridge over the Yangtze River in Wuhan

武汉二七长江大桥为双向八车道城市快速路桥，设计车速80km/h，桥面有效宽度为29.5m。主桥采用三塔双索面结合梁斜拉桥，跨度布置为90m+160m+616m+616m+160m+90m。斜拉桥采用半飘浮支承体系，中塔横梁顶设置竖向支座及纵向限位挡块；边塔横梁处设置双向活动支座，在边塔横梁两侧设置四套纵向阻尼装置。主梁采用I形结合梁，梁宽32.3m，桥梁中心线处梁高3.5m，混凝土板厚26cm。斜拉索为镀锌钢绞线拉索。斜拉索在主梁上采用锚拉板结构。全桥共264根拉索，索距13.5m，最大索力8000kN，拉索由79根镀锌钢绞线组成。桥塔为花瓶形钢筋混凝土结构，塔高均为209m。主塔墩均采用高桩承台钻孔灌注桩基础，3～5号墩基础分别由22根φ2.8m钻孔桩、18根φ3.4m钻孔桩、28根φ2.8m钻孔桩组成。该桥的建成刷新了多塔斜拉桥与结合梁斜拉桥跨度两项世界纪录。

Erqi Bridge over the Yangtze River in Wuhan is an urban freeway bridge with 29.5m in the width. It has eight traffic lanes in dual direction with the design vehicle speed of 80km/h. The main bridge is a cable-stayed bridge with three towers, double cable planes and concrete steel composite girders, arranged as six spans, i.e., 90m+160m+616m+616m+160m+90m. The structure is a type of half floating system. The middle tower has vertical supports and longitudinal movement restraint blocks on diaphragm, and each side tower has only vertical supports and four sets of longitudinal dampers on each side of diaphragms. The main girder employs I-shaped composite sections with 32.3m in width. The section depth is 3.5m at centerline of the bridge with 26cm concrete deck. There are 264 cables in total, each of which is composed of 79 galvanized steel wire cables. The cables are connected to girders with steel tensile anchorage plates with 13.5m spacing. The towers are vase-shaped concrete structures with 209m in height. The tower foundations are rise pile cap with bored piles.

桥　　名：	武汉二七长江大桥
桥　　型：	三塔结合梁斜拉桥
主　　跨：	2×616m
桥　　址：	湖北省武汉市
完成日期：	2011 年
设计单位：	中铁大桥勘测设计院集团有限公司
施工单位：	中铁大桥局股份有限公司
	中交第二航务工程局有限公司

（部分图片提供者：黄爱民）

Name: Erqi Bridge over the Yangtze River in Wuhan
Type: Triple-tower steel and concrete composite girder cable-stayed bridge
Main span: 2×616m
Location: Wuhan, Hubei Province
Completion: 2011
Designer(s): China Railway Major Bridge Reconnaissance & Design Institute Co., Ltd.
Contractor(s): China Major Bridge Engineering Co, Ltd.
　　　　　　　　CCCC Second Harbor Engineering Co., Ltd.

宁波清水浦大桥
Qingshuipu Bridge in Ningbo

宁波清水浦大桥是宁波绕城公路东段项目的控制性工程，大桥位于宁波市区东部，连接北仑区和镇海区，桥位距甬江出海口约10km，双向八车道高速公路。

主桥为五跨连续半飘浮体系，桥跨布置为54m+166m+468m+166m+54m，边跨位于岸上。主梁采用钢—混凝土结合梁，左右分幅，单幅主梁形式为双边钢箱＋预制混凝土桥面板。单幅主梁宽22m（不包括风嘴），梁高2.3m。索塔采用双菱形联塔，塔高141.5m。索塔采用群桩基础，每个承台下布置66根ϕ2.2m钻孔灌注桩，最大桩长123.5m。

混凝土桥面板采取综合防裂措施，一般措施有纵向预应力、梁端斜拉索采用钢锚箱锚固、预制桥面板至少存放6个月才能安装，特殊措施有预制桥面板采用C60聚丙烯纤维混凝土、湿接缝采用C60纤维素纤维混凝土，成桥后，桥面板上下表面采用硅化剂涂装。

Qingshuipu Bridge in Ninbo is located in east Ningbo City and connects Beilun District and Zhenhai District. It is 10km away from the sea estuary of the Yong River. The bridge has eight traffic lanes in dual direction.

The main bridge structure is a five spans continuous half floating system, i.e., 54m+166m+468m+166m+54m. The main bridge has two steel concrete composite girders. Each girder has double box section with precast concrete deck. Each girder has 22m in width and 2.3m in height. The towers are double-diamond shape with 141.5m in height. Each footing is supported by 66 ϕ 2.2m bored piles and the maximum length of piles is 123.5m.

To avoid cracks in concrete deck, the general measurements treatments are used, which include arranging longitudinal strands, using steel anchor box to anchorage cables on girders, and installing precast concrete deck after six months of casting. The special measures treatments include using polypropylene fiber C60 concrete for precast deck and fiber C60 concrete in wet joints, and painting silicification agent on the upper and bottom surfaces of concrete deck.

桥　　名：宁波清水浦大桥
桥　　型：四塔双幅结合梁斜拉桥
主　　跨：468m
桥　　址：浙江省宁波市
完成日期：2011 年
设计单位：浙江省交通规划设计研究院
施工单位：中交第一公路工程局有限公司

Name: Qingshuipu Bridge in Ningbo
Type: Four-tower twin steel and concrete composite girder cable-stayed bridge
Main span: 468m
Location: Ningbo, Zhejiang Province
Completion: 2011
Designer(s): Zhejiang Provincial Institute of Communication Planning, Design & Research
Contractor(s): CCCC First Highway Engineering Co., Ltd.

新疆果子沟大桥
Guozigou Bridge in Xinjiang

桥　　名：新疆果子沟大桥
桥　　型：双塔钢桁梁斜拉桥
主　　跨：330m
桥　　址：新疆维吾尔自治区伊宁市
完成日期：2011 年
设计单位：中国公路工程咨询集团有限公司
施工单位：中交第二航务工程局

Name: Guozigou Bridge in Xinjiang
Type: Double-tower steel truss girder cable-stayed bridge
Main span: 330m
Location: Yining, Xinjiang Uygur Autonomous Region
Completion: 2011
Designer(s): China Highway Engineering Consulting Group Co., Ltd.
Contractor(s): CCCC Second Harbor Engineering Co., Ltd.

新疆果子沟大桥为新疆G045线赛里木湖至果子沟口段公路改建工程的一座大型桥梁，位于果子沟与将军沟交汇处，桥面宽度26.93m，桥面距谷底约180m。

大桥为双塔双索面钢桁梁斜拉桥，跨径布置为170m+330m+170m，基础采用钻孔桩，哑铃形承台，主塔为阶梯形钢筋混凝土框架结构，塔柱采用单箱单室截面，采用C50 混凝土。主梁采用钢桁架，桥面板采用预制混凝土桥面板。斜拉索平面扇形布置，梁上索距12m，塔上索距2.1m。

果子沟大桥是新疆首座大跨度斜拉桥，为高寒、高震、高海拔及复杂风环境山区桥梁建设提供了新的思路，同时也为果子沟风景区增添了一道亮丽的人文景观。

Guozigou Bridge is located at the junction of Guozigou and Jiangjungou with 26.93m deck width and the deck is 180m high from valley bottom. It is a large bridge from Sailimu Lake to Guozigou highway of G045 line in Xinjiang Municipality.

It is a cable-stayed bridge with double-towers, double cable planes and steel truss girders, arranged as 3 spans, i.e., 170m+330m+170m. The foundation is dumbbell-shaped footing with bored piles. The main tower is a stepped-frame concrete structure with single box sections of C50 concrete. The concrete deck is precasted. The cables distribute in fan shape with 12m spacing on the girder and 2.1m spacing on the towers.

The bridge is the first cable-stayed bridge in Xinjiang, which provides novel ideas and concepts for building bridges in the mountain area with conditions of cold weather, frequent earthquake, high altitude and complex wind environment.

安庆长江铁路大桥
Anqing Railway Bridge over the Yangtze River

　　安庆长江铁路大桥是南京至安庆城际铁路和阜阳至景德镇铁路的重要组成部分，为四线铁路桥梁，两线客运专线，两线 I 级干线。宁安线设计时速 200km/h 以上，下游引桥 160km/h，预留 200km/h。桥梁设计荷载为两线中—活载，两线 ZK 活载。

　　越江主桥采用双塔钢桁梁斜拉桥，跨度布置为 101.5m+188.5m+580m+217.5m+159.5m+116m。大桥开工时为在建跨度最大的高速铁路桥梁，采用了包括：固定支座加阻尼器的结构支承体系、Q420qE 新钢种（部分）、三片主桁加劲梁结构、钢正交异性板整体铁路桥面、新型栓焊组合式双幅拉板索梁锚固结构、大吨位液压阻尼器等新技术。

The bridge is four-lane railway bridge with two lanes for high speed passenger lines and two lanes for Class I railway lines, which is the important part of urban railway between Nanjing and Anqing and railway between Fuyang and Jingdezhen. The design speed is 200km/h for Ningan line, 160km/h now but 200km/h for reserved condition for the approach bridge of lower reaches. The design loads include two-lane Class I load and two-lane ZK live load.

The main bridge across the Yangtze River is a cable-stayed bridge with double-towers and steel truss girder, arranged as 6 continuous spans, i.e., 101.5m+188.5m+580m+217.5m+ 159.5m+116m. The bridge used to be the largest span railway bridge during construction. It applied many new technologies including fixed bearings with dampers, new Q420qE steel materials, three-member main trusses with stiffened beams, integral orthotropic steel railway deck, double tension plates anchorage system with mixed bolting and welding, and large tonnage hydraulic dampers.

Name: Anqing Railway Bridge over the Yangtze River
Type: Double-tower steel truss girders cable-stayed bridge
Main span: 580m
Location: Anqing, Anhui Province
Completion: 2012
Designer(s): China Railway Major Bridge Reconnaissance & Design Institute Co., Ltd.
Contractor(s): China Major Bridge Engineering Co., Ltd.

嘉绍大桥
Jiashao Bridge

  嘉绍大桥是嘉兴至绍兴跨越钱塘江河口段的一座特大型桥梁，采用六塔斜拉桥结构，桥跨布置为 70m+200m+5×428m+200m+70m=2680m。索塔采用独柱形式，上部结构采用四索面分幅钢箱梁结构。单幅箱梁为栓焊流线型扁平钢箱梁，梁高 4.0m，单幅梁宽 24m，两幅梁间横梁长 9.8m，全幅总宽 55.6m。

  嘉绍大桥处于钱塘江河口的尖山河段，是钱塘江涌潮发展壮大的位置，桥址处河床宽浅、潮强流急、涌潮汹涌，最大涌潮潮高可达 3m，最大流速超过 7.5m/s；河床底质起动流速低，易冲易淤，深槽摆动幅度达到 2.3km 以上。嘉绍大桥设计采取了多项新技术，采用全新的多塔斜拉桥索塔造型和塔梁支撑体系：塔身独柱形，横梁采用 X 形空间托架，塔梁之间设置纵向双排支座。这种新型索塔和结构体系解决了采用小规模索塔来提高多塔斜拉桥主梁竖向刚度的关键技术难题。首次提出在多塔斜拉桥跨中位置设置释放轴向变形的"刚性铰"构造，科学合理地解决了多塔斜拉桥超长主梁温度变形问题。

Jiashao Bridge is a large bridge connecting Jiaxing and Shaoxing by crossing the Qiantang River. It is a six-tower cable-stayed bridge with span combination of 70m+200m+5×428m+200m+70m. The towers are single-column shape and the superstructure has four cable planes with two individual steel box girders. Each girder is the bolted and welded steel box with flat streamline section in shape. The height is 4.0m and the width is 24m with diaphragm spacing of 9.8m.

Jiashao Bridge is located in the Jianshan area of the mouth estuary of Qiantang River. The riverbed is wide and shallow with strong tide and rapid current. The maximum altitude of tide is up to 3m with speed over 7.5m/h. The bottom sediment speed of the riverbed is low, so it is easy to be scoured and deposited, and swing amplitude of the deep channel can be up to 2.3km. The new technologies adopted including: (1) It employed new support system for towers and girders. The multiple-tower cable-stayed bridge type has single-column towers, X-shaped braces in diaphragms, and double-row longitudinal supports between towers and girders. This new structural system solved the key issue of improving girder stiffness with small size towers; (2) It firstly presented to arrange rigid hinges to release axial deformation at the middle span, which solved the problem of the deformation due to temperature for extra-long girders.

桥　　名：嘉绍大桥
桥　　型：六塔钢箱梁斜拉桥
主　　跨：5×428m
桥　　址：浙江省绍兴市
完成日期：2013年
设计单位：中交公路规划设计院有限公司
施工单位：中交第二航务工程局有限公司
　　　　　广东省长大公路工程有限公司

Name: Jiashao Bridge
Type: Six-towers steel box girder cable-stayed bridge
Main span: 5×428m
Location: Shaoxing, Zhejiang Province
Completion: 2013
Designer(s): CCCC Highway Consultants Co., Ltd.
Contractor(s): CCCC Second Harbor Engineering Co., Ltd.
　　　　　　　　Guangdong Provincial ChangDa Highway Engineering Co., Ltd.

郴州赤石大桥
Chishi Bridge in Chenzhou

郴州赤石大桥为汝城至郴州高速公路中的一座大桥，桥址位于湖南省宜章县赤石乡渔溪村，设计车速80km/h，主桥全宽为28m。

主桥为四塔预应力混凝土双索面斜拉桥，跨径布置为165m+3×380m+165m。中塔采用塔墩梁固结体系，两边塔采用塔墩固结、塔梁半飘浮体系。主梁为预应力混凝土箱梁，主桥各塔均布置23对索，拉索纵向呈扇形布置；主塔为双曲线索塔，呈H形，最高主塔桥面至承台顶高185.7m，主塔总高达285.6m。

赤石大桥采用了空心薄壁索塔结构，外形美观。

Chishi Bridge in Chenzhou is a large bridge on the highway from Rucheng to Chenzhou. It is located at Chishi Town, Yizhang County, Hunan Province. The design speed is 80km/h, and the bridge width is 28m.

The main bridge is PC cable-stayed bridge with four-tower and double cable planes, and the spans are arranged as 165m+3×380m+165m. The main girder is PC box section. There are 23 pairs of cables which spread in fan shape along the bridge. The main towers are the H-shaped hyperbola towers with height of 285.6m and the deck is 185.7m above the foundation.

Chishi Bridge employs hollow thin wall tower sections, and looks very beautiful.

Name: Chishi Bridge in Chenzhou
Type: Four-tower PC girder cable-stayed bridge
Main Span: 3×380m
Location: Chenzhou, Hunan Province
Completion: 2013
Designer(s): Hunan Provincial Communication Planning and Design Institute
Contractor(s): China Railway Major Bridge Engineering Group Co.,Ltd.

九江长江大桥
Jiujiang Bridge over the Yangtze River

桥　　名：九江长江大桥
桥　　型：双塔混合梁斜拉桥
主　　跨：818m
桥　　址：江西省九江市
完成日期：2013年
设计单位：江西省交通设计院
　　　　　湖北省交通规划设计院
施工单位：中铁大桥局集团有限公司

Name: Jiujiang Bridge over the Yangtze River
Type: Double-tower steel and concrete hybrid girder cable-stayed bridge
Main Span: 818m
Location: Jiujiang, Jiangxi Province
Completion: 2013
Designer(s): Jiangxi Provincial Communcation Design Institute
　　　　　　　　Hubei Provincial Communcation Planning and Design Institute
Contractor(s): China Railway Major Bridge Engineering Group Co.,Ltd.

九江长江大桥位于九江阎家渡码头上游约1km处跨越长江，连接江西省九江市与湖北省黄梅县。大桥按高速公路双向六车道标准建设，主桥桥面宽38.9m。

主桥采用双塔双索面单侧混合梁斜拉桥，跨径组合为70m+75m+84m+818m+233.5m+124.5m。基础采用钻孔灌注桩，主塔为H形，设三道横梁，南索塔高230.854m，北索塔高242.308m，桥面以上塔高均为201.6m。主跨及北岸边跨主梁采用封闭式流线型扁平钢箱梁，南岸边跨采用单箱多室斜腹板等截面预应力混凝土箱梁，钢梁与混凝土梁的结合段设在主跨内距南塔32.5m处。斜拉索空间平行布置。

结合桥位要求，本桥采用了单侧混合梁、不对称高低塔的总体布置方案，边跨混凝土箱梁全宽38.9m，采用了顶、底板带有小次梁的整体式单箱三室结构。

Jiujiang Bridge over the Yangtze River is located 1km upstream from Yanjiadu Pier of the Yangtze River. It connects Jiujiang City, Jiangxi Province and Huangmei County, Hubei Province. The bridge is designed according to the standard of six traffic lanes in dual direction with a 38.9m width.

The main bridge is a cable-stayed bridge with double-towers, double cable planes and hybrid girders arranged as six spans, i.e., 70m+75m+84m+818m+233.5m+124.5m. The foundation employs bored piles. The main towers are H-shaped with three diaphragms, and the south tower is 230.854m in height and the north one is 242.308m. Both towers are 201.6m high above the bridge deck. The girders of the main span and north side spans is closed steel box section with streamline shape, while the girder of south spans is PC single-box multiple-cell section. The hybrid segment of the steel girder and the concrete girder is 32.5m away from the south tower in the main span. The cables spread in parallel.

The bridge employs the scheme which includes PC girders on one side and unsymmetrical towers because of the location requirements. The total width of the concrete girder at side spans is 38.9m, which uses three-cell single box section, and the flanges have small stiffening beams.

粉房湾长江大桥
Fenfangwan Bridge over the Yangtze River

桥　　名：粉房湾长江大桥
桥　　型：双塔双层钢桁梁斜拉桥
主　　跨：464m
桥　　址：重庆市
完成日期：2013年
设计单位：重庆市交通规划勘察设计院
施工单位：中国建筑股份有限公司

Name: Fenfangwan Bridge over the Yangtze River
Type: Double-tower double-deck steel truss girder cable-stayed bridge
Main Span: 464m
Location: Chongqing
Completion: 2013
Designer(s): Chongqing Communication Planning and Design Institute
Contractor(s): China State Construction Co.,Ltd.

粉房湾长江大桥位于重庆市江津区，是江津区连接重庆主城区的快速通道。大桥为公路与城市轻轨两用桥，上层为双向六车道公路桥面，下层为双线轻轨桥面。

大桥为双塔四索面双层公轨两用斜拉桥，跨径布置为216.5m+464m+216.5m。主桥钢桁梁采用桁架和正交异性桥面板组合体系。主塔采用矩形承台，下设9根直径3.0m的钻孔灌注桩。索塔采用墩塔固结的钢筋混凝土和部分施加预应力的混凝土结构，南北塔身结构形式和高度均相同，塔柱全高均为188.3m，拉索布置为扇形双索面，每塔单索面为14根，全桥拉索共224根。

粉房湾长江大桥建成通车后，可缩短江津城区至重庆主城距离17km。

Fenfangwan Bridge over the Yangtze River is located at Jiangjin District, Chongqing City, which is on the expressway connecting Jiangjin District and Chongqing. The bridge is used for both highway and light rails, the upper lever of the bridge has six traffic lanes in dual direction and the lower lever is for two light rails.

The bridge is a cable-stayed bridge with two towers and four cable planes, arranged as three spans, i.e., 316.5m+464m+216.5m. The main bridge employs the system of steel truss girders and orthotropic steel deck. The foundations of the main towers use rectangular pile cap with 9 ϕ 3m bored piles. The towers and girders are reinforcement concrete and prestressed concrete structures, and fixed each other. Both the north tower and the south tower have the same height of 188.3m. There are 224 cables seperate in two fan planes that each plane of each tower has 14 cables.

The bridge can shorten a distance of 17km between Jiangjin District and Chongqing.

宁波甬江铁路大桥
Ningbo Railway Bridge over the Yong River

宁波甬江铁路大桥位于浙江省宁波市,桥址处主河槽宽180m,下游64.8m处有已建成通车的主跨468m宁波绕城公路叠合梁斜拉桥。

主桥采用53m+50m+50m+66m+468m+66m+50m+50m+53m钢箱混合梁斜拉桥,半飘浮体系。混凝土主梁伸入中跨24.5m,其余中跨采用钢箱主梁。混凝土主梁采用支架逐孔现浇施工,钢箱主梁采用节段吊装。钢—混结合段采用阶梯状填充混凝土前后承压板式钢—混接头,整个结合段长14.05m。斜拉索采用平行钢丝拉索,空间双索面扇形布置,全桥共100对。索塔采用钻石形结构,全高177.9m,内置式钢锚箱。索塔桩基础采用直径3m的钻孔灌注桩,最大桩长132.5m,首次在铁路大直径超长桩中采用桩端后压浆技术。

Ningbo Railway Bridge over the Yong River is located in Ningbo, Zhejiang Province and serves as the railway hub. It is known as the first and largest railway cable-stayed bridge in the world with hybrid box girders. There is a 468m highway cable-stayed bridge with composite beams in operation downstream of 64.8m.

The width of river channel at the location of the bridge is 180m, and the span arrangement of the bridge is 53m+50m+50m+66m+468m+66m+50m+50m+53m. The bridge structure adopts semi-floating system. 100 pairs of parallel wire stayed cables are arranged in spatial double cable planes. The pylon is designed in diamond shape with a height of 177.9m. Steel anchorage box is installed inside the pylons.

Both steel and concrete box girders are adopted in the main span, with 24.5m concrete girder at both ends and 419m steel girder in the middle. For the 14.05m joint segment, filling concrete in stepladder shape, together with bearing plates, are adopted.

A cast-in-place construction method on falsework is introduced for the concrete girder, and a segmental lifting method for steel girder. Bored piles with diameters of 3m, among which the longest is 132.5m, are adopted as the pylon foundations. It is the first adoption of pile-end grouting technology in large-diameter and super-long railway piles.

Name: Ningbo Railway Bridge over the Yong River
Type: Double-tower steel and concrete hybrid girder cable-stayed bridge
Main span: 468m
Location: Ningbo, Zhejiang Province
Completion: 2013
Designer(s): China Railway Siyuan Survey and Design Group Co., Ltd.
Contractor(s): China Tiesiju Civil Engineering Group Co., Ltd.

台州椒江二桥
The Second Jiao River Bridge in Taizhou

台州椒江二桥位于浙江省台州市东部临海市和椒江区境内，在椒江口老鼠屿处跨越椒江，路线全长8.22km，双向六车道公路。

主桥跨径布置为70m+140m+480m+140m+70m=900m。台风和淤泥质覆盖层厚度大是本桥两大技术难点：台风是本桥所在区域重大灾害性气象要素，桥梁设计基本风速为45m/s，本桥首次采用半封闭钢箱结合梁，即带风嘴流线型边箱与混凝土顶板结合的结合梁，主梁含风嘴全宽42.5m，中心线处高度3.5m。与以往结合梁斜拉桥的施工工艺不同，本桥施工采用先预制钢混结合节段，后整体安装的施工工法。桥位基岩埋藏深度达120~135m，覆盖层中淤泥质土厚度约46m，通过比较嵌岩端承桩、摩擦桩和沉井三种基础形式，最后采用嵌岩端承桩，每个索塔基础采用30根2.5~2.8m变直径端承嵌岩钻孔灌注桩基础，最大桩长达139m。

The Second Jiao River Bridge in Taizhou, Zhejiang Province, is located at Linhai and Jiaojiang districts. The whole route is 8.22km with six traffic lanes in dual direction.

The main bridge is composed of five spans, i.e., 70m+140m+480m+140m+70m. There are technical difficulties, typhoon and thick silt covers. For the bridge construction, typhoon is the main catastrophic phenomena. The design wind speed of the bridge is 45m/s. The bridge is the first one in China to employ semi-close composite steel box girders that have concrete deck and streamlined side box with wind nose. The girder with wind nose is 42.5m wide and 3.5m high in bridge centerline. The composite girders are prefabricated and then installed integrally. The bedrock is 120m to 135m below the ground surface, and the thickness of silt in the cover is about 46 m. Compared with rock-end bearing piles, friction piles and caissons, the rock-end bearing piles are used for the foundations. Each tower foundation has 30 piles with diameters between 2.5m and 2.8m, and the maximum length of pile is 139m.

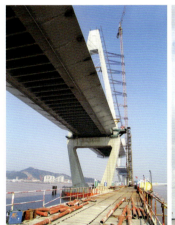  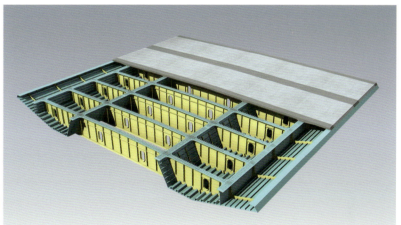

Name: The Second Jiao River Bridge in Taizhou
Type: Double-tower steel and concrete composite girder cable-stayed bridge
Main span: 480m
Location: Taizhou, Zhejiang Province
Completion: 2013
Designer(s): Tongji Architectural Design (Group) Co., Ltd.
  Taizhou City Traffic Investigation and Design Institute
Contractor(s): CRBC International Co., Ltd.
  CCCC First Highway Engineering Co., Ltd.

第四篇　拱式桥
Chapter 4　Arch Bridges

引言

拱桥是我国最常见的桥型之一，已有两千年以上的建造历史。公元605年隋朝工匠李春所建造的赵州桥，是一座敞肩拱桥（今称空腹拱桥），被英国李约瑟博士列为中国26项重大发明之一，成为古代中国桥梁的传世典范。

改革开放以前，由于钢材匮乏，造价经济的石拱桥、混凝土拱桥是公路桥梁广泛采用的桥型。1990年主跨120m的湖南乌巢河大桥仍采用可以就地取材的石拱桥，1997年在山西晋城又建造了跨度146m的丹河桥，但此时大跨度石拱桥建造已很不经济且施工难度增大，不宜为追求跨度纪录而继续发展。

20世纪90年代，一种用料省、造价低、施工简便的新型拱桥——钢管混凝土拱桥开始兴起，并迅速在全国各地推广，从最初跨度仅115m的四川旺苍桥不断增大至主跨360m的广州丫髻沙大桥，还创造了利用钢管混凝土拱为劲性骨架，再立模浇筑钢筋混凝土的箱形拱桥的施工工艺，成功建造了主跨420m的重庆万州长江大桥。然而，钢管混凝土拱桥在构造、施工、养护、力学性能分析方面也逐渐暴露出一些问题，影响结构耐久性，需研究解决。

进入21世纪以来，拱桥的跨越能力、结构体系、建筑材料和施工技术得到了快速发展。近十年来，我国修建了十多座跨度超过400m的大跨度拱桥，包括550m的上海卢浦大桥（2003年）和552m的重庆朝天门长江大桥（2009年）；结构体系出现了梁和拱、刚构和拱等多种不同组合结构的拱桥体系，系杆拱桥中以钢缆拉索代替桥面系梁作为平衡拱肋主要推力的技术，促进了大跨度系杆拱桥的应用；建筑材料上，近年修建了多座大跨钢箱拱、钢桁拱桥，钢管混凝土拱桥经过不断改进仍继续发挥作用，并且开始使用高强度等级（C80）混凝土；施工技术方面，无支架施工技术、拱肋的竖转加平转施工技术和大段拱肋浮运顶升施工技术的采用，促进了复杂地形和困难水域地区大跨度拱桥的应用。值得一提的是拱桥也是近年修建高速铁路桥梁的主要桥型之一，如宜万铁路宜昌长江大桥为混凝土连续刚构和钢管混凝土拱组合桥，由于拱梁组合桥梁竖向刚度大，能满足大跨度桥梁高速行车的要求，又有施工方便等优点，这种桥型在随后我国高速铁路中等跨度桥梁建设中得到广泛采用。

应当指出的是，在我国西部山区地形和地质条件有利时，拱桥仍应是主要考虑桥型。当前中国有一些跨谷桥为追求跨度纪录，或者由于设计者的错误理念，在适合修建拱桥的地方，选择了不合理、不经济的其他桥型方案，这是需要总结和反思的。

本画册中入选的拱桥有18座，仅次于斜拉桥，包括7座钢管混凝土拱桥，5座钢箱拱桥，5座钢桁拱桥和1座混凝土箱拱桥。上海卢浦大桥、重庆菜园坝长江大桥、南京大胜关铁路桥是21世纪初中国拱桥的杰出代表，得到了国际同行的赞许。

Introduction

Arch bridges are the most common type of bridge in China. The Zhaozhou Bridge, which was built in 605 by Lichun, a craftsman in the Sui Dynasty, is an open spandrel arch bridge. This bridge is regarded by Dr. Joseph Lee as one of the 26 major Chinese inventions, and has come to epitomize the technological achievements of ancient China.

Before the reform and opening-up policy of 1978, stone, plain concrete and reinforced concrete were widely used to build arch bridges for highways due to the lack of steel in China. Stone was still used up to 1990 as a major material in arch bridge construction. The Wuchao River Bridge in Hunan Province, which broke the record for masonry arches with a main span of 120m, was thought to be the last major stone arch bridge in the world. This record was broken in 1997, however, by the 146m masonry span of the Danhe River Bridge in Jincheng, Shanxi Province. Although the cost of stone bridges is low, their construction presents significant risks relative to other materials. Thereafter, it is not appropriate to construct large-span stone arch bridges for the purpose of breaking the world record.

In the 1990s, a new type of arch bridge, the concrete-filled steel tubular arch, gained popularity due to its lower cost and ease of construction. This type of bridge soon spread widely across China. The span of this newer type of bridge has increased from the 115m span of the Wangcang Bridge in Sichuan to the 360m span of the Yajisha Bridge in Guangzhou. The 420m span of the Wanzhou Bridge in Chongqing was built using a concrete-filled steel tube as a pilot truss upon which was cast an outer layer of reinforced concrete. In spite of these successes, concrete-filled steel tubular arches have exhibited problems related to construction, maintenance, and structural behaviour which give rise to concerns regarding long-term performance. These problems require further study.

In the 21st century, rapid developments in structural systems, materials, and methods of construction led to further increases in span length. In the recent decade, more than 10 arch bridges have been built with spans greater than 400m, including the Lupu Bridge in Shanghai with a main span of 550m and the Chaotianmen Bridge in Chongqing with a main span of 552m. Several structural systems were developed, including continuous steel truss arch combined with a truss, steel arch combined with rigid frame, and concrete-filled steel tubular arch combined with continuous girder. The use of steel cables to replace tie beams in tied arches has improved the application of long span tied arch bridges in regions of flat topography. Many long span steel box arch bridges and steel truss arch bridges have been built, and concrete-filled steel tube arch bridges are still in use with constant improvements. High-strength concrete such as C80 has come into use. Arch bridges are also widely used for high-speed railway bridges with moderate spans, such as the Yichang Bridge over the Yangtze River, which is an arch bridge with a continuous rigid frame combined with concrete-filled steel tube. The vertical stiffness of the arch-beam system in long span bridges is high enough to satisfy the requirement for high speed trains. Given its relative ease of construction, this type of arch bridge has become widely used for high-speed railway bridges with moderate spans in China.

In the western regions of China, where the landform and geological conditions are favorable, arch bridges should still be chosen as the major bridge type. However, due to the misguided pursuit of record spans or a poor choice of structural concept, some bridges across valleys are incorrectly built as other types of bridges. These decisions should be the subject of careful review and reflection.

Eighteen arch bridges have been selected for this chapter. This number is second only to cable-stayed bridges in this book. There are seven concrete-filled steel tubular arch bridges, five steel box arch bridges, five steel truss arch bridges, and one concrete box rib arch bridge. The collection includes the Lupu Bridge, the Caiyuanba Bridge in Chongqing, and the Dashengguan Railway Bridge, three outstanding representatives of arch bridges in China in the early 21st century that have earned worldwide recognition.

卢浦大桥
Lupu Bridge

卢浦大桥是一座横跨上海黄浦江的大跨径钢箱拱肋中承式拱桥，西岸与南北高架相连，东岸与外环线相通。大桥采用双向六车道标准，桥面使用宽度29.8m，桥下通航净空46m×340m。

主桥全长750m，为100m+550m+100m中承提篮式陀螺形钢箱拱，拱肋平面倾斜度1:5，矢高100m，矢跨比为1/5.5，拱肋单箱宽5m，箱高从跨中6m增加到拱脚9m，桥面以上部分的两片拱肋之间由25道一字形风撑连接，桥面以下由8道K形风撑连接。主梁采用正交异性桥面板钢箱梁，主跨为分离双箱，边跨为单箱多室，主梁通过吊杆或立柱支撑在拱肋上。全桥共28组吊杆，每组4根，拱上立柱8对。恒载水平推力由设置在主梁两侧钢箱梁内的32根水平拉索承担，拉索锚固于边跨尾端。

边跨拱肋、加劲梁及主跨桥面以下拱肋采用满堂支架拼装，形成锚孔，采用临时塔悬臂吊装主梁以上的拱肋，主拱合龙后张拉临时水平拉索，利用吊杆节段拼装主跨加劲梁，主梁合龙后将临时水平拉索转换为箱梁内的永久拉索，形成系杆拱。

卢浦大桥除合龙段拱肋采用一端栓接、一端焊接外，其余拱肋、立柱和加劲梁均采用焊接连接。

Lupu Bridge is a tied arch bridge with steel arch ribs over the Huangpu River in Shanghai, connecting the North-South Viaduct on the west bank and the Outer Ring Road on the east bank. It has six traffic lanes in dual direction and the navigation clearance is 46m×340m.

The span arrangement of Lupu Bridge is 100m+550m+100m, totally 750m. The arch rise is 100m, and the rise-to-span ratio is 1/5.5. The cross section of the arch rib is a steel box with spiral changes along the axis, and the inclination of the arch plane is 1:5. The section width is 5m, and the depth rises from 6m at the crown to 9m at the springing. The two arch ribs are connected by 25 straight wind bracings above the deck and 8 K-shaped wind bracings below the deck. The main girder has a cross-section of steel boxes with orthotropic steel decks. The horizontal cables in the main girder are adopted to balance the horizontal thrust.

The side spans are constructed by the full scaffold method, and the main arch is temporarily supported by cables and towers. The horizontal cables are tensioned after the closure of the main arch.

桥　　名：卢浦大桥
桥　　型：中承式钢箱拱桥
主　　跨：550m
桥　　址：上海市
完成日期：2003 年
设计单位：上海市政工程设计研究总院（集团）有限公司
　　　　　上海市城市建设设计研究总院
施工单位：上海建工集团股份有限公司

Name: Lupu Bridge
Type: Half through steel box tied arch bridge
Main span: 550m
Location: Shanghai
Completion: 2003
Designer(s): Shanghai Municipal Engineering Design Institute (Group) Co., Ltd.
　　　　　　　Shanghai Urban Construction Design and Research Institute
Contractor(s): Shanghai Construction Group Co., Ltd.

巫山长江大桥
Wushan Bridge over the Yangtze River

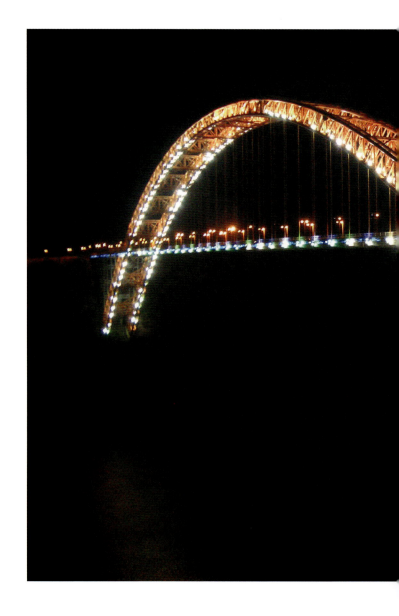

　　巫山长江大桥是一座中承式钢管混凝土拱桥，位于长江三峡段的巫峡入口处，连接重庆巫山和湖北建始两县，被称为"渝东门户桥"。桥长612.2m，由6×12m（引桥）+492m（主跨）+3×12m（引桥）组成，双向四车道，桥面净宽19m，通航净空300m×18m。

　　主拱由两片相互平行的钢管混凝土拱肋组成，净跨460m，拱高128m，矢跨比1/3.6。每片拱肋由4根弦杆和横联、竖联钢管组成的桁架构成，弦杆内灌注C60混凝土，肋宽4.14m，肋高由拱顶7.0m变化到拱脚14.0m。两拱肋中距19.70m，桥面以上设置K形横撑，桥面以下设置米字形横撑，均由钢管桁架组成。横梁均为预应力混凝土组合截面梁，桥面为简支变连续预应力混凝土π形梁。采用分离式钢筋混凝土拱座，置于稳定完整的弱风化基岩上。

　　大桥主拱肋采用临时索塔斜拉扣挂悬臂拼装，解决了吊装质量大、高度高、混凝土泵送困难的技术难题。

Wushan Bridge over the Yangtze River is a half through concrete-filled steel tubular arch bridge located in the entrance of Wuxia Gorge. The span arrangement is 6×12m+492m+3×12m with four traffic lanes in dual direction and the navigation clearance is 300m×18m.

The main arch ribs are made up of four parallel concrete-filled steel tubes with a rise-to-span ratio of 1/3.6. The width of the ribs is 4.14m and the height changes from 7.0m at the crown to 14.0m at the springing. The wind bracings are made up of steel truss with a K shape above the deck and a 米 shape below the deck. The deck is made up of PC slabs with π-shaped section and erected as simplify-supported structures and then converted to a continuous structure. The main arch ribs are constructed with the cantilever erection method with temporary cables and towers.

桥　　名：巫山长江大桥	**Name:** Wushan Bridge over the Yangtze River
桥　　型：中承式钢管混凝土拱桥	**Type:** Half through concrete-filled steel tube arch bridge
主　　跨：460m	**Main span:** 460m
桥　　址：重庆市巫山县	**Location:** Wushan County, Chongqing City
完成日期：2004 年	**Completion:** 2004
设计单位：四川省交通运输厅公路规划勘察设计研究院	**Designer(s):** Sichuan Provincial Transport Department Highway Planning, Survey, Design and Research Institute
施工单位：四川公路桥梁建设集团有限公司	**Contractor(s):** Sichuan Road & Bridge (group) Co., Ltd.

重庆万州长江大桥
Wanzhou Bridge over the Yangtze River in Chongqing

重庆万州长江大桥位于三峡库区的万州城区，是达万铁路与宜万铁路相连接的跨江节点工程。该桥主桥为三跨连续钢桁拱—桁梁组合结构铁路桥，跨径布置为168.7m+360.0m+168.7m，设计活载为中活载。

桥梁边跨为平弦钢桁梁，桁高16m，桁宽16m。中跨采用刚性拱柔性梁的新型桁拱结构，矢高59m，矢跨比1/6.1，采用H形截面刚性吊杆，间距12m。为解决吊杆的风振问题，吊杆腹板和翼板上均开设长圆孔。桥面系采用纵横梁体系，横梁高2.2m，纵梁高1.48m，两片纵梁间设置联结系。主跨两墩为10m×19m的矩形空心墩，墩高分别为54m及59m，基础分别采用钻孔桩基础和嵌入基岩的扩大基础。

万州长江大桥是单线、客货共线的大跨度刚性拱柔性梁的拱—桁梁组合结构，其刚度设计标准以及钢桁拱梁拼装中的合龙技术为同类桥梁修建提供了重要参考。

Wanzhou Bridge over the Yangtze River is located in Wanzhou, Chongqing City. The main bridge is a continuous steel truss arch and truss girder composite structure railway bridge with a span arrangement of 168.7m +360.0m+168.7m.

The girder in the side spans is a steel truss with a 16m width and a 16m height. The bridge is a rigid arch and flexible girder structural system, and the arch ribs are also steel trusses. The arch in the main span rises 59m and the rise-to-span ratio is 1/6.1. The suspenders have H-shaped sections. To avoid the wind-induced vibration, oblong holes with half-circle ends are added along the suspenders. The deck consists of the longitudinal and transverse beams.

The bridge is built for both passenger trains and cargo trains. Its design standard of the structural stiffness and the closure technique in the construction with the cantilever assembling method are referenced by subsequent bridges.

桥　　名：重庆万州长江大桥
桥　　型：中承式钢桁拱桥
主　　跨：360m
桥　　址：重庆市万州区
完成日期：2005年
设计单位：中铁大桥勘测设计院有限公司
施工单位：中铁大桥局集团有限公司
　　　　　中铁山桥集团有限公司

Name: Wanzhou Bridge over the Yangtze River in Chongqing
Type: Half through steel truss arch bridge
Main span: 360m
Location: Wanzhou District, Chongqing City
Completion: 2005
Designer(s): China Railway Major Bridge Reconnaissance & Design Institute Co., Ltd.
Contractor(s): China Railway Major Bridge Engineering Group Co., Ltd.
　　　　　　　　China Railway Shanhaiguan Bridge Group Co., Ltd.

广州新光大桥

Xinguang Bridge in Guangzhou

桥　名：	广州新光大桥
桥　型：	中承式刚架拱桥
主　跨：	428m
桥　址：	广东省广州市
完成日期：	2006 年
设计单位：	中铁工程设计咨询集团有限公司
	四川省交通运输厅公路规划勘察设计研究院
施工单位：	贵州省桥梁工程总公司
	中铁山桥集团有限公司

Name: Xinguang Bridge in Guangzhou
Type: Half through arch bridge with integral piers
Main span: 428m
Location: Guangzhou, Guangdong Province
Completion: 2006
Designer(s): China Railway Engineering Consulting Group Co., Ltd.
　　　　　　　Sichuan Provincial Transport Department Highway Planning, Survey, Design and Research Institute
Contractor(s): Guizhou Bridge Engineering Group Co., Ltd.
　　　　　　　China Railway Shanhaiguan Bridge Group Co., Ltd.

广州新光大桥为广州新光快速路上跨越珠江主航道的一座特大桥梁，主桥为177m+428m+177m的中承式三跨连续刚架钢桁拱桥，双向六车道，桥宽37.62m。

主跨矢高为104m，矢跨比为1/4，桁式拱肋上、下弦均为箱形断面。拱肋腹杆为H形截面。主跨桥面结构是由钢横梁、钢纵梁、钢筋混凝土桥面板组成的半飘浮式桥面系。大桥主墩处的三角刚构系梁采用实体矩形截面，斜腿为正拱，边拱的延续，斜腿中间部分为箱形截面。边跨系杆拱采用较重的钢筋混凝土桥面，产生较大的支承反力，使V形刚构能平衡推力。主墩基础施工采用了薄封底钢板桩围堰法，基础均采用嵌岩钻孔桩。

新光大桥主跨拱肋施工中采用了低位组拼、大段整体浮运、整体垂直提升方法架设施工，提升高度为85m，质量达3078t。

Xinguang Bridge over the Pearl River is located in Guangzhou, Guangdong Province. It is a half through three span continuous steel truss arch bridge with integral piers, with a span arrangement of 177m+428m+177m. The total width is 37.62m and designed for six traffic lanes in dual direction.

The rise of the arch in the main span is 104m and the rise-to-span ratio is 1/4. The deck in the main span is a composite structure, which is composed of longitudinal and transverse steel beams and reinforced concrete deck slabs. Reinforced concrete girders are used in the side spans to balance the weight of main span. The foundations of main piers are composed of bored piles and constructed with cofferdams. The arch ribs are assembled at a lower position and then vertically lifted to the proper elevation.

茅草街大桥
Maocaojie Bridge

茅草街大桥是湖南省 S204 省道跨越淞澧洪道、藕池河西支、南茅运河及沱江的一座特大桥。桥面为双向四车道，全宽 16m，通航净空 300m×18m。

跨越淞澧洪道的主桥为 80m+368m+80m 三跨中承式系杆拱桥。主跨拱肋矢高 71.2m，矢跨比 1/5，为钢管混凝土桁架拱肋。每片拱肋由 4 根弦管和横联、竖联钢管组成的桁架构成，内灌 C50 混凝土，肋宽 3.2m，高度由拱脚处 8m 变化到拱顶处 4m，拱肋间距 19.3m。边跨为钢筋混凝土拱肋。全桥共设置 14 道横撑，由空钢管桁架组成。桥面采用钢混结合梁，由钢横梁、钢纵梁、预制钢筋混凝土 π 形板组成，其上现浇铣削钢纤维混凝土及沥青混凝土铺装层。边跨、主跨拱脚均固结于拱座，在两边跨端部之间设置钢绞线系杆，通过边跨拱肋平衡主跨拱肋产生的水平推力。

主跨拱肋采用临时塔斜拉扣挂法施工，单肋单节段吊装，全桥共 60 个吊装节段，最大节段吊重为 70t。

Maocaojie Bridge is located in Hunan Province on the S204 highway. The bridge has four traffic lanes in dual direction with a total width of 16m and the navigation clearance is 300m×18m.

The main bridge is a half through tied arch bridge with a span arrangement of 80m+368m+80m. With a rise of 71.2m and a rise-to-span ratio of 1/5, each concrete-filled steel tubular truss arch rib in the main span has a width of 3.2m, a height of 8m at the spring and 4m at the crown, and is composed of four chords. The ribs in the side spans are made from reinforced concrete. There are fourteen transverse braces between the two ribs. The deck system combines steel longitudinal and transverse members and prefabricated reinforced concrete deck with a π shape. Steel strands are stretched and anchored at both ends of side spans to balance the thrust.

The arch ribs are divided into 60 segments and erected with temporary towers and stayed cables.

桥　　名：茅草街大桥	**Name:** Maocaojie Bridge
桥　　型：中承式钢管混凝土拱桥	**Type:** Half through concrete-filled steel tube tied arch bridge
主　　跨：368m	**Main span:** 368m
桥　　址：湖南省益阳市	**Location:** Yiyang, Hunan Province
完成日期：2006年	**Completion:** 2006
设计单位：四川省交通运输厅公路规划勘察设计研究院	**Designer(s):** Sichuan Provincial Transport Department Highway Planning, Survey, Design and Research Institute
施工单位：四川路桥建设股份有限公司	**Contractor(s):** Sichuan Road & Bridge Construction Co., Ltd.

东平大桥
Dongping Bridge

东平大桥位于佛山市禅城区南部，是跨越东平河的城市主干道桥梁，双向八车道，桥面设计宽度48.6m。

主桥是一座钢筋混凝土连续梁—中承式钢箱拱协作体系拱桥，主跨跨径300m、边跨跨径95.5m。拱圈竖向由主、副拱肋组成，主跨主拱肋计算跨径292.9m，矢跨比1/4.55，副拱位于桥面以上，连接拱顶和边跨悬臂端，在悬臂转体施工时承担拉力。主、副拱均采用箱形截面，横桥向三道拱肋。主拱肋截面高3.0~7.2m，宽1.2m；副拱肋截面高为2.0m，宽1.2m。三片拱肋间共设置14道异形管横撑。边跨箱形拱肋内灌注C40混凝土压重。桥面梁由主、次纵梁和主、次横梁组成梁格，梁格上设置8mm厚钢板，再现浇12cm厚钢纤维混凝土，形成钢—混凝土组合桥面板。吊杆为镂空的H型钢刚性吊杆。

主跨主拱肋采用卧拼竖提转体方法拼装，完成后的主拱、副拱及边拱形成自平衡体系，再通过平面转体合龙两个半拱。

Dongping Bridge is located in Foshan, Guangdong Province. It is a composite structural system with a continuous girder and a steel box arch. The span arrangement is 95.5m+300m+95.5m and the width is 48.6m designed for eight traffic lanes in dual direction.

The main arch comprises three ribs. Each rib consists of the main and sub arch limbs with steel box cross sections. The main-arch limbs in the main span are half through catenary arches with fixed ends. The sub-limbs linking the arch crown and the bridge ends are above the deck and subjected to the tensile force during the swing construction. Fourteen transverse braces are installed between the three arch planes. The deck system is a composite structure composed of longitudinal and transverse beams and steel fiber reinforced concrete slabs. The suspenders are made with H-shaped profiled bars.

The main arch ribs are assembled on the ground and swing vertically to form a balanced cantilever, then the two cantilevers swing horizontally to form the final arch.

Name: Dongping Bridge
Type: Half through steel box tied arch bridge
Main Span: 300m
Location: Foshan, Guangdong Province
Completion: 2006
Designer(s): Sichuan Provincial Transport Department Highway Planning, Survey, Design and Research Institute
Contractor(s): Road and Bridge Southern China Engineering Co., Ltd.
　　　　　　　　Shanghai Tongxin Mechanical & Electrical Control Technology Co., Ltd.

太平湖大桥
Taiping Lake Bridge

桥　　名：太平湖大桥
桥　　型：中承式钢管混凝土拱桥
主　　跨：336m
桥　　址：安徽省黄山市
完成日期：2006年
设计单位：安徽省交通规划设计研究院有限公司
施工单位：广西壮族自治区公路桥梁工程总公司

Name: Taiping Lake Bridge
Type: Half through concrete-filled steel tube arch bridge
Main Span: 336m
Location: Huangshan, Anhui Province
Completion: 2006
Designer(s): Anhui Tramsport Consulting & Design Institute Co., Ltd.
Contractor(s): Guangxi Road & Bridge Engineering Corporation

　　太平湖大桥位于安徽省黄山区太平湖柳家梁峡谷风景区，跨越太平湖，为双向四车道高速公路桥梁，桥宽 30.8m。

　　主桥采用中承式钢管混凝土提篮拱桥，主拱跨径 336m，矢高 68m，矢跨比 1/4.94。拱肋为等宽度变高度、矩形截面的钢管混凝土桁架结构。拱肋截面宽 3.0m，高度从拱顶 7.28m 变化到拱脚 11.28m。单片拱肋采用 4 根内填混凝土的钢管组成上下弦管，弦管之间由钢腹管相连。全桥拱肋之间共设 24 道横撑，其中桥面以上为 X 形横撑，桥面以下为背靠背 K 形横撑。主桥桥面系为整体漂浮体系，桥面横梁采用工字形钢梁，纵梁采用混凝土 π 形梁。拱座基础采用分离式明挖扩大基础。

　　钢管桁架主拱肋采用悬臂扣索法拼装施工。在施工中成功解决了提篮拱空中姿态调整的技术难题，变双肋吊扣为单肋吊扣，大大降低了起吊重量。

Taiping Lake Bridge is located in the scenic area of Taiping Lake, Huangshan, Anhui Province. The bridge is 30.8m wide and designed for four traffic lanes in dual direction.

The bridge is a half through concrete-filled steel tube arch bridge. The main arch spans 336m and rises 68m. The rise-to-span ratio is 1/4.94. The width of arch rib section is 3.0m and the height varies from 7.28m at the crown to 11.28m at the springing. Each rib is made up of four steel tube chords. Twenty-four transverse braces are installed with X shape above the deck and K shape below the deck. The main girder is a whole floating system with longitudinal and transverse beams and π-shaped deck. The foundation is a spread foundation.

The arch is erected by the cantilever method with temporary tower and stay cables. With the improvement of lifting technique, the leaned arch ribs are lifted and anchored separately to reduce the lifting force.

菜园坝长江大桥
Caiyuanba Bridge over the Yangtze River

　　菜园坝长江大桥地处重庆市主城区中心地带，主桥是刚构、钢桁梁、提篮式钢箱系杆拱组合结构体系的拱式桥梁，全长800m，跨度布置为88m+102m+420m+102m+88m，上层设双向六车道加双侧人行道，桥面净宽30.5m；下层设双线城市轻轨，桥面净宽8.6m。

　　边跨采用Y形刚构，由前后悬臂、主横梁、前后次横梁、前后主横梁及系杆索锚固件等组成。刚构前悬臂为10m×6m～5.2m×3.6m的变截面空心薄壁结构，从前悬臂顶缘中心向下15m长为实心构造；刚构后悬臂为10m×6m～4m×3.6m的变截面空心薄壁结构，从后悬臂顶缘中心向下10m长为实心构造。

　　主跨为提篮拱结构，系梁跨度320m，矢高为56.44m，主拱肋内倾角为10.67°。主拱为宽2.4m、高4m的钢箱结构，拱肋之间设6道钢箱横撑。钢桁梁采用正交异性桥面板与桁架的组合结构，整体节点和整体节段设计。桁梁高11.2m，顶宽39.8m，底宽13m，标准节段长16m。主桥墩身采用14m×9m～12m×6.2m的变截面空心薄壁结构。

　　菜园坝长江大桥采用正交异性板钢桁梁整体节段安装技术，中跨系杆与边跨系杆分开设置，独立锚固，三套相对独立的拉索体系可在施工过程中及成桥后对大桥主体结构进行内力与线形的调整与控制。大桥造型简洁、刚柔共举。

Caiyuanba Bridge over the Yangtze River is located downtown of Chongqing. The main bridge structure is the combination of rigid frame, steel truss and steel tied arch bridge. The span arrangement is 88m+102m+420m+102m+88m. A double-layer deck is designed with six traffic lanes in dual direction on the upper deck and two light rail lanes on the lower deck.

The side spans of the bridge are two Y-shaped rigid frames. The main span is an X arch rising 56.44m. The arch ribs incline towards each other with an angle in relation to vertical line of 10.67°. The tie beam is 320m long. The width of the arch rib is 2.4m and the height is 4m. Six steel transverse braces with box sections are installed. The main girder is composed of orthotropic decks and a truss girder. The truss girder is 11.2m high and 39.8m wide at the top and 13m wide at the bottom.

The three tie beams in the side spans and the main span are anchored separately as three segments to control the deflection and internal force in the whole structure.

桥　名：菜园坝长江大桥
桥　型：中承式混合箱拱桥
主　跨：420m
桥　址：重庆市
完成日期：2007 年
设计单位：招商局重庆交通科研设计院有限公司
　　　　　林同棪国际工程咨询（中国）有限公司
施工单位：中铁大桥局集团有限公司
　　　　　中铁山桥集团有限公司

Name: Caiyuanba Bridge over the Yangtze River
Type: Half through hybrid box rib arch bridge
Main span: 420m
Location: Chongqing
Completion: 2007
Designer(s): China Merchants Chongqing Communications Research and Design Institute Co., Ltd.
　　　　　T.Y.Lin Engineering Consulting(China) Co., Ltd.
Contractor(s): China Railway Major Bridge Engineering Group Co., Ltd.
　　　　　China Railway Shanhaiguan Bridge Group Co., Ltd.

支井河大桥
Zhijinghe Bridge

支井河大桥位于湖北省巴东县野三关镇，是沪蓉国道主干线上的一座特大桥，桥梁全长 545.54m，跨越不对称 V 形支井河峡谷，桥面宽度 24.5m。

主桥为跨径 430m 的上承式钢管混凝土无铰拱桥，矢高 78.18m，矢跨比 1/5.5。主拱由两片平行布置的拱肋组成，拱肋是由 4 根钢管混凝土主弦杆和箱形钢腹杆组成的空间桁架，拱顶截面高度 6.5m，拱脚 13m，拱肋宽度 4m，两肋间距 13m，通过 20 道米字形横撑相连。主梁采用预应力混凝土连续小箱梁，横向八片梁，简支变连续。两岸拱座均位于悬崖上，采用整体式钢筋混凝土结构。

支井河大桥因受到施工空间及运输条件的限制，拱肋共分成 30 个节段，以小单元散件运抵现场，利用结点板高强螺栓连接后，采用"先栓后焊，栓焊结合"的连接方式组拼成整体。结合地形特点，大桥的吊装采用跨度 756m 的无塔缆索起重机进行。

Zhijinghe Bridge is located in Badong, Hubei Province. The bridge crosses the asymmetric V-shaped Zhijinghe Gorge, and it is 545.54m long and 24.5m wide.

The main span is a concrete-filled steel tubular arch bridge with a main span of 430m. The arch rises 78.18m and the rise-to-span ratio is 1/5.5. The arch is composed of two parallel ribs spaced 13m. Each rib is a spatial truss made up of concrete-filled steel tube chords and steel box web members. The width of the rib is 4m and the height varies from 6.5m at the crown to 13m at the springing. The integral RC arch abutments are supported on the cliff.

Limited by the construction space and the transportation condition, each arch rib is divided into 30 segments, and each segment is further divided into several members that can be conveniently delivered to the construction site. The members are connected with high-strength bolts and then are welded together. The lifting is finished by a unique cable crane without towers.

Name: Zhijinghe Bridge
Type: Concrete-filled steel tube arch bridge
Main Span: 430m
Location: Badong County, Hubei Province
Completion: 2008
Designer(s): CCCC Second Highway Consultants Co., Ltd.
Contractor(s): China Railway 13th Bureau Group Co., Ltd.

小河大桥
Xiaohe Bridge

　　小河大桥是沪蓉国道跨越峡谷的桥梁，位于湖北省恩施市。主桥采用上承式钢管混凝土拱桥。桥面距河底190m，全长504m，受所接隧道分幅布置制约，采用桥面结构分幅布置、主拱圈连为一体的设计思想，单幅桥面宽12.5m。

　　主拱肋计算跨径338m，矢高67.6m，矢跨比1/5。拱肋高度从拱脚处7.9m变化到拱顶处4.9m。每道拱肋由6根直径1100mm的钢管组成弦杆，内灌C60混凝土。全桥在拱肋间设置17道米字形横撑，每道横撑为空钢管桁架结构。拱上建筑为三联6×20m桥面连续空心板结构，为便于安装，拱上立柱也采用钢管混凝土结构，每个立柱由六根 ϕ450mm×10mm 钢管组成双排排架，内灌C50混凝土。主拱座为整体式钢筋混凝土结构，直接支撑在山体岩石上。

　　全桥采用缆索吊机吊装，拱肋采用临时塔斜拉扣挂悬臂拼装。

Xiaohe Bridge, located in Enshi, Hubei Province, is a deck type concrete-filled steel tube arch bridge. The distance from the deck to the bottom of the river is 190m. The total length of the bridge is 504m. The arch is integral, while the deck is divided into two parts to meet the need of connecting the adjacent tunnels directly. Each deck is 12.5m wide.

The arch spans 338m, rises 67.6m and has a rise-to-span ratio of 1/5. The height of the arch rib ranges from 7.9m at the springing to 4.9m at the crown. Each rib is a truss composed of six ϕ 1100mm steel tubular chords filled with C60 concrete. There are 17 lateral braces between the two ribs. Each column supported on the arch is a frame composed of six ϕ 450mm steel tubes.

All components of the bridge are lifted by a cable crane. The arch ribs are erected by the cantilever method with temporary towers and stay cables.

桥　　名：小河大桥
桥　　型：上承式钢管混凝土拱桥
主　　跨：338m
桥　　址：湖北省恩施市
完成日期：2008 年
设计单位：湖北省交通规划设计院
施工单位：中铁港航局集团第二工程有限公司

Name: Xiaohe Bridge
Type: Concrete-filled steel tube arch bridge
Main span: 338m
Location: Enshi, Hubei Province
Completion: 2008
Designers(s): Hubei Communication Planning & Design Institute
Contractor(s): The Second Co., Ltd. of China Railway Port Channel Engineering Group

朝天门大桥
Chaotianmen Bridge

朝天门大桥在重庆朝天门下游1.7km处的溉澜溪、青草坪之间横跨长江，是公轨两用特大跨江城市桥梁，全长4886m。主桥长932m，采用190m+552m+190m三跨连续中承式钢桁拱桥，双层桥面布置，上层为双向六车道和两侧人行道，下层中间为双线轻轨，两侧为双向2车道。

主桥采用三跨连续钢桁系杆拱结构，除北岸侧主墩设固定支座外，其余桥墩处均设纵向滑动支座，中墩的支座反力达到145000kN，采用铸钢球形铰抗震支座，其设计寿命100年。中跨钢桁系杆拱，矢跨比为1/4.3，两侧边跨为变高度桁梁，主桥宽度36.5m。中跨下层系杆内配置了体外预应力束，使上下水平系杆截面形式统一。桁架杆件采用Q420qD、Q370qD和Q345qD三种强度的钢材混合设计。中墩顶的主支承节点采用整体节点，以减小节点板的厚度。

钢桁梁从边墩开始利用临时墩拼装，到达主墩后，再悬臂拼装主跨拱圈，最后在跨中合龙，为保证成桥后的内力与线形达到一次落架状态，边墩高度、主墩支座位置在架设过程中均可调。

Chaotianmen Bridge over the Yangtze River is located 1.7km downstream from Chaotianmen in Chongqing. It is designed with double-layer decks. Its upper deck has six traffic lanes in dual direction, and the lower one has two light rail lanes in the middle and two traffic lanes on the two sides.

The main bridge is a three span half through steel truss tied arch bridge with a main span of 552m and two side spans of 190m. The whole structure works like a three span continues beam with fixed bearings on the top of the north main pier. The reaction force imposed on each bearing on the main pier is 145000kN. The truss made up of two truss planes is 36.5m wide. The arch has the rise-to-span ratio of 1/4.3. External prestressed cables are arranged in the lower chords of the deck truss in the middle span.

The truss girders in the side spans are erected by the cantilever method with auxiliary piers. The arch in the main span is assembled with the aids of temporary towers and stay cables. The level and longitudinal location of every bearing are adjustable during the erection process to control the internal force and deflection of the truss.

下层钢系杆内的水平预应力索
Longitudinal prestressing strands in the lower steel tie

桥　　名：朝天门大桥
桥　　型：中承式钢桁拱桥
主　　跨：552m
桥　　址：重庆市
完成时间：2009年
设计单位：中铁大桥勘测设计院有限公司
　　　　　招商局重庆交通科研设计院有限公司
施工单位：中交第二航务工程局有限公司

Name: Chaotianmen Bridge
Type: Half through steel truss arch bridge
Main Span: 552m
Location: Chongqing
Completion: 2009
Designer(s): China Railway Major Bridge Reconnaissance & Design Institute Co., Ltd.
　　　　　　　China Merchants Chongqing Communications Research and Design Institute Co., Ltd.
Contractor(s): CCCC Second Harbor Engineering Company Ltd.

南京大胜关长江大桥
Dashengguan Bridge over the Yangtze River in Nanjing

　　南京大胜关长江大桥主桥为六跨连续钢桁梁中承式铁路拱桥，全桥孔跨布置为108m+192m+336m+336m+192m+108m，桥宽40.4m，其中两孔336m的主跨为钢桁架拱式结构，其他孔跨为下承式连续钢桁梁结构。基础采用钻孔桩，主墩桩长102～112m，设计活载为六线铁路，包括两线高速铁路，两线快速客运专线，两线轻轨交通。

　　大桥横桥向为三片平面主桁结构，主桁间距2×15m。高速铁路、客运专线分别位于三片桁架组成的两个空间之中，轻轨则布置在两侧桁架外挑悬臂上。主跨桁拱拱顶处拱圈桁高12m，拱脚处拱圈桁高47.9m，桁拱矢跨比为1/4。主拱吊杆采用八边形截面钢制构件吊杆，具有较好的气动外形。边跨连续梁结构为等高桁梁，桁高16m，拱圈桁架与边跨连续桁梁均采用三角形桁式，节点纵向间距均为12m。行车桥面为采用闭口纵肋的正交异性钢桥面板结构，钢桥面板和主桁下弦杆焊接形成板桁组合结构以增强主梁竖向刚度。桥面板上现浇有150mm厚混凝土道碴槽，上覆6cm防水层，道碴槽板宽9.4m及9.8m，用焊接栓钉与钢桥面板结合。

　　南京大胜关长江大桥主桥在结构设计上具有高速、大跨、拱梁组合结构体系和多线荷载作用的特点。

Dashengguan Bridge over the Yangtze River in Nanjing is a six-span continuous steel truss half through railway arch bridge. The span arrangement is 108m+192m+336m+336m+192m+108m. The width of its deck is 40.4m including two high speed railway lanes, two passenger railway lanes and two light rail lanes. The two 336m main spans are tied truss arches, and the side spans are continuous trusses.

The bridge is composed of three main trusses, and the distance between two trusses is 15m. The high speed railway lanes and the passenger railway lanes are located in the spaces between the trusses, while the light-rail lanes are situated on the cantilever connected to the trusses. The arch cross section is 12m high at the crown and 47.9m at the springing. The rise-to-span ratio of the arch is 1/4. The height of the continuous truss in the side spans is 16m. All the arches and the continuous side spans are triangle type trusses. The longitudinal distance between every two joints is 12m.

This bridge is featured with the arch-beam composite structural system and the multi-lane railway load.

桥　　名：	南京大胜关长江大桥
桥　　型：	连续钢桁拱桥
主　　跨：	336m
桥　　址：	江苏省南京市
完成日期：	2009年
设计单位：	中铁大桥勘测设计院有限公司
施工单位：	中铁大桥局集团有限公司
	中铁山桥集团有限公司
	中铁宝桥股份有限公司

Name: Dashengguan Bridge over the Yangtze River in Nanjing
Type: Continuous steel truss arch bridge
Main span: 336m
Location: Nanjing, Jiangsu Province
Completion: 2009
Designer(s): China Railway Major Bridge Reconnaissance & Design Institute Co., Ltd.
Contractor(s): China Railway Major Bridge Engineering Group Co., Ltd.
　　　　　　　China Railway Shanhaiguan Bridge Group Co., Ltd.
　　　　　　　China Railway Baoji Bridge Group Co., Ltd.

巫山大宁河大桥
Wushan Bridge over the Daning River

桥　名：巫山大宁河大桥
桥　型：上承式钢桁拱桥
主　跨：400m
桥　址：重庆市巫山县
完成日期：2009年
设计单位：中交第二公路勘察设计研究院有限公司
施工单位：贵州省桥梁工程总公司
　　　　　国营武昌造船厂

Name: Wushan Bridge over the DaningRiver
Type: Steel truss arch bridge
Main Span: 400m
Location: Wushan County, Chongqing City
Completion: 2009
Designer(s): CCCC Second Highway Consultant Co., Ltd.
Contractor(s): Guizhou Bridge Engineering Group Co., Ltd.
　　　　　　　　Wuchang Shipbuilding Industry Co., Ltd.

巫山大宁河大桥位于杭州至兰州公路线中的重庆巫山至奉节段，桥梁全长681m。主桥主跨为400m上承式钢桁架拱桥，大桥设四车道，桥面净宽24.5m。

主拱净矢高80m，矢跨比1/5，大桥主拱肋采用三片等高桁架结构，桁高10m，桁架上下弦杆采用箱形断面，腹杆采用工字形或箱形断面，上下横联采用工字形断面。拱上立柱采用钢排架结构，横向三根立柱与三片桁架相对应，设横向交叉提高立柱稳定性。拱上立柱纵向间距27m，立柱采用钢箱结构。拱上桥面行车道结构采用跨径27m钢—混凝土组合的连续梁结构。

大宁河大桥拱肋由三片平面钢桁架拱肋组成，是全焊式特大跨度上承式钢桁架拱桥。

Wushan Bridge over the Daning River, located in Wushan County, Chongqing City, is a steel truss arch bridge with a main span of 400m. The total length of the bridge is 681m, and the width of the deck is 24.5m including four traffic lanes.

The arch has a net rise of 80m and a rise-to-span ratio of 1/5. The main arch rib is composed of three pieces 10m high steel trusses. The chords of each truss has a box shape section, while the web member has an I-shaped or box shape section, and the lateral bracing has a H-shaped section. The columns supported on the arch are composed of steel frames with box sections, and the longitudinal distance between every two columns is 27m.

Wushan Bridge over the Daning River is featured with three pieces fully welded steel truss arches.

宜万铁路宜昌长江大桥
Yiwan Railway Bridge over the Yangtze River in Yichang

  宜万铁路宜昌长江大桥位于湖北省宜昌市境内,主桥采用连续刚构柔性拱组合结构,桥跨布置为130m+2×275m+130m,该桥为双线铁路桥,设计荷载为中活载,设计车速为160km/h。

  主梁采用单箱双室预应力混凝土梁,箱梁中墩支点处梁高14.5m,边墩支点及跨中处高4.8m,外腹板为斜腹板,桥面宽14.4m。拱肋为钢管混凝土,计算跨径264m,矢高52.8m,矢跨比为1/5.0,两片拱肋中心距12.15m。吊杆顺桥向间距10m,每吊点设双吊杆,顺桥向布置。边主墩采用双薄壁墩结构,壁厚3.0m,实心截面;中主墩采用空心单柱墩,壁厚1.5m,墩高均为38.5m,基础均为钻孔嵌岩桩。

  大桥将连续刚构和钢管混凝土拱两种结构结合在一起,具有整体刚度大、施工方便等优点,是最近几年我国高速铁路桥梁建造广泛采用的一种桥型。

Yiwan Railway Bridge over the Yangtze River, located in Yichang, Hubei Province, is a composite structure of PC continuous bridge with integral piers and concrete-filled steel tube arch bridge. The span arrangement is 130m+2×275m+130m. The bridge has a two-line railway and the design speed is 160km/h.

The girder of the bridge is a double-cell single-box PC beam. The height of the girder is 14.5m at the main piers and 4.8m at the mid-span. The width of the deck is 14.4m. The stiffening arch spans 264m and rises 52.8m. The arch rib is composed of concrete-filled steel tubes. The distance between the two ribs is 12.15m and the longitudinal distance between every two suspenders is 10m. The central main pier is a single column with hollow sections, while the two side main piers are both double thin walls with solid sections.

This bridge has strong stiffness and the construction is convenient. This bridge type has been widely adopted in the high speed railways recently in China.

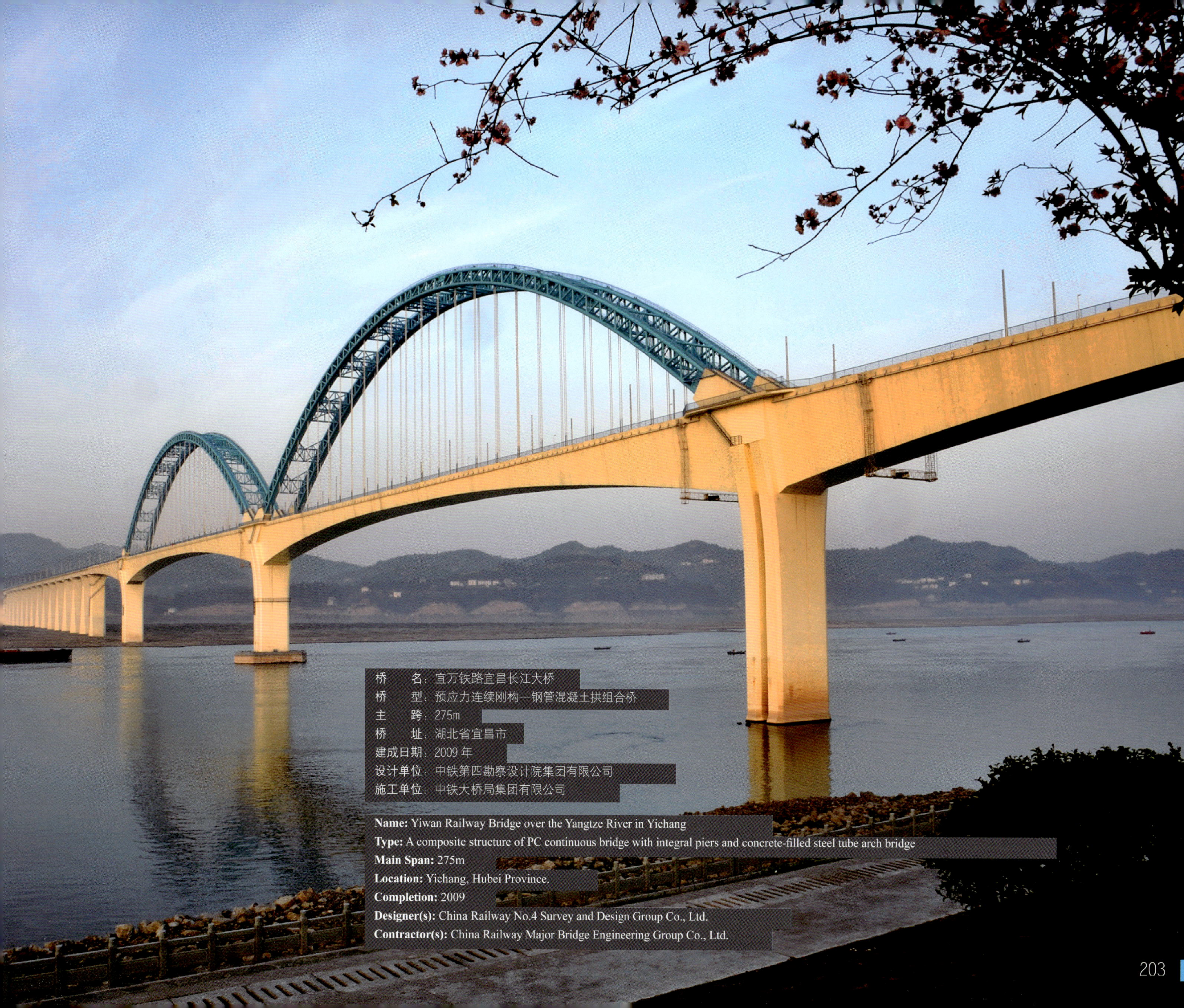

桥　　名：宜万铁路宜昌长江大桥
桥　　型：预应力连续刚构—钢管混凝土拱组合桥
主　　跨：275m
桥　　址：湖北省宜昌市
建成日期：2009 年
设计单位：中铁第四勘察设计院集团有限公司
施工单位：中铁大桥局集团有限公司

Name: Yiwan Railway Bridge over the Yangtze River in Yichang
Type: A composite structure of PC continuous bridge with integral piers and concrete-filled steel tube arch bridge
Main Span: 275m
Location: Yichang, Hubei Province.
Completion: 2009
Designer(s): China Railway No.4 Survey and Design Group Co., Ltd.
Contractor(s): China Railway Major Bridge Engineering Group Co., Ltd.

宁波明州大桥
Mingzhou Bridge in Ningbo

宁波明州大桥（东外环甬江大桥）是宁波市中心城快速路网跨越甬江的特大型桥梁，主桥采用中承式拱梁组合体系的双肢钢箱系杆拱桥，跨径布置为100m+450m+100m。大桥设双向八车道，桥宽45.8m，设计车速80km/h。

拱肋分为上、下两肢，为全焊矩形钢箱截面，上下肢结合段采用凸形断面，矢跨比为1/5。边跨拱肋与中跨拱肋保持在一个平面内，横向倾斜度为1:5。加劲梁采用正交异性桥面板全焊钢箱梁方案，边跨采用闭口断面，中跨采用开口断面。车行道部分桥面板厚14mm，采用U形加劲肋。其余部分桥面板、腹板、底板均采用球扁钢加劲肋。吊杆间距9m。主墩基础采用70根 ϕ1500mm 钻孔灌注桩。

宁波明州大桥是国内特大跨度钢箱系杆拱桥之一，外形上拱肋采用双肢造型，桥梁造型具有新意。

Mingzhou Bridge over the Yongjiang River is located in Ningbo, Zhejiang province. The main bridge is a half through composite steel box girder tied arch bridge. The span arrangement is 100m+450m+100m. The width of the deck is 45.8m including eight traffic lanes in dual direction. The design speed is 80km/h.

The arch rib has upper and lower limbs, and the cross section of each limb is a fully welded steel box. The rise-to-span ratio of the arch is 1/5. The deck is made of steel truss with orthotropic steel plate. The 14mm thick steel deck plate is reinforced with U-shaped stiffeners. The foundation of each main pier is composed of 70 bored piles.

Mingzhou Bridge is one of the largest tied arch bridges with steel box ribs in China. It features the shape of its two-limb arch ribs.

桥　　名：宁波明州大桥
桥　　型：中承式钢箱拱桥
主　　跨：450m
桥　　址：浙江省宁波市
完成日期：2011 年
设计单位：上海市政工程设计研究总院（集团）有限公司
施工单位：上海建工（集团）总公司
　　　　　中交第二航务工程局有限公司

Name: Mingzhou Bridge in Ningbo
Type: Half through steel box arch bridge
Main span: 450m
Location: Ningbo, Zhejiang Province
Completion: 2011
Designer(s): Shanghai Municipal Engineering Design Institute Group Co., Ltd.
Contractor(s): Shanghai Construction Group Co., Ltd.
　　　　　　　　CCCC Second Harbor Engineering Company Ltd.

广元昭化嘉陵江大桥
Zhaohua Bridge over the Jialing River in Guangyuan

广元昭化嘉陵江大桥位于广元市昭化镇，大桥全长864m，主桥为跨度364m的上承式钢管劲性骨架外包混凝土箱形拱桥，桥面宽度27.5m。拱圈净跨径为350m，净矢高83.33m，矢跨比为1/4.2。拱圈为双拱肋，之间以横联连接，拱肋为单箱双室箱形截面，内包型钢与钢管混凝土组成桁架的劲性骨架，拱上立柱横向为双柱，采用空心薄壁结构，空心立柱横桥向宽2.5m，纵桥向墩顶宽1.6m，纵桥向按80：1的比例向下变宽，空心墩壁厚为35cm。行车道梁采用跨径28m预应力混凝土简支带翼小箱梁，每孔横向8片梁，梁高1.6m。

拱圈采用劲性骨架法施工。该劲性骨架为型钢与钢管混凝土组成的桁架结构，骨架构造由传统的空间结构改为平面桁架，简化了施工程序，便于模板安装和移动，从而减少外包混凝土工期并保证施工质量。

Zhaohua Bridge over the Jialing River is located in Guangyuan, Sichuan Province. It is a RC box arch bridge with a main span of 364m. The total length of the bridge is 864m and the width of the deck is 27.5m. The arch has a rise of 83.33m. The rise-span ratio is 1/4.2. The two arch rings are connected with lateral bracings. Each arch ring has a single box section with two cells. There are stiff skeleton frames made up of concrete-filled steel tubular truss inside of the concrete walls of each arch ring.

The arch ring is erected by using the stiff skeleton frame, which is made of trusses in vertical planes rather than traditional spatial truss. This makes the installation and move of the formwork much easier than before. Consequently, it reduces the time for concrete casting and promotes the construction quality.

桥　　名：广元昭化嘉陵江大桥
桥　　型：上承式混凝土箱拱桥
主　　跨：364m
桥　　址：四川省广元市
完成日期：2011 年
设计单位：四川省交通运输厅公路规划勘察设计研究院
施工单位：四川公路桥梁建设集团有限公司

Name: Zhaohua Bridge over the Jialing River in Guangyuan
Type: Reinforced concrete box rib arch bridge
Main span: 364m
Location: Guangyuan, Sichuan Province
Completion: 2011
Designer(s): Sichuan Provincial Transport Department Highway Planning, Survey, Design and Research Institute
Contractor(s): Sichuan Road & Bridge(group) Co., Ltd.

肇庆南广铁路西江特大桥
Nanguang Railway Bridge over the West River in Zhaoqing

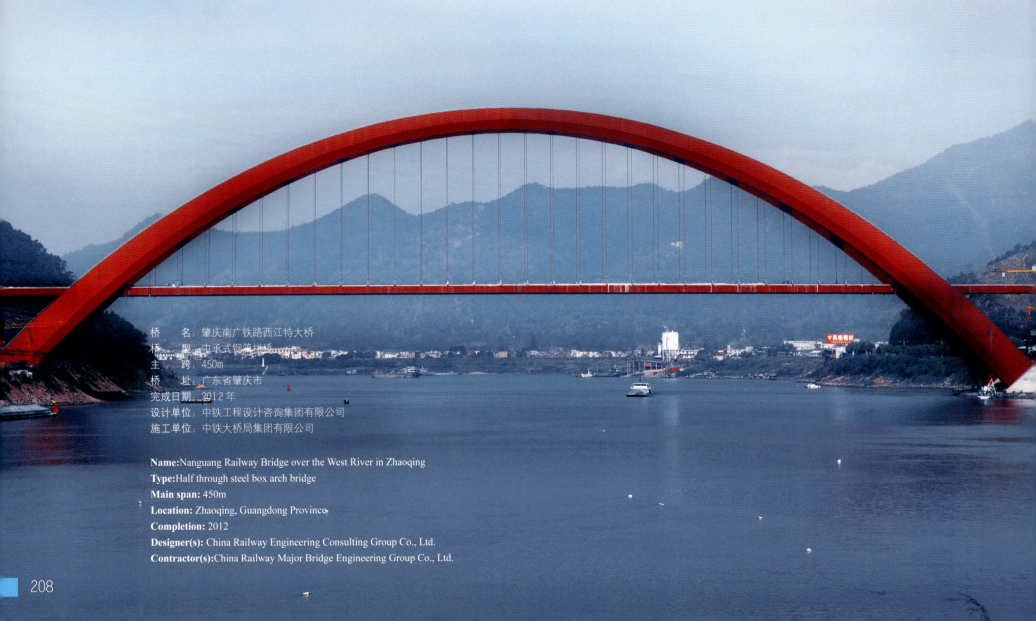

桥　　名：肇庆南广铁路西江特大桥
桥　　型：中承式钢筋拱桥
主　　跨：450m
桥　　址：广东省肇庆市
完成日期：2012年
设计单位：中铁工程设计咨询集团有限公司
施工单位：中铁大桥局集团有限公司

Name: Nanguang Railway Bridge over the West River in Zhaoqing
Type: Half through steel box arch bridge
Main span: 450m
Location: Zhaoqing, Guangdong Province
Completion: 2012
Designer(s): China Railway Engineering Consulting Group Co., Ltd.
Contractor(s): China Railway Major Bridge Engineering Group Co., Ltd.

肇庆南广铁路西江特大桥位于西江三榕峡上游，桥梁全长618.3m，主跨为450m的中承式钢箱提篮式拱桥，设计最高车速为250km/h，双线、客货共线，满足开行双层集装箱列车要求。

主拱矢跨比为1/4，拱肋内倾角为4.8°，拱肋为钢箱结构，截面尺寸为1.5m×5m。两拱肋之间通过K形横撑和一字横撑连成整体，全桥共设置18组横撑。桥面系由钢横梁、主纵梁、次纵梁以及钢筋混凝土桥面板组成。桥面板为20cm厚C50钢筋混凝土预制板和20cm厚C50钢筋混凝土后浇层构成，桥面系为半飘浮式桥面结构体系。

肇庆南广铁路西江特大桥是我国目前仅有的高速铁路大跨中承式钢箱提篮式拱桥，它标志我国高速铁路拱式桥跨越能力的重大提升。

Nanguang Railway Bridge over the West River in Zhaoqing is located in the upstream of the Sanrong Gorge. It is a half through steel box arch bridge with a main span of 450m. The total length of the bridge is 618.3m and the design speed is 250km/h.

The arch bridge has a rise-to-span ratio of 1/4. The two arch ribs incline towards each other with a 4.8°. Each of the arch ribs has 1.5m×5m steel box cross sections. The two arch ribs are connected with 18 K-shaped or straight lateral bracings. The deck system is a semi-floating structure and composed of steel lateral beams, main longitudinal girders, secondary longitudinal girders and RC deck plates.

Nanguang Railway Bridge over the West River in Zhaoqing is the only long span half through steel box arch bridge in Chinese high speed railway system presently. It indicates the new application of the arch type bridge in China for high speed railway.

波司登合江长江大桥
Bosideng Hejiang Bridge over the Yangtze River

波司登合江长江大桥位于四川省泸州市合江县，是国家高速公路网成渝地区环线上的一座特大桥，全长841m，桥面宽30.6m，按照双向六车道设计。

主桥为钢管混凝土中承式拱桥，跨径518m，净矢跨比1/4.5。拱圈由两道钢管混凝土桁架拱肋组成，每肋宽度为4m，高度由拱顶8m变化到拱脚16m，上下弦杆钢管内填充C60混凝土，通过横联、竖向钢管构成桁架。拱肋中距28.6m，桥面以上拱肋间设闭口K形横撑，桥面以下设钢管混凝土桁架横撑。吊杆和拱上立柱间距14.3m，桥面系由两道主纵梁、三道次纵梁及横梁组成，纵横梁均采用工字形截面，桥面板为钢—混凝土组合桥面板。拱座采用分离式双座，基础埋置于弱风化岩层内。

主跨拱桥采用无支架缆索吊装、斜拉扣挂法施工。扣塔的安装采用组合式摇臂吊机分解组塔方法，该方法源自输电铁塔的架设。

钢—混组合桥面板
Steel-concrete composite deck

Bosideng Bridge over the Yangtze River is located in Luzhou, Sichuan Province. This bridge is 841m long and 30.6m wide. It is designed for six traffic lanes in dual direction.

The concrete-filled steel tube half through arch bridge has a main span of 518m. The rise-span ratio of the arch is 1/4.5. Each arch ring is 4m wide and composed of two concrete-filled steel tubular trusses. The height of the trusses is 8m at the crown and 16m at the springing. The upper and lower chords of the trusses are filled with C60 concrete. The distance between the two arch rings is 28.6m. The two arch rings are connected with K-shaped lateral bracings.

The arches are erected by the cantilever method with temporary towers and stayed cables.

跨中拱肋合龙
Closure of the arch ribs in the middle span

桥　　名：波司登合江长江大桥
桥　　型：中承式钢管混凝土拱桥
主　　跨：518m
桥　　址：四川省泸州市
完成日期：2012年
设计单位：四川省交通运输厅公路规划勘察设计研究院
施工单位：广西壮族自治区公路桥梁工程总公司

Name: Bosideng Hejiang Bridge over the Yangtze River
Type: Half through concrete-filled steel tube tied arch bridge
Main span: 518m
Location: Luzhou, Sichuan Province
Completion: 2012
Designer(s): Sichuan Provincial Transport Department Highway Planning, Design and Research Institute
Contractor(s): Guangxi Road & Bridge Engineering Corporation

第五篇　梁式桥
Chapter 5　Girder Bridges

引言

梁式桥是中小跨度桥梁的首选桥型，也是桥梁总长度中比例最高的桥型。第二次世界大战后，作为现代桥梁工程三大标志性成果之一的预应力技术也主要用于梁式桥。从1952年德国Finsterwalder用挂篮悬臂浇筑工艺建成了第一座突破100m的Worms莱茵河桥（$L=114.2m$）起，预应力混凝土连续梁桥不断发展，20世纪60年代又出现了带挂孔的预应力混凝土T形刚构桥。跨度124m的柳州桥（1968年）、跨度144m的福州乌龙江桥（1971年）和主跨达174m的重庆长江大桥（1980年）是改革开放前中国梁式桥的代表作。

瑞士C.Menn教授在20世纪70年代创造了双薄壁墩预应力混凝土连续刚构桥，并于1979年建成了世界第一座主跨107m的Fegire桥。他利用双薄壁墩的柔性解决了温度、徐变收缩作用问题，取消了连续梁的支座，方便了悬臂施工，减小了支点处的负弯矩，为提高梁式桥的跨越能力创造了条件。

此后，预应力混凝土连续刚构桥的跨度很快突破了200m。到1985年，澳大利亚门道桥的跨度已达到了260m。中国在20世纪80年代建造广东番禺洛溪大桥时首次成功采用了主跨180m的连续刚构桥（1988年）。此后，贵州六广河大桥（主跨240m，建成于1993年）、黄石长江大桥（主跨3×245m，1996年）、广东虎门珠江大桥辅航道桥（主跨270m，1997年）、济南黄河二桥（主跨210m，1999年）、重庆黄花园嘉陵江大桥（主跨250m，1999年）、泸州长江二桥（主跨252m，2000年）等相继建成，连续刚构桥成为20世纪90年代中国内河上许多大桥的首选桥型。预应力混凝土连续刚构桥曾经出现的裂缝和跨中下挠问题，也通过研究正逐步得到解决，使这一适合200m以上跨度的梁式桥继续向前发展。

进入21世纪以来，预应力混凝土连续刚构桥仍得到业内人士的青睐，全国各地建成了许多200m以上的梁式桥。

本画册中入选的14座梁式桥中，有12座连续刚构桥（跨度从185m至330m）和2座连续梁桥。其中，重庆石板坡大桥复线桥因受老桥（重庆长江大桥2×174m）桥墩位置的限制必须采用330m的主跨。林同棪国际公司首创了"钢—混凝土混合连续刚构体系"，中段采用质量较轻的钢梁使支点的负弯矩相当于280m的全预应力混凝土连续刚构，从而克服了困难，进一步提高了梁式桥跨越能力。

两座入选的连续梁桥也各具特色：其中11跨120m的山东鄄城黄河大桥（2009年）采用了波形钢腹板的预应力混凝土连续梁桥；崇启大桥（2011年）为多跨185m的连续钢箱梁桥。这些桥梁充分体现出中国的梁式桥技术已赶上世界先进水平。

Introduction

Girder bridges are the preferred structural system for bridges in the short and medium span ranges, and are the most common bridge type over the entire range of span lengths. Following World War II, the primary application to bridge construction of prestressing technology (one of the three great achievements in modern bridge engineering) was for girder bridges. Beginning in 1952, the German Ulrich Finsterwalder used the balanced cantilever method to build the Bridge over the Rhine at Worms. Its span of 114.2m was the first concrete girder span to exceed 100m. Since then, the technology of prestressed concrete continuous girder bridges has been in constant development. The 1960s saw the emergence of prestressed concrete girder bridges with integral piers with a suspended span. The Liuzhou Bridge (completed in 1968) with a span of 124m, the Bridge over the Wulong River in Fuzhou (1971) with a span of 144m and the Chongqing Bridge over the Yangtze River (1980) with a main span of 174m are representative examples of Chinese girder bridges built before China's economic reform and opening-up.

In the 1970s, Swiss Professor Christian Menn invented the prestressed concrete continuous girder bridge with double-leaf integral thin-walled piers. This development was first applied to the Fegire Bridge (1979) which had a main span of 107m. The flexibility of the two thin columns of a given pier enables them to accommodate shortening of the superstructure due to concrete creep, shrinkage, and decrease in temperature, thus eliminating the need for bearings between superstructure and piers. This arrangement can also facilitate cantilever construction and reduce negative moments in the girder over the piers. These advantages created more possibilities for increasing the feasible span range of girder bridges.

Going forward, prestressed concrete continuous bridges with integral piers quickly spanned over 200m. By 1985, the record for this type of bridge was claimed by the 260 m main span of the Gateway Bridge in Australia. Integral piers for long span girder bridges were first used in China on the Luoxi Bridge in Fanyu, Guangdong. This bridge, completed in 1988, had a main span of 180m. Following this, girder bridges became the preferred type for long span bridges in China in the 1990s. Notable examples from this period include the Bridge over the Liuguang River in Guizhou (240m span, completed in 1993), the Huangshi Bridge over the Yangtze River in Hubei (three spans of 245m, 1996), the auxiliary channel crossing of the Bridge over the Pearl River in Humen, Guangdong (270m span, 1997), the Second Bridge over the Yellow River in Jinan (210m span, 1999), the Huanghuayuan Bridge over the Jialing River in Chongqing (250m span, 1999) and the second Luzhou Bridge over the Yangtze River (252m span, 2000). The problems of cracking and unexpected sagging at mid-span in this type of bridge are being addressed through on-going research, which will enable even more applications for girder bridges with spans beyond 200m.

Prestressed concrete continuous bridges with integral piers have remained popular into the 21st century, and many bridges of this type have been constructed in every part of China. Among the fourteen girder bridges selected for this book, there are twelve prestressed concrete continuous bridges with integral piers with spans ranging from 185m to 330m, and two continuous girder bridges supported on bearings. The longest spanning of these is the Shibanpo Parallel Bridge over the Yangtze River in Chongqing. Because it is located immediately adjacent and parallel to the previously built Chongqing Bridge over the Yangtze River, its 330m main span was chosen to provide pier locations consistent with those of the existing bridge. The designer, T. Y. Lin International Group Ltd., used a 108m steel girder for the central portion of the main span, thus producing the world's first steel-concrete hybrid continuous bridge with integral piers. The light weight of the steel portion reduces negative moment at the supports to values corresponding to a similar bridge built entirely of concrete with a 280m main span. The new bridge thus provides a suitable counterpart to its older neighbor and extends the feasible span range of girder bridges.

The two continuous girder bridges supported on bearings included in this book have unique characteristics of their own. The bridge over the Yellow River in Juancheng, Shandong (eleven spans of 120m, completed in 2009) is a prestressed concrete continuous girder bridge with corrugated steel webs. The Chongqi Bridge over the Yangtze River in Shanghai, completed in 2011, is a continuous steel box girder bridge with 4 main spans of 185m. These bridges fully reflect that Chinese achievements in girder bridge design and construction have caught up with the advanced world.

云南红河大桥
Honghe Bridge in Yunnan

云南红河大桥位于云南省元江县，是国道213线元江—磨黑高速公路上的一座特大桥梁。主桥长度769m，双向四车道，桥面宽22.5m。

主桥结构为5跨一联的预应力混凝土连续刚构，跨越超过170m的V形深谷，分跨为58m+182m+265m+194m+70m，第一跨位于半径800m的缓和曲线内。主梁为直腹板单箱单室结构，桥墩均采用双柱式薄壁结构，高度最低的1号墩为21.85m，最高的3号墩达到121.5m；中墩采用群桩或扩大基础，梁端为重力式桥台。

箱梁中跨底板内设计了平衡底板预应力钢束向下径向力的钢筋，并在跨中合龙段内设置了一道横隔板；为了增大2、3号高墩的稳定性，双薄壁墩柱间设置了两道横隔板。

为了减少温度、混凝土徐变收缩及车辆制动对1号墩的不利作用，边跨合龙前采用悬臂端预压，次边跨和中跨合龙前采用对顶等控制措施，从而有效减小了双柱墩的轴力差和墩顶弯矩，也有助克服主跨箱梁下挠。

The Honghe Bridge located in Yuanjiang County, Yunnan Province, is on Yuan-Mo expressway of No.213 State Highway. Its main bridge has a total length of 769m and a width of 22.5m for four traffic lanes in dual direction.

The main bridge over a 170m deep valley is a PC continuous bridge with integral piers. It has five spans of 58m+182m+265m+194m+70m. The first span is on the transition curve of 800m radius. The cross section of the girder is a single-cell box with vertical webs. All Piers are twin columns thin-wall structures. The Pier 1 is the shortest (21.85m), while the Pier 3 the highest (121.5m). The group pile or spread foundation is used for piers while the abutments at the ends of the bridge are gravity ones.

In the central span, the special reinforcements are arranged in the bottom slab to balance the downward radial forces caused by curved prestressing tendons. Furthermore, a diaphragm is set up at the closure segment at mid-span. Two thin-walled pier shafts is set up to improve the stability of the piers No.2 and No.3.

Long-term temperature effect, concrete shrinkage and creep, and vehicle breaking force of the girder will have some adverse effects to pier No.1. Some special methods were adopted during the closure process to reduce them, such as loading at the end of side span cantilevers, and applying opposite longitudinal force to middle spans cantilevers before closure. These methods also helped to reduce the long-term deflections of the mid-span.

Name: Honghe Bridge in Yunnan
Type: PC continuous bridge with integral piers
Main Span: 265m
Location: Yuanjiang County, Yunnan Province
Completion: 2003
Designer(s): Yunnan Provincial Institute of Communications Planning, Design and Research
Beijing Jianda Road and Bridge Consultant Co., Ltd.
Contractor(s): CCCC Second Harbor Engineering Company Ltd.

福建宁德下白石大桥
Xiabaishi Bridge in Ningde

桥　名：	福建宁德下白石大桥
桥　型：	预应力混凝土连续刚构桥
主　跨：	260m
桥　址：	福建省宁德市
完成日期：	2003 年
设计单位：	中交第一公路勘察设计研究院有限公司
施工单位：	湖南路桥建设集团公司

Name: Xiabaishi Bridge in Ningde
Type: PC continuous bridge with integral piers
Main Span: 260m
Location: Ningde, Fujian Province
Completion: 2003
Designer(s): CCCC First Highway Consultants Co., Ltd.
Contractor(s): Hunan Road and Bridge Construction Group Corp.

福建宁德下白石大桥位于福建省宁德市下白石镇，是国道主干线同江至三亚高速公路福建省境内福宁高速公路上的一座特大桥。主桥长 810m，宽 24m，双向六车道。

主桥结构为四跨预应力混凝土连续刚构，分跨为 145m+2×260m+145m，横向上下行两幅结构分离。主梁为直腹板单箱单室结构，梁高从根部 14m 至跨中 4.2m 按 1.6 次抛物线变化，高跨比分别为 1/18.6 和 1/61.9。

为便于腹板混凝土浇筑，箱梁纵向预应力钢束在 80% 的梁段均未设置下弯束，仅在 0 号块两侧的 8 个梁段内设置了下弯钢束，有利于抵抗根部范围的主拉应力。7 号墩基岩埋藏较浅，设计成墙式嵌岩基础，不设承台，减少了基岩开挖量。主墩墩身主筋采用了环氧涂层钢筋。

The Xiabaishi Bridge in Ningde, Fujian Province, has a total length of 810m. It is on Fu-Ning Expressway, a part of the State-Highway connecting Tongjiang in Heilongjing Province and Sanya in Hainan Province. The main bridge is a four-span (145m+2×160m+145m) PC continuous bridge with integral piers. Two separate single-cell box girders, with a height of 14m at pier top and 4.2m at mid-span, are used to up- and down-ward carriageways of 12m wide each.

To facilitate the concrete casting of webs, the longitudinal prestressing tendons are straight within the 80% length of the box. Only in 4 segments on each side of the pier, the tendons are bent down to resist principle tensile-stresses thereof. As the rock surface is shallow at Pier 7, the wall type foundation embedded in rock is adopted to reduce rock excavation. The epoxy coated reinforcement is used for main piers.

广州琶洲珠江大桥
Pazhou Bridge over the Pearl River in Guangzhou

桥　名：广州琶洲珠江大桥	**Name:** Pazhou Bridge over the Pearl River in Guangzhou
桥　型：预应力混凝土V形支撑连续刚构桥梁	**Type:** PC continuous bridge with integral V-shaped piers
主　跨：160m	**Main Span:** 160m
桥　址：广东省广州市	**Location:** Guangzhou, Guangdong Province
完成日期：2003年	**Completion:** 2003
设计单位：中铁第一勘察设计院集团有限公司	**Designer(s):** China Railway First Survey and Design Institute Group Ltd.
施工单位：广东省长大公路工程有限公司	**Contractor(s):** Guangdong Provincial Changda Highway Engineering Co., Ltd.

广州琶洲珠江大桥位于广州市，是一座跨越珠江的城市快速道路特大桥梁。主桥长570m，宽30.0m，双向八车道；桥下具备千吨级船舶通航能力。

主桥为五跨V形墩刚构—连续梁组合结构，分跨为70m+135m+160m+135m+70m，横向上下行两幅结构分离。主梁为直腹板单箱单室结构，主跨V形墩高度为20m，箱形结构，基础设计为支承式基桩。

V形墩及其上梁段是设计和施工的关键。箱梁按三向预应力结构设计，悬臂浇筑施工最大节段重量不超出2000kN；V形墩支架现浇的施工荷载主要由内设劲性骨架承担；主墩基桩采用挖孔施工法，其余桥墩基桩为钻机和冲机成孔法。

The Pazhou Bridge over the Pearl River in Guangzhou, Guangdong Province is a large urban expressway bridge. Its main bridge is 570m long and 30m wide for eight traffic lanes in dual direction. The navigational clearance can meet the requirement for 1000t vessels.

The main bridge is a five-span (70m+135m+160m+135m+70m) PC continuous bridge with integral V-shaped piers. Two separate single-cell box girders are used for both up- and down-ward carriageways.

Three directional prestressing tendons are adopted for the box girders. The maximum weight of the box segments during cantilever casting is limited to 2000kN.

The construction load during V-shaped pier casting is supported by stiff steel-frames within the pier. The end-bearing piles of the main pier are excavated, while others are bored or punched.

广州海心沙珠江大桥
Haixinsha Bridge over the Pearl River in Guangzhou

广州海心沙珠江大桥位于广州市，是广州市仓头至龙穴岛快速路上的一座特大型桥梁。主桥长526m，宽33m，双向八车道。

主桥结构为预应力混凝土连续刚构，分跨为138m+250m+138m，横向上下行两幅结构分离。主梁为直腹板单箱单室结构，主跨主墩高度为34m，薄壁结构。基础设计为嵌岩桩。

在施工中仿照斜拉桥的施工监控原理，通过参数识别进行预应力钢束的动态调整设计，并通过参数变异计算预留体内和体外预应力备用钢束，以在需要时调整内力。

桥　　名：广州海心沙珠江大桥
桥　　型：预应力混凝土连续刚构桥
主　　跨：250m
桥　　址：广东省广州市
完成日期：2004年
设计单位：广东省公路勘察规划设计院股份有限公司
施工单位：中铁大桥局集团有限公司

Name: Haixinsha Bridge over the Pearl River in Guangzhou
Type: PC continuous bridge with integral piers
Main Span: 250m
Location: Guangzhou, Guangdong Province
Completion: 2004
Designer(s): Guangdong Highway Design Institute Co., Ltd.
Contractor(s): China Railway Major Bridge Engineering Group Co., Ltd.

The Haixinsha Bridge over the Pearl River in Guangzhou, with a total length of 526m, connects the Cangtou and Longxue Island.

The main bridge is a three-span (138m+250m+138m) PC continuous bridge with integral piers. Two separate single-cell box girders with vertical webs are used for up- and down-ward carriageways of 16.5m wide each. The main piers are twin columns thin-wall structure with the height of 34m, and the foundations are socketed piles.

The construction-control principles used in cable-stayed bridges are applied to the prestressing-adjustment based on the identified parameters during the construction. Furthermore, if necessary, the prestressing for both internal and external spare tendons could be adjusted.

重庆石板坡长江大桥复线桥
Shibanpo Parallel Bridge over the Yangtze River in Chongqing

主梁为单箱单室结构,预应力混凝土结构和钢结构混合设计,主跨中段108m采用了钢箱梁,主跨还考虑后期可补加体外预应力钢束。为降低混凝土收缩徐变效应,也对材料提出了具体性能指标与工艺要求。以上设计方案既克服了混凝土连续刚构自重大、跨越能力有限的难题,也为解决该类桥梁跨中下挠等病害进行了有益实践。

A steel box girder of 108m long is adopted for the middle part of the main-span, while the PC girder is adopted for other parts of the bridge. It has been considered that the external tendons can be added to the main span during the service stage. Specific criteria and technology of the materials used are adopted to reduce the creep and shrinkage of concrete. These measures mentioned above not only improve the spanning capability of heavy concrete bridges with integral piers, but also provide practical example for the deflection control at mid-span of this kind of bridge.

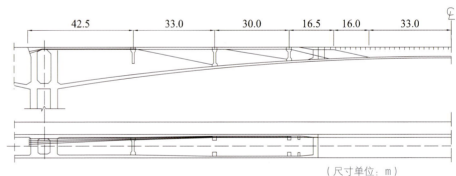

(尺寸单位:m)

重庆石板坡长江大桥复线桥位于原旧桥上游,是一座城市主干道Ⅰ级特大桥。桥梁全长1103.5m,宽19m,单向四车道;桥下通航净空18m×290m。该复线桥结构为钢—混凝土混合连续刚构,由北向南分跨为87.75m+4×138m+330m+133.75m。

The Shinbanbo Parallel Bridge over the Yangtze River in Chongqing is located upstream of the old one. It is a one-way four-lane bridge with a total length of 1103.5m and a deck width of 19m. The navigation clearance is 18m×290m. The bridge is a steel-concrete hybrid continuous bridge with integral piers, which has the spans of 87.75m+4×138m+330m+133.75m from the north to the south.

以强大的托架为支承，三次分层浇筑混凝土，严格的水化热控制和有效的养护，解决了高度16m主墩箱梁0号块大体积混凝土的施工难题。

To solve the construction problem of 16m-high pier-top segment, the concrete was cast three times. At the same time, strict control of hydration heat and effective curing were adopted.

钢混接头　Connection Joint of Steel and Concrete

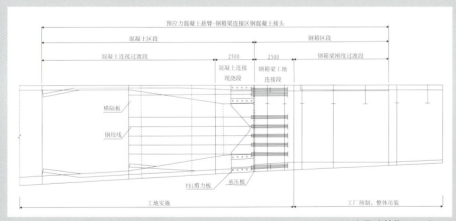

（尺寸单位：mm）

钢与混凝土箱梁接头设计采用了PBL剪力板、预应力和普通钢筋及钢—混结合段内填充混凝土等构造措施，并通过大比例模型试验方式检验其受力的可靠性。

Several connection devices such as PBL shear-plate, prestressing tendons, steel reinforcement and filling concrete in the vicinity of steel girders etc., have been used to ensure good connections between the PC girders and steel girder at mid-span. The reliability of these measures was verified by large scale model testing.

利用混凝土箱梁悬臂端设置的体外定位劲性骨架，有效控制了与钢箱梁连接接头的各向位移及转角偏差，保证了主跨钢箱梁的合龙精度。

With positioning stiffening frame installed at the cantilever ends of the concrete box girder, the displacement and angle deviation of the joint section were effectively controlled. The closure accuracy of the steel girder in the mid-span was ensured.

　　基于周密的施工组织，完成了预制长103m重14000kN钢箱梁的整体浮运、转向及定位；旋转抬头、平行上升、恢复水平的出水方案，克服了钢箱梁底面出水瞬间强大的吸附力；计算机控制液压千斤顶吊装系统和横向偏移调整技术，确保了钢箱梁连续平稳提升和精确合龙。

The 103m, 14000kN steel box girder were floated to the site with full length. To reduce the huge water absorption force when the girder is lifted up out of the water, the following hoisting process was adopted. Firstly, rotate the girder and lift one end of the girder out of water. Secondly, lift two ends of the girder simultaneously until the whole girder getting out of the water. Finally, adjust the steel girder to be horizontal. To ensure the girder being lifted continuously and smoothly and the closure accuracy of the girders, computer controlled hydraulic jack lifting system and lateral deviation adjustment method were adopted during the construction.

桥　　名：重庆石板坡长江大桥复线桥	**Name:** Shibanpo Parallel Bridge over the Yangtze River in Chongqing
桥　　型：钢—混凝土混合连续刚构桥	**Type:** Steel-concrete hybrid continuous bridge with integral piers
主　　跨：330m	**Main Span:** 330m
桥　　址：重庆市	**Location:** Chongqing
完成日期：2006年	**Completion:** 2006
设计单位：林同棪国际（重庆）工程咨询有限公司	**Designer(s):** T.Y.Lin International (Chongqing) Engineering Consulting Co., Ltd.
施工单位：重庆桥梁工程有限责任公司	**Contractor(s):** Chongqing Bridge Engineering Co., Ltd.

滨州黄河公铁两用大桥
Binzhou Railway-Highway Bridge over the Yellow River

滨州黄河公铁两用大桥位于山东北镇黄河公路大桥下游3.3km处。主桥长度780m，为上下两层桥。

主桥结构为五孔平弦连续钢桁梁，分跨为120m+3×180m+120m。上层为公路桥，桥宽19m，双向四车道；下层桁高18m，桁宽11m，为单线铁路。

该桥为黄河上的首座公铁两用大桥，由于航道及凌汛的需要，其跨度定为180m，为目前国内平弦钢梁桥的最大跨度，也刷新了亚洲同类桥型的最大跨度纪录。由于钢梁跨度大，弦杆内力变化大，钢梁杆件首次采用变高度截面形式。

The Binzhou Railway-Highway Bridge over the Yellow River is located 3.3km downstream from Beizhen Yellow River Bridge in Shandong Province. Two-level deck is used. The upper one is for dual 4-lane highway with the width of 19m, while the lower one for single-track railway. The 780m long main bridge consists of five-span (120m+3×180m+120m) continuous steel truss with constant height of 18m and width of 11m.

It is the first Railway-Highway Bridge across the Yellow River. To meet the requirement for navigation and ice-flooding, the main span length reaches 180m, the longest one for constant-height steel truss in China as well as in Asia. Due to the extra-long span length the uneven cross sections for the truss members are adopted for the first time.

桥　　名：滨州黄河公铁两用大桥
桥　　型：连续钢桁梁桥
主　　跨：180m
桥　　址：山东省滨州市
完成日期：2007 年
设计单位：中铁大桥勘测设计院集团有限公司
施工单位：中交第三公路工程局有限公司
　　　　　中铁大桥局集团有限公司

Name: Binzhou Railway-Highway Bridge over the Yellow River
Type: Continuous steel truss bridge
Main Span: 180m
Location: Binzhou, Shandong Province
Completion: 2007
Designer(s): China Railway Major Bridge Reconnaissance & Design Institute Co., Ltd.
Contractor(s): CCCC Third Highway Engineering Co., Ltd.
　　　　　　　　China Railway Major Bridge Engineering Group Co., Ltd.

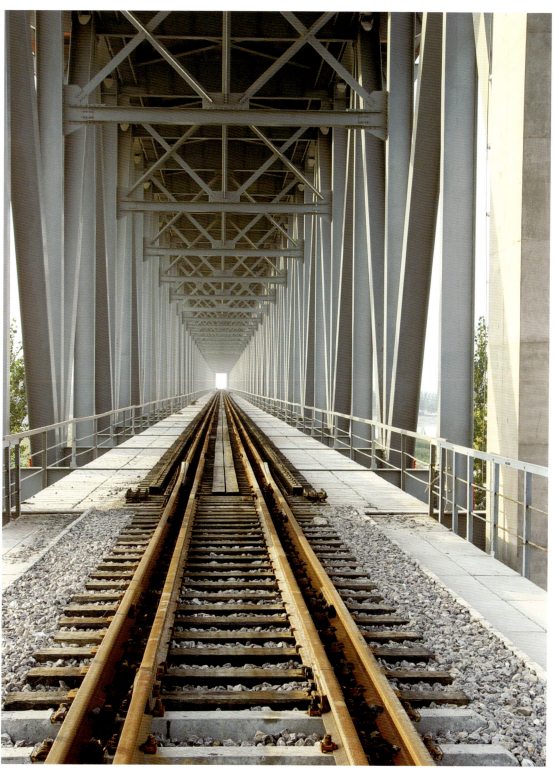

重庆嘉华嘉陵江大桥
Jiahua Bridge over the Jialing River in Chongqing

桥　　名:	重庆嘉华嘉陵江大桥
桥　　型:	预应力混凝土连续刚构桥
主　　跨:	252m
桥　　址:	重庆市
完成日期:	2007年
设计单位:	上海市政工程设计研究总院
	重庆市交通规划勘测设计院
施工单位:	中铁八局集团有限公司

Name: Jiahua Bridge over the Jialing River in Chongqing
Type: PC continuous bridge with integral piers
Main Span: 252m
Location: Chongqing
Completion: 2007
Designers(s): Shanghai Municipal Engineering Design Institute
　　　　　　　Chongqing Communications Planning, Survey & Design Institute
Contractor(s): China Railway No.8 Engineering Group Co., Ltd.

重庆嘉华嘉陵江大桥是一座位于重庆市南北主轴线上的城市快速道路桥梁。桥梁长528m，宽37.6m，双向八车道，两侧设人行道；通航净空10m×180m。

桥梁结构为三跨预应力混凝土连续刚构，分跨为138m+252m+138m。上部横向采用上下行两幅分离的直腹板单箱单室结构，主跨桥墩为横向分离的单箱单室结构并设有防撞分水棱，承台与支承式桩基础上下行采用整体式结构。

为克服箱梁开裂和下挠问题，考虑后期可补加体外预应力钢束；仔细进行了耐久性设计，并采用自动喷淋系统养护高性能混凝土；优化了挂篮悬臂施工工艺，使一次浇筑混凝土重量超过3200kN，合龙前采取对顶措施调整了结构内力。

The Jiahua Bridge over the Jialing River is on the urban expressway in Chongqing. It has a total length of 528m and a deck width of 37.6m for dual 8-lane highway with sidewalks on both sides. The navigational clearance is 10m ×180m.

The main bridge is a three-span (138m+255m+138m) PC continuous bridge with integral piers. Two separate single-cell box girders with vertical webs are used for up- and down-wards vehicles relatively. An integrated pile foundation and a pile cap with an anti-collision ridge are adopted for separate girders.

To avoid unexpected cracks and deflection of the girder, the external prestressing tendons can be applied to the girder during bridge operation. The durability of the bridge has been deliberately considered. Through optimizing the cantilever construction technology, 3200kN concrete could be cast all at once. By jacking apart the opposite cantilevers before closure, the internal forces of the structure were adjusted.

四川汉源大树大渡河大桥
Dashu Bridge over the Dadu River in Hanyuan

四川汉源大树大渡河大桥位于四川省汉源县瀑布沟水电站库区内,横跨大渡河。主桥长521m,宽10.5m,两个车道,通航等级Ⅴ级。

主桥结构为三跨预应力混凝土连续刚构,分跨为133m+255m+133m。主梁为直腹板单箱单室结构。从中跨跨中至箱梁根部,箱高从4m至16m以半立方抛物线变化;桩基深80m,墩高100m。

大桥竖向预应力束采用高强钢绞线和低回缩量锚具,以降低预应力损失。由于大桥2号主墩桩基需要穿越超过50m厚度透镜状砂层的复杂地质,建设中采用了"钻孔跟进护筒方案"穿越砂层。

The Dashu Bridge over the Dadu River in Hanyuan County, Sichuan Province, has a total length of 521m and a width of 10.5m for two lanes.

The main bridge is a three-span (133m+255m+133m) PC continuous bridge with integral piers, with one single-cell box section of 10.5m wide and 16m high at supports and 4.0m high at mid-span in the shape of a half cubic parabola. The piles are 80m deep while the piers are 100m high.

The high-strength strands and low-retraction anchorages are used for prestressing tendons to reduce prestress losses. In order to penetrate 50m deep lenticular sand layer, the method of Boring with Immediate Pipe Casing is adopted for pile foundation construction.

Name: Dashu Bridge over the Dadu River in Hanyuan
Type: PC continuous bridge with integral piers
Main Span: 255m
Location: Hanyuan County, Sichuan Province
Completion: 2009
Designer(s): Sichuan Provincial Transport Department Highway Planning, Survey, Design and Research Institute
Contractor(s): Sichuan Road & Bridge (group) Co., Ltd.

广珠城际容桂水道铁路桥
Guangzhu Intercity Railway Bridge over the Ronggui Water Channel

广珠城际容桂水道铁路桥位于广东省佛山市顺德区境内。主桥长593m，宽11.6m，梁高5.5~11m。

主桥结构为四跨预应力混凝土连续刚构，分跨为108m+2×185m+115m，横向上中下游三幅结构分离。主梁为直腹板单箱单室结构。为目前国内、也是全世界主跨度最大的铁路无砟轨道连续刚构桥。

大桥所经过的河道地基稀软，只能承受60kN/m² 的压力，故3个主墩的桩基深度达75m，直接穿越30m厚的花岗岩层。为有效控制各种荷载工况下结构的变形，主梁采用低徐变、抗开裂的高性能混凝土，设计了可后补的体外预应力钢束，以改善跨中截面应力状态，降低后期徐变下挠。

The Guangzhu Intercity Railway Bridge over the Ronggui Water Channel is located in Foshan, Guangdong Province. It is the largest non-ballast railway bridge in the world.

Its main bridge is a four-span (108m+2×185m+115m) PC continuous bridge with integral piers, with the cross section of one single-cell box of 11.6m wide and with a height from 5.5m to 11m.

Since the soil bearing capacity at the bridge foundation site is very low (only 60kN/ m^2), the 75m deep piles are used for three of the piers. In order to control the structure deformation under various load cases, the low-creep and high-crack-resistance concrete is adopted for the main girder. Furthermore, external tendons were reserved.

桥　　名：广珠城际容桂水道铁路桥
桥　　型：预应力混凝土连续刚构桥
主　　跨：185m
桥　　址：广东省佛山市
完成日期：2010年
设计单位：中铁第四勘察设计院集团有限公司
施工单位：中铁三局集团第二工程有限公司

Name: Guangzhu Intercity Railway Bridge over the Ronggui Water Channel
Type: PC continuous bridge with integral piers
Main Span: 185m
Location: Foshan, Guangdong Province
Completion: 2010
Designer(s): China Railway Siyuan Survey and Design Group Co., Ltd.
Contractor(s): The Second Engineering Co., Ltd. of the Third Engineering Group of China Railway

重庆鱼洞长江大桥
Yudong Bridge over the Yangtze River in Chongqing

桥　　名：重庆鱼洞长江大桥
桥　　型：预应力混凝土连续刚构桥
主　　跨：260m
桥　　址：重庆市
完成日期：2011年
设计单位：招商局重庆交通科研设计院有限公司
施工单位：中国铁建股份有限公司

Name: Yudong Bridge over the Yangtze River in Chongqing
Type: PC continuous bridge with integral piers
Main Span: 260m
Location: Chongqing
Completion: 2011
Designer(s): China Merchants Chongqing Communications Research & Design Institute Co., Ltd.
Contractor(s): China Railway Construction Corporation Limited

重庆鱼洞长江大桥南起重庆市巴南区鱼洞经济开发区，北至大渡口区。主桥长810m，宽41.6m，为长江上最宽的跨江大桥。

主桥结构为四跨预应力混凝土连续刚构，分跨为145m+2×260m+145m，横向上下游两幅结构分离。主梁为直腹板单箱单室结构。大桥中间两条轨道、两边各三个车道，这种在两边跑汽车，中间跑轻轨的布置在全国是首例。

大桥施工中采用了国内最重的1800kN级挂篮进行悬臂作业，成功浇筑了最重达5100kN的悬臂梁段。为解决复杂地质条件下围堰的渗漏水问题，首次将膏浆帷幕止水新技术成功应用于桥梁深水基础施工。为避免洪水对高支架的影响，采用了先中后边的合龙顺序。

The Yudong Bridge over the Yangtze River in Chongqing with a total length of 810m is on the expressway of the southwest urban area of the city.

The main bridge is a four-span (145m+2×260m+145m) PC continuous bridge with integral piers. A two-cell box is adopted for the whole deck width of 41.6m, the widest deck among bridges crossing the Yangtze River. It is also the first time in the country to have a layout with two tracks of light railway in the middle and three lanes of highway on both sides.

The balanced cantilever casting method using suspended scaffolds of 1800kN heavy, the heaviest in China, is successfully used to cast segments up to 5100kN. To solve the cofferdam leakage problem under complicated geological conditions, the waterproof paste curtain technique is applied for deep-water foundation construction for the first time. The mid-span closure was before that of side spans.

山东鄄城黄河公路大桥
Juancheng Bridge over the Yellow River in Shandong

山东鄄城黄河公路大桥位于山东省与河南省交界处,是德州至商丘高速公路上一座跨越黄河的公路桥梁。主桥长1460m,宽28m,双向四车道;桥下通航净空8m×35m。主桥采用13跨波形钢腹板预应力混凝土连续箱梁结构,分跨为70m+11×120m+70m,横向上下行两幅结构分离。单幅主梁采用波形钢腹板单箱单室结构,下部结构为柱形空心墩、钻孔灌注桩基础。

波形钢腹板在工厂制造,现场采用栓接和焊接相结合的方式组拼;腹板与顶、底板结合采用打孔、穿筋及焊接纵向钢筋的埋入式抗剪连接件。箱梁按纵横双向预应力设计,纵向体内预应力钢束布置在顶、底板内,可更换设计的体外钢束采取折线布置并主要承受车辆荷载等作用,顶板横向布置体内预应力钢束。

箱梁利用桥面吊机逐段拼接波形钢腹板、浇筑顶底板混凝土;采用先边跨合龙、再中跨合龙的施工次序,合龙前采用型钢骨架临时固结,并通过水箱配重调整确保合龙口两侧梁端无相对竖向位移。

The Juancheng Bridge over the Yellow River in Shandong on Dezhou-Shangqiu Highway is located on the border of Shandong and Henan Provinces. Its main bridge is 1460m long and 28m wide for dual-carriageways of 4 lanes each. The navigational clearance is 8m×35m. The main bridge is a thirteen-span (70m+11×120m+70m) PC continuous box girder bridge with corrugated steel webs. Two separate single-box girders with vertical corrugated steel webs are used for superstructure and rectangular hollow piers and bored piles foundation for substructure.

The corrugated steel webs were fabricated in factories and assembled on site with the method of bolting and welding. Longitudinal and transverse prestressing tendons were used in the box girders, while the longitudinal internal prestressing tendons were arranged in the top and bottom slabs. Replaceable external prestressing tendons in polyline were designed mainly to carry the live loads. Transverse internal prestressing tendons were arranged in the deck slab.

The derrick cranes were used to assemble the corrugated steel webs in segments and cast top and bottom concrete slabs. The mid-span closure was constructed after side span closure. The steel frame was installed to fix the cantilever ends of the meeting girders temporarily before closure and water tanks were used as counterweight to make sure that there was no relative vertical displacement between the two ends.

Name: Juancheng Bridge over the Yellow River in Shandong
Type: PC continuous box girder bridge with corrugated steel webs
Main Span: 120m
Location: Juancheng, Shandong Province
Completion: 2011
Designer(s): China Highway Engineering Consulting Corporation
Henan Haiwei Engineering Consulting Co., Ltd.
Contractor(s): CCCC Second Highway Engineering Co., Ltd.

崇启大桥
Chongqi Bridge

崇启大桥位于长江口北港水域,属于上海至西安国家高速公路。主桥长944m,宽33.2m,分成两幅,双向六车道;桥下满足30000kN级海轮通航要求。

主桥采用六跨连续钢箱梁结构,分跨为102m+4×185m+102m。上部结构上下行两幅分离,下部结构承台及基础整体构造。单幅主梁采用变截面直腹板单箱单室结构,箱梁内设置横肋和斜撑,支点处设实腹式横隔板,桥面板采用U肋加劲正交异性结构;基础采用大直径钢管打入桩。

单幅主梁采用分段制造、浮吊架设工艺。全长分为12个节段,顶板接缝采用焊接,其余均用高强螺栓连接;最大节段长度为185m,重量27000kN(含临时结构)。

The Chongqi Bridge over the Yangtze River in Shanghai, with a total length of 944m, is on the State-Highway from Shanghai to Xi'an. The 33.2m-wide deck consists of two separate girders for six traffic lanes in dual direction. The navigation clearance meets the requirements of 30000kN vessels.

The main bridge with six spans of 102m+4×185m+102m is a continuous steel box girder bridge. The integral cap and foundation of piles is adopted for substructure. One single-cell box with varying height is used for the girder cross section. There are transverse ribs and bracings in the box and, in addition, the solid diaphragms at the supports. The orthotropic plate with U-shaped ribs is used for top slab of the box girder. The large-diameter steel pipe are adopted for foundations.

Each steel box girder is divided into 12 segments prefabricated in factory and erected on site by floating crane. The maximum segment length is 185m, with the weight of 27000kN.

桥　　名：崇启大桥
桥　　型：连续钢箱梁桥
主　　跨：185m
桥　　址：上海市崇明县和江苏省启东市
完成日期：2011 年
设计单位：中交公路规划设计院有限公司
施工单位：中交第二航务工程局有限公司

Name: Chongqi Bridge
Type: Continuous steel box girder bridge
Main Span: 185m
Location: Chongming County, Shanghai and Qidong, Jiangsu Province
Completion: 2011
Designer(s): CCCC Highway Consultants Co., Ltd.
Contractor(s): CCCC Second Habor Engineering Company Ltd.

（部分图片提供者：王刚）

雅泸高速腊八斤大桥
Labajin Bridge on Ya'an-Lugu Expressway

桥　　名：雅泸高速腊八斤大桥
桥　　型：预应力混凝土连续刚构桥
主　　跨：200m
桥　　址：四川省荥经县
完成日期：2011 年
设计单位：四川省交通运输厅公路规划勘察设计研究院
施工单位：四川雅西高速公路有限责任公司

Name: Labajin Bridge on Ya'an-Lugu Expressway
Type: PC continuous bridge with integral piers
Main Span: 200m
Location: Xingjing, Sichuan Province
Completion: 2011
Designer(s): Sichuan Provincial Transport Department Highway Planning, Survey, Design and Research Institute
Contractor(s): Sichuan Yaxi Expressway Co., Ltd.

雅沪高速腊八斤大桥位于四川省荥经县石滓乡境内，是雅安－泸沽高速公路上一座特大型桥梁。主桥长610m，宽24.2m，双向六车道。

主桥结构为四跨预应力混凝土连续刚构，分跨为105m+2×200m+105m，横向上下行两幅结构分离。主梁为直腹板单箱单室结构。中跨跨中梁高3.8m，墩顶梁高12.75m，以1.8次抛物线变化。主墩高182.5m，有"亚洲第一高墩"之称。

该桥结合交通运输部西部科研课题"钢管混凝土组合桥墩技术研究"成果，主桥和引桥桥墩均采用钢管混凝土劲性骨架与外包混凝土形成的组合柱，并首次成功采用C80混凝土自密实灌注工艺，具有自重轻、承载能力高、延性好的特点。

The Labajin Bridge on Ya'an-Lugu Expressway in Xingjing County, Sichuan Province has a total length of 610m and a deck width of 24.2m for six traffic lanes in dual direction.

The main bridge is a four-span PC continuous bridge with integral piers, with four spans of 105m+2×200m+105m. It is divided into two parallel bridges upstream and downstream respectively.

The deck uses a single-cell single-box section of 12.1m wide with vertical webs. The depth of the girder varies from 12.75m at the supports to 3.8m at the mid-span in the shape of a 1.8 parabola. The height of the pier shafts are 182.5m, which are known as "the Highest Piers in Asia".

Based on the achievements of the research project "The Research of Steel Tube Concrete Composite Piers" supported by the Ministry of Communications of China, this bridge used steel tube concrete composite pier shafts in the main bridge as well as the approach spans. In addition, C80 concrete with self-compact casting technique was firstly used to achieve less self-weight, higher carrying capacity and better ductility.

雅泸高速黑石沟大桥
Heishigou Bridge on Ya'an-Lugu Expressway

桥　　名：雅泸高速黑石沟大桥
桥　　型：预应力混凝土连续刚构桥
主　　跨：200m
桥　　址：四川省荥经县
完成日期：2012年
设计单位：四川省交通运输厅公路规划勘察设计研究院
施工单位：中国路港集团有限公司

Name: Heishigou Bridge on Ya'an-Lugu Expressway
Type: PC continuous bridge with integral piers
Main Span: 200m
Location: Xingjing County, Sichuan Province
Completion: 2012
Designer(s): Sichuan Provincial Transport Department Highway Planning, Design And Research Institute
Contractor(s): China Lugang Group Co., Ltd.

雅泸高速黑石沟大桥位于四川省荥经县境内，跨越约200m的深沟。主桥长425m，宽24.8m，分成两幅，双向四车道。

主桥结构为四跨不对称预应力混凝土连续刚构，分跨为55m+120m+200m+105m，上部横向采用上下行两幅分离的直腹板单箱单室结构；双幅桥墩为中段带桁架横向联系的双空心柱构造，最大高度155m，基础为上下行整体式结构。墩柱采用钢管混凝土劲性骨架与外包混凝土形成的钢管组合柱，以满足震后可修、大震不垮的要求，并充分发挥其承载力。

墩柱钢管骨架分段制造、逐段安装并随即在钢管内灌注混凝土，然后进行外包混凝土施工，先期形成的钢管混凝土骨架为后续施工提供了支架。

The Heishigou Bridge on Ya'an-Lugu Expressway in Xingjing County, Sichuan Province, crosses a valley of 200m deep. It is 425m in length, and 24.8m in width for four traffic lanes in dual direction.

The main bridge is a four-span PC continuous bridge with integral piers with asymmetric spans of 55m+120m+200m+105m. Two girders with a single-cell box section with vertical webs are used for the deck. Two separate hollow columns connected by truss bracings are used for the piers with maximum height of 155m. However the foundation for two columns is integrated. The columns are made of steel tube segments filled in and wrapped around by concrete to meet the earthquake requirement.

The steel tube segments were fabricated and assembled on site. Concrete were pumped into the tubes and casted around the tubes forming the final cross section. The completed steel tube segments are used as false work for the concrete construction.

第六篇 城市桥梁
Chapter 6　Urban Bridges

引言

在2012年第二十届桥梁学术会议上，邓文中先生的大会主题报告"美观何价"，引起了争论。城市桥梁作为一种景观标志，其美学价值应比一般公路桥梁有更高的要求和考虑。由于城市桥梁的跨度相对较小，投资也较低，为了使桥梁的景观给人以美感，或希望成为城市的标志，会选择并非最经济的方案，因此也增加了结构和施工费用。邓文中先生在结语中强调："美观不是怪异，美观不一定昂贵。"在一座城市的许多桥梁中，从整体规划出发，为个别桥梁的标志性景观要求，适当增加美的附加费用，并且为专家和市民所接受，是值得的。

《桥梁》杂志在会后又约请了一些专家在"桥梁会客厅"栏目进行了讨论。总的看来，首先，专家们都反观怪异，怪异不是美，而是丑，必须坚决反对；其次，对桥梁的美学考虑要"适当"，要有一个度，以旧金山新海湾大桥为例，市民募集了一定的附加费用，要求设计得美一些，也是有度的，只占总造价的很小比例；再次，标志性工程只能是"个别"的，不能每座桥都要求标志性，大多数桥梁还是要强调经济与功能；最后，城市桥梁的美学价值应当由使用它的市民来评判，要尊重民众的意见，而且还必须经得起时间的检验。

本画册入选的17座城市桥梁中桥型种类齐全，有1座自锚式悬索桥、7座斜拉桥、2座矮塔斜拉桥、4座拱式桥和3座梁式桥，其中有1座开启桥和1座人行桥，代表了大多数评选专家审美取向。随着中国人民物质生活的提高和城市化进程的加快，21世纪将会建造更多的城市桥梁。随着我国桥梁工程师自身美学修养的不断提高，在满足适用和安全的前提下，将会设计出更美观的桥梁，给广大人民提供长久的美的享受。

Introduction

Mr. M.C.Tang's keynote address "The Value of Elegance", presented at the 20th Bridge Conference in China, aroused controversy. Due to their symbolic role, urban bridges demand greater consideration to aesthetics than common highway bridges. Considering the shorter spans and lower cost of urban bridges, owners sometimes prefer concepts that are not the cheapest, to transform a bridge into a symbol of the city. This increases the cost of materials and adds complexity to construction. In his presentation at the same conference, Mr. M.C.Tang emphasized that: "aesthetics is not weird, and aesthetics may not be expensive." Among the bridges in a city, it is worthwhile to add appropriate additional fees for aesthetic purpose, from the perspective of the overall planning and for the sake of symbolic value of specific bridges. This rationale can be easily accepted by experts and citizens alike.

After the conference, the Chinese journal *Qiaoliang* (*Bridge*) invited some experts to discuss this topic in a special issue. From the discussion, it emerged that the experts were generally against unorthodox and awkward visual forms for bridges, regarding them devoid of aesthetic value. The experts also held the general opinion that aesthetic considerations in design should be "appropriate", i.e., there is a limit to the aesthetic treatment of bridges. For example, the design of the new Oakland Bay Bridge in San Francisco required additional funds to achieve the desired aesthetic objectives, but this additional cost was a small percentage of the overall construction cost. The experts further considered that elevating bridges to "symbolic" status should only be done in exceptional cases. Most bridges should emphasize economy and function. Finally, it was agreed that the aesthetic value of urban bridges should be judged by the citizens using it. Their ideas should be considered and the bridge must be capable of standing the test of time.

The 17 urban bridges included in this picture book include a wide variety of types. There is one self-anchored suspension bridge, seven cable-stayed bridges, two extradosed prestressed concrete bridges, four arch bridges, and three girder bridges, including one movable bridge and one pedestrian bridge. These structures represent the aesthetic tendency of most jury experts. With the improvement of the material well-being of Chinese people and the increasing pace of urbanization, the 21st century will see more urban bridges. With the consistent improvement of the aesthetic abilities of our country's bridge engineers, more bridges will be built that are not only safe and usable, but which also will provide long-term aesthetic enjoyment for the people.

复兴大桥
Fuxing Bridge

桥　　名：复兴大桥
桥　　型：钢管混凝土系杆拱桥
主　　跨：190m
桥　　址：浙江省杭州市
完成日期：2004 年
设计单位：杭州市城建设计研究院有限公司
施工单位：广西壮族自治区公路桥梁工程总公司

Name: Fuxing Bridge
Type: Tied concrete-filled steel tube arch bridge
Main span: 190m
Location: Hangzhou, Zhejiang Province
Completion: 2004
Designer(s): Hangzhou Architectural & Civil Engineering Design Institute Co., Ltd.
Contractor(s): Guangxi Road & Bridge Engineering Corporation

复兴大桥又名钱江四桥，位于杭州市钱江一桥下游 4.3km 处，北起复兴立交，南至中兴立交。大桥全长 1145m，主桥为多跨双层组合钢管混凝土系杆拱桥，跨径组合为 2×85m+190m+5×85m+190m+2×85m。其中两主孔为跨径 190m 的下承式和中承式系杆组合桁架式钢管混凝土拱桥，另有 9 孔跨径 85m 的上、下承拱梁组合钢管混凝土拱桥。

　　复兴大桥的结构特色在于巧妙地利用大小拱结合形成了新型钢管混凝土系杆拱桥，并采用多跨连拱，双层路面结构。上层桥面设双向六条机动车快速行车道，下层设地铁、公交车专用道及行人、非机动车通道和八个观景平台。

Fuxing Bridge, also known as the 4th Bridge over the Qiantang River, is located 4.3km downstream from the First Bridge over the Qiantang River in Hangzhou. This bridge has a total length of 1145m from the Fuxing Overpass in the north to the Zhongxing Overpass in the south. The main bridge is multi-span double-deck tied concrete-filled steel tube (CFST) arch bridge. Its span layouts are 2×85m+190m+5×85m+190m+2×85m. The two main spans, which are both 190m long, are through and half-through truss-CFST-combined arch bridges. Other 9 spans, which are all 85m long, are deck-up and through CFST-arch-girder-combined bridge.

The special characteristics of this bridge are the compound use of large and small arches, the usage of continuous arches, and the adoption of double-deck structure. In the upper deck, there are six freeway lanes in dual traffic. While in the lower deck, there are several special lanes designed for subway and bus, passenger lanes and non-motorized vehicle lanes. Moreover, 8 platforms are also designed to be placed in the lower deck for sightseeing.

（部分图片提供者：柯伟）

长沙洪山大桥
Hongshan Bridge in Changsha

桥　　名：长沙洪山大桥
桥　　型：无背索斜拉桥
主　　跨：206m
桥　　址：湖南省长沙市
完成日期：2004 年
设计单位：湖南大学
施工单位：中铁大桥局集团有限公司

Name: Hongshan Bridge in Changsha
Type: Cable-stayed bridge with inclined pylon and no back stay
Main span: 206m
Location: Changsha, Hunan Province
Completion: 2004
Designer(s): Hunan University
Contractor(s): China Railway Major Bridge Engineering Group Co., Ltd.

长沙洪山大桥是长沙市北二环线上跨浏阳河的一座特大桥梁，南接四方坪立交，北接捞刀河特大桥，跨径布置为206m+30.3m，是一座竖琴式无背索斜塔斜拉桥。

主梁采用超长悬臂钢—混凝土结合梁结构，呈脊骨梁形式。桥面设双向六车道，每侧3个车道位于13m长的悬臂梁之上。在施工阶段采用预弯预应力措施合理控制混凝土板的受力状态。倾斜的桥塔利用桥塔自重平衡主梁恒载与一半活载，受力合理。

The Hongshan Bridge in Changsha, with the spans of 206m+30.3m, is a cable-stayed bridge with inclined pylon and no back stay. It is located on the second North Ring in Changsha and crosses the Liuyang River, connecting the Sifangping Overpass in the south and the Bridge over the Laodao River in the north.

The main girder, with a spine shaped cross section, is designed as a steel-concrete composite beam with super long cantilevers. There are 6 vehicle lanes on the deck, with three lanes on each side on the cantilever region which is 13m long. During the construction period, the pre-bending and pre-stressing technique is adopted to control the stress state of the concrete slabs. The design concept for the inclined pylon of the cable-stayed bridge is that the self-weight of the pylon should balance the dead load of the main span and half of the live load to achieve a reasonable stress state in the pylon.

天津大沽桥
Dagu Bridge in Tianjin

大沽桥坐落在天津市和平区与河北区交界处的海河上，是天津市海河综合开发工程中第一座新建桥梁。

大沽桥全长154m，跨径布置为24m+106m+24m，桥面宽为30～59m，双向六车道，是一座敞开式空间四索面系杆拱桥，大小拱肋均为倾斜的钢箱结构，大拱高39m，外倾18°，小拱高19m，外倾22°。车行道桥面结构为24m宽正交异性板钢箱梁，车行道与人行道之间采用镂空设计，外侧为圆弧形观景平台，满足行人的亲水期望。

非对称拱的设置突破了常规拱桥的二维平面受力模式，四索面吊杆布置保证了结构安全，从而不需设置风撑，同时呈现出独特优美的造型；镂空梁增强了亲水性的景观效果，同时满足桥梁横向受力的要求。

The Dagu Bridge in Tianjin is located in the border area of the Heping District and the Hebei District over the Haihe River. It is the first newly constructed bridge in the Haihe River Comprehensive Development Project.

The full length of the Dagu Bridge is 154m and the spans are arranged as 24m+106m+24m. Its deck is 30~59m wide with six lanes in dual direction. This bridge is a tied arch bridge with four spatial cable planes and no upper connection braces. The arch ribs of the big and small arches are designed as inclined steel-box structures. The big arch is 39m high with an outward inclination of 18°, while the small arch is 19m high with an outward inclination of 22°. The bridge deck is a 24m wide orthotropic steel-box girder. A hollow space is designed between the traffic lanes and the sidewalks. In each lateral side of the bridge, there is an arc-shaped sightseeing platform to meet the pedestrian's expectation of closing to water.

The adoption of asymmetrical arches breaks through the two-dimensional load bearing pattern of conventional arch bridges. The system of four cable planes not only ensures the safety of the structure without wind braces, but also shows a particularly graceful shape. The hollow space with the transverse beams can enhance the landscape effect of closing to water, and also satisfy the requirement of the bridge for carrying transverse loads.

桥　　名：天津大沽桥
桥　　型：敞开式空间四索面系杆拱桥
主　　跨：106m
桥　　址：天津市
完成日期：2005年
设计单位：林同棪国际工程咨询（中国）有限公司
　　　　　天津城建设计院有限公司
施工单位：天津城建集团有限公司

Name: Dagu Bridge in Tianjin
Type: Tied arch bridge with four spatial cable planes and no upper braces
Main span: 106m
Location: Tianjin
Completion: 2005
Designer(s): T.Y. Lin International Engineering Consulting (China) Co., Ltd.
　　　　　　　Tianjin Urban Construction Design Institute Co., Ltd.
Contractor(s): Tianjin Urban Construction Group Co., Ltd.

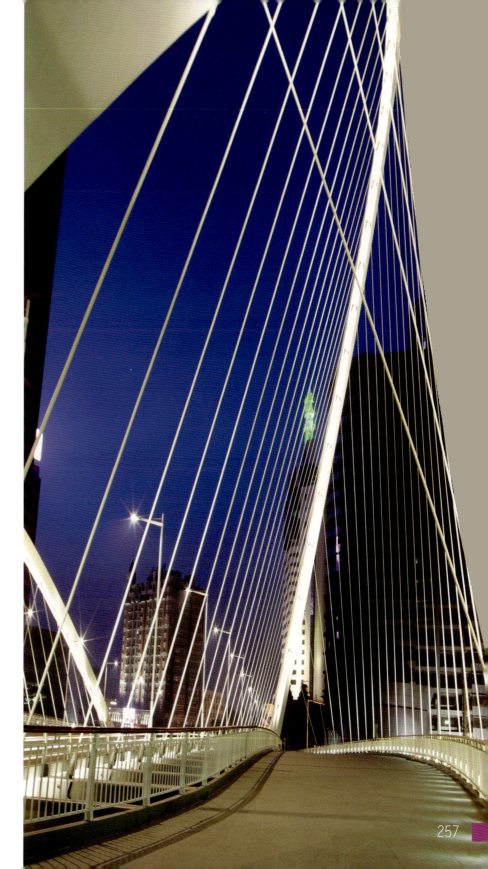

舟山新城大桥
Xincheng Bridge in Zhoushan

舟山新城大桥是浙江临城新区规划的"四横六纵"城市主干道交通网中的重要跨海通道，连接长峙岛与舟山本岛。

主桥与引桥全长1277m，梁宽16.4m，设计为双向四车道。桥梁跨径布置为6×30m+6×30m+36m+148m+36m+8×30m+7×30m。主桥为中承式钢管混凝土系杆拱桥，主跨拱肋采用钢管混凝土结构，为悬链线拱轴线，拱高37m，矢跨比1/4，拱肋采用实腹哑铃式变截面，横撑采用箱形变截面结构。

The Xincheng Bridge in Zhoushan, Zhejiang Province, is an important cross-sea routeway which is a part of the planned "Four Horizontal & Six Vertical" city transportation network in Lincheng New District. This bridge connects the Changzhi Island and the Zhoushan Main Island.

The total length of the bridge is 1277m, including the main bridge and the approach bridges. The deck is 16.4m wide, with dual-way two traffic lanes. The spans of the bridge are arranged as 6×30m+6×30m+36m+148m+36m+8×30m+8×30m+7×30m. The main bridge is a half-through basket bowstring arch with the central span of 148m. The arch ribs are fabricated as concrete-filled steel tubes. The arch axis is a catenary. The rise of the arch is 37m and the rise-to-span ratio is 1/4. The cross section of ribs is designed as solid dumbbell type with variable depth. Between the ribs, several transverse braces with variable box sections are installed.

桥　　名：	舟山新城大桥
桥　　型：	中承式钢管混凝土系杆拱桥
主　　跨：	148m
桥　　址：	浙江省舟山市
完成日期：	2005年
设计单位：	中交公路规划设计院有限公司
施工单位：	中铁大桥局集团有限公司

Name: Xincheng Bridge in Zhoushan
Type: Half-through tied concrete-filled steel tube arch bridge
Main span: 148m
Location: Zhoushan, Zhejiang Province
Completion: 2005
Designer(s): CCCC Highway Consultants Co., Ltd.
Contractor(s): China Railway Major Bridge Engineering Group Co., Ltd.

开封黄河大桥
Kaifeng Bridge over the Yellow River

开封黄河大桥位于河南省开封市东北，主桥上部结构为七塔八跨双索面预应力混凝土矮塔斜拉桥，桥跨布置为85m+6×140m+85m=1010m。主桥采用塔梁固结、墩梁分离连续结构。塔高38m，塔的高跨比为1/3.68。主梁采用单箱三室斜腹板箱梁，根部梁高5.5m，跨中梁高2.7m。

为增加桥下透视效果，使主桥上下部结构相协调，每个主墩采用两个分离的箱形墩柱，横桥向分别在墩顶和承台设置系梁加强墩柱的横向联结。为增加美观性，墩身采用设有凹棱的多边形箱形截面。

The Kaifeng Bridge over the Yellow River in Henan is located in the northeast of Kaifeng City. The main bridge is an extradosed prestressed concrete bridge with 7 pylons and 8 spans which are arranged as 85m+6×140m+85m. Its main girders fixed with the pylons are placed on the top of the piers, resulting in a continuous system with 7 pylons and 8 spans. The height of pylons is 38m, and the ratio of the pylon height to the main span is 1/3.68. The main girder has a single box section with inclined webs. The depth of the main beam at the supports and at the mid-span are 5.5m and 2.7m, respectively.

In order to increase the perspective effect under the bridge to make the upper and lower parts of the bridge in a good harmony with each other, each of the piers is designed as two separated piers with box section. Transvers beams are installed at the top of the piers and the pile cap to enhance the lateral connection. The box with polygon lines is adopted as the section of the piers to increase the aesthetic effect.

桥　　名：开封黄河大桥
桥　　型：矮塔斜拉桥
主　　跨：6×140m
桥　　址：河南省开封市
完成日期：2006年
设计单位：河南省交通规划勘察设计院有限责任公司
施工单位：中铁大桥局集团有限公司

Name: Kaifeng Bridge over the Yellow River
Type: Extradosed prestressed concrete bridge
Main span: 6×140m
Location: Kaifeng, Henan Province
Completion: 2006
Designer(s): Henan Provincial Communications Planning Survey & Design Institute Co., Ltd.
Contractor(s): China Railway Major Bridge Engineering Group Co., Ltd.

青藏铁路拉萨河大桥
Qinghai-Tibet Railway Bridge over the Lhasa River

青藏铁路拉萨河大桥是青藏铁路进入拉萨市的单线铁路桥,大桥距拉萨市中心 5km,是青藏铁路的标志性工程之一。

青藏铁路拉萨河大桥为五跨三拱下承式拱梁组合结构,主桥全长 324m,跨度布置为 36m+72m+108m+72m+36m,桥梁全宽 8.1m。

主桥预应力混凝土主纵梁采用矩形截面,梁高在顶面按曲线变化。为减小拱肋的厚重感,中孔拱肋采用双层叠拱,每片拱肋由上下 2 根钢管和竖杆组成。边拱采用哑铃形截面。

主桥桥墩采用变截面双圆柱墩,像牦牛的骨骼充满力度,并与上部结构优美的曲线风格相统一;引桥桥墩采用雪莲花式的变截面圆柱形墩,具有浓厚的西藏当地乡土人情风味。

考虑该桥所处的特殊地理位置和气候条件,大桥设计中引入了少维修和免维护的设计理念,采用纤维混凝土拱脚、混凝土外涂装及钢结构长效涂装等综合措施来提高桥梁耐久性。采用先梁后拱、大节段吊装法施工。

The Qinghai-Tibet Railway Bridge over the Lhasa River, located 5km far from the center of Lhasa, is a single track railway bridge. This bridge is one of the symbolic projects of the Qinghai-Tibet Railway.

The bridge is a concrete-filled steel tube through arch bridge with prestressed concrete continuous girder. The total length of the bridge is 324m, with three arches and five spans which are arranged as 36m+72m+108m+72m+36m. The width of the deck is 8.1m.

The rectangle section is adopted for the prestressed concrete girder of the main bridge. The bottom of the beam is on the same horizontal line, while the top is on a curved line from the mid-span to the

supports of the beam. In order to decrease the messiness feeling of the arch ribs, the middle arch is designed as a double stacked arch, which consists of two steel tubes and vertical links. The dumbbell shape is chosen for the section of the side arches.

The piers of the main bridge are designed as double circular columns with variable section, just like the strong skeleton of the yaks. This design can be also in good harmony with the graceful style of the superstructure. The piers of the approach bridges have the circular variable section showing the shape of snow lotus herb, which stands for the local favor of the Tibet.

Considering the special geographical and climatic conditions in the bridge site, the concepts of fewer repairs and free of maintenance were employed in the design of the bridge. The durability of the bridge is enhanced by several comprehensive measures such as the fiber reinforced concrete arch foot, the outer coating of concrete and long term coating system for the steel structures. The construction methods of "Beam Construction ahead of Arch" and the large segment lifting are adopted for this bridge

桥　　名：青藏铁路拉萨河大桥	**Name:** Qinghai-Tibet Railway Bridge over the Lhasa River
桥　　型：钢管混凝土拱连续梁组合结构	**Type:** Concrete-filled steel tube arch bridge with prestressed concrete continuous girder
主　　跨：108m	**Main span:** 108m
桥　　址：西藏自治区拉萨市	**Location:** Lhasa, Tibet
完成日期：2006 年	**Completion:** 2006
设计单位：铁道部第三勘察设计院集团有限公司	**Designer(s):** The Ministry of Railways Third Survey Design Institute Group Co., Ltd.
施工单位：中铁大桥局集团有限公司	**Contractor(s):** China Railway Major Bridge Engineering Group Co., Ltd.

广州猎德大桥
Liede Bridge in Guangzhou

桥　　名：广州猎德大桥
桥　　型：自锚式悬索桥
主　　跨：219m
桥　　址：广东省广州市
完成日期：2009 年
设计单位：西南交大土木工程设计有限公司
施工单位：中交第二航务工程局有限公司

Name: Liede Bridge in Guangzhou
Type: Self-anchored suspension bridge
Main span: 219m
Location: Guangzhou, Guangdong Province
Completion: 2009
Designer(s): Southwest Jiaoda Civil Engineering Design Co., Ltd.
Contractor(s) : CCCC Second Harbor Engineering Company Ltd.

广州猎德大桥位于广州大桥与华南大桥之间，北岸与猎德路相接，南岸与新港东路立交相接。大桥为独塔空间双索面自锚式悬索桥，跨径布置47m+167m+219m+47m，全长480m。桥塔采用贝壳状三维曲面造型，高128m。大断面单箱钢箱加劲梁顶推施工工艺，"珠江之贝"三维曲面清水混凝土索塔施工工艺以及非对称空间自锚式缆索系统施工工艺，是大桥施工技术特点。

The Liede Bridge in Guangzhou is located between the Guangzhou Bridge and the Huanan Bridge over the Pearl River, connecting the Liede Road in the north bank and the Xingang East Overpass in the south bank. The bridge is designed as a self-anchored suspension bridge with single pylon and double cable planes, with the spans of 47m+167m+219m+47m and 480m in total. The pylon, which is 128m high, has a three-dimensional surface with conchoidal shape. The special construction techniques of this bridge include, launching technique of the single steel box stiffening beam with large cross section, construction technique of the pylon which has the special three-dimensional non-coated surface of "Shell of the Pearl River" and the installation technique of the asymmetrical spatial self-anchored main cable system.

福建三明台江大桥
Sanming Bridge over the Taijiang River in Fujian

福建三明台江大桥位于三明市三元区，跨越台江连接三明市即将开发的东西两岸。大桥为钢拱塔预应力混凝土梁斜拉桥。跨径布置为50m+60m+2×110m+60m+50m，全长440m。钢拱塔高82.2m，采用梯形钢箱断面和圆弧形拱轴线。斜拉索按照在塔上由高到低、在梁上由近到远的方式锚固，形成空间螺旋曲面。斜拉索在梁上的锚固点集中在桥面中心线上，且纵桥向间距不等。

拱形塔和空间索面造型别致，富有动感和韵律感。

The Sanming Bridge over the Taijiang River in Fujian is located in the Sanyuan District of Sanming City, linking the east and west banks of the Taijiang River, which are to be developed. The bridge is a cable-stayed bridge with steel arch pylon and prestressed concrete beam. The spans are arranged as 50m+60m+2×110m+60m+50m and 440m in total. The steel arch pylon is 82.2m high and has a section of trapezoidal steel box. The shape of the arch axis is designed as a circular arc. The cables of this bridge are anchored on the centerline of the deck in a single row and with unequal spacing. The cable planes of the bridge look like four helical surfaces.

The special shape of the arch pylon and spatial cable planes makes the bridge full of sense of movement and rhythm.

桥　　名：福建三明台江大桥
桥　　型：钢拱塔斜拉桥
主　　跨：110m
桥　　址：福建省三明市
完成日期：2010年
设计单位：林同棪国际工程咨询（中国）有限公司
施工单位：中铁八局集团有限公司

Name: Sanming Bridge over the Taijiang River in Fujian
Type: Cable-stayed bridge with steel arch pylon
Main span: 110m
Location: Sanming, Fujian Province
Completion: 2010
Designer(s): T. Y. Lin International Engineering Consulting (China) Co., Ltd.
Contractor(s): China Railway 8th Engineering Group Co., Ltd.

宁波外滩大桥
Waitan Bridge in Ningbo

桥　　名：宁波外滩大桥
桥　　型：异型斜拉桥
主　　跨：225m
桥　　址：浙江省宁波市
完成日期：2010 年
设计单位：上海市政工程设计研究总院（集团）有限公司
施工单位：四川公路桥梁建设集团有限公司

Name: Waitan Bridge in Ningbo
Type: Special-shaped cable-stayed bridge
Main span: 225m
Location: Ningbo, Zhejiang Province
Completion: 2010
Designer(s): Shanghai Municipal Engineering Design Institute (Group) Co., Ltd.
Contractor(s): Sichuan Road & Bridge (group) Co., Ltd.

宁波外滩大桥属于宁波市"五路四桥"建设工程之一，西起大庆南路，跨甬江，东至曙光路。主桥采用独塔四索面异型斜拉桥结构，跨径布置为225m+90m。加劲梁采用平弯分离式钢箱梁，两箱梁间通过横梁联系，加劲梁外侧设有人行道和悬挑人行桥，可作为行人在江面上观光的亲水平台，单侧桥面宽达21.4m。索塔采用斜塔结构，高98m，与后斜杆构成人字形，并与水平杆相连形成三角形结构。

异型桥塔水平杆采用支架法施工，用龙门吊机吊运就位；前塔柱采用"竖拼竖转"法施工；后斜杆采用"先卧拼后整体提升、平移"法施工。

The Waitan Bridge in Ningbo is included in the so called "Five Roads, Four Bridges" construction project in Ningbo. This bridge, crossing the Yongjiang River, starts from Daqing South Road in the west and ends in the Shuguang Road in the east. The main bridge is a special-shaped cable-stayed bridge with single pylon and four cable planes. The spans are arranged as 225m+90m. The stiffening girder has a section of two separated boxes. These boxes are connected by lateral beams. Sidewalks and cantilevered pedestrian deck installed outside the stiffening girder can provide the passengers a sightseeing platform over the river. The width of deck on each side reaches 21.4m. The pylon is an inclined structure, with the height of 98m, showing a herringbone shape combining with the back inclined strut, which is made of steel and fixed to the pylon at the top. They form a triangle together with two horizontal struts.

The horizontal struts were installed on scaffoldings and lifted by gantry crane to the site. The inclined pylon was constructed by the method of "Vertical Assembly, Vertical Rotation". The back strut was constructed by the method of "Horizontal assembly, lift and move".

重庆嘉悦嘉陵江大桥
Jiayue Bridge over the Jialing River in Chongqing

重庆嘉悦嘉陵江大桥连接渝北区与北碚区,为双索面矮塔斜拉桥,跨径布置为66m+75m+75m+145m+250m+145m,全长756m。桥塔为Y形结构,全高100m,桥面以上高32m。加劲梁共有两层,车辆与行人上下分流,下层两侧为各宽3.5m的观光长廊。主梁为单箱单室大悬臂断面形式,箱梁底板宽12m,顶板宽28m,每侧支撑在横梁上的悬臂翼缘长度为8.0m。箱梁梁高采用变截面,从靠近桥塔根部的7.0m变化至跨中的5.0m。

桥塔塔身采用翻模法施工,桥面以上桥塔由于结构外倾,施工中设置水平对拉刚架,以保证桥塔的稳定并控制变形。

The Jiayue Bridge over the Jialing River connects the Yubei District and the Beibei District. It is an extradosed prestressed concrete bridge with double cable planes. The spans are arranged as 66m+75m+75m+145m+250m+145m, and 756m in total. The pylons are designed as Y shape with a height of 100m in total and 32m above the deck. The stiffening girder has two decks for vehicles and pedestrians, respectively. A sightseeing corridor, which is 3.5m wide, is designed on the side of the lower deck. The main beam has a single cell box section with long cantilevers. The width of the box is 12m at the bottom and 28m at the top. The length of the cantilever flange which supports on the lateral beams on each side of the main beam is 8.0m. The main beam has a variable cross section with the depth gradually decreasing from 7.0m at the supporting area around the pylon to 5.0m at the mid-span in the shape of a parabola.

The pylon shafts were constructed by the turnover mold method. Since the pylon above the deck is inclined outwards, horizontal tensioning frames were installed to ensure the stability of the pylon and control the displacement during construction.

Name: Jiayue Bridge over the Jialing River in Chongqing
Type: Extradosed prestressed concrete bridge
Main span: 250m
Location: Chongqing
Completion: 2010
Designer(s): T. Y. Lin International Engineering Consulting (China) Co., Ltd.
Contractor(s): Chongqing Construction Bridge Engineering Company Ltd.

太原跻汾桥
Jifen Bridge in Taiyuan

太原跻汾桥位于太原市长风商务区中轴线上，跨越汾河，与汾河东西两岸公园相衔接。桥梁将原规划中并行的两座人行桥通过纽带的设计理念连接到了一起，形成了一座极具特色的双弧交叉空间交错桥面人行桥。双弧交叉的桥面与连续变化连接杆件，巧妙地形成了一个DNA分子的空间结构。

南北两线主桥跨径布置均为41m+125m+56m，采用V形刚构连续梁。主梁为钢箱梁结构，梁宽7.6m，两线主桥在跨中设有平台连接。人行桥基频仅为1.125Hz，为了保证桥梁使用性能、安全性能和行人舒适性，针对桥梁实际运营中可能出现的超过舒适度要求的大振幅侧向振动的状况，结构设计中预留了设置黏滞阻尼器和调频质量阻尼器两个备选方案。

The Jifen Bridge in Taiyuan is located in the central axis of the Changfeng Business District in Taiyuan, crossing the Fenhe River. This bridge connects the parks located in the east and west banks of the Fenhe River. The original design concept of connecting two parallel pedestrian bridges together is adopted to form a very special pedestrian bridge with double crossed arcs. The double crossed arc decks and continuously varied connecting members form a spatial structure of a DNA molecule.

The spans of the north and south main bridges are both arranged as 41m+125m+56m. The bridge with V-shaped pier connected with continuous beam is adopted as the final scheme. The main beam has a section of steel box with a width of 7.6m. Platforms are installed to laterally connect the two main bridges. The fundamental frequency of this pedestrian bridge is 1.125Hz. Considering the possible large lateral vibration which may exceeds the requirement of comfort during the service period, two kinds of dampers, which are viscous damper and tuned mass damper, are proposed in the structural design to ensure the service performance, safety performance of the bridge as well as the passenger's comfort.

桥　　名：太原跻汾桥
桥　　型：V形刚构连续梁桥
主　　跨：125m
桥　　址：山西省太原市
完成日期：2010年
设计单位：同济大学建筑设计研究院（集团）有限公司
施工单位：中交第一航务工程局有限公司

Name: Jifen Bridge in Taiyuan
Type: Continuous girder bridge with integral V-shaped piers
Main span: 125m
Location: Taiyuan, Shanxi Province
Completion: 2010
Designer(s): Architectural Design & Research Institute of Tongji University
Contractor(s): CCCC First Harbor Engineering Company Ltd.

（部分图片提供者：祁颋）

塘沽响螺湾海河开启桥
Xiangluowan Movable Bridge over the Haihe River in Tanggu

桥　名：塘沽响螺湾海河开启桥
桥　型：立转式悬臂开启钢桥
主　跨：76m
桥　址：天津市
完成日期：2010年
设计单位：天津市市政工程设计研究院
施工单位：中铁十四局集团第三工程有限公司

Name: Xiangluowan Movable Bridge over the Haihe River in Tanggu
Type: Vertical rotating cantilever movable steel bridge
Main spans: 76m
Location: Tianjin
Completion: 2010
Designer(s): Tianjin Municipal Engineering Design & Research Institute
Contractor(s): China Railway Shisiju Group Third Engineering Co., Ltd.

塘沽响螺湾海河开启桥位于天津市滨海新区，为一座立转式开启桥。桥下通航净宽68m，未开启时净空大于7.0m，开启时净空大于31m，满足Ⅵ级航道要求。

主桥全长105.94m，跨径布置为14.97m+76m+14.97m，桥面宽为20m，设双向四车道。

主桥为立转式悬臂开启体系，主要由基础、桥墩、主梁、配重、开启装置组成。桥梁主跨悬臂部分采用变截面钢箱梁，梁高从根部的4.0m渐变至跨中1.5m；配重部分采用球墨铸铁，单侧主梁配重600t。桥面铺装采用8mm花纹钢板，纹高1.6mm。

主桥开启采用动力为600kW的动力转动装置，设置于两个塔基之中，采用支撑轴承加转动轴承实现平衡加转动功能，转动半径为12m，梁端转动角度为85°。采用立转式开启稳定性高，开启时间短，总开启的时间为315s，总的关闭时间为265s。

The Xiangluowan movable bridge over the Haihe River in Tanggu is located in the Binhai new district in Tianjing. This bridge is a vertical rotating movable bridge. It is an important passage for the communication between the two sides of the Haihe River. The navigational clearance of this bridge is 68m wide, 7.0m high when closed and 31m when open, satisfying the requirement of level VI for navigation.

The main bridge has three spans which are arranged as 14.97m+76m+14.97m, and 105.94m in total. The deck is 20m wide, with four vehicle lanes in dual direction.

The main bridge, which is mainly composed of foundation, pier, main girder, counterweight and opening devices, has a vertical rotating cantilever system. The cantilever region of the main span uses a steel box beam with variable cross section. The depth of the beam gradually decreases from 4m at the support to 1.5m at the mid-span. The counterweight uses the ductile cast iron, 600t on each side of the main beam. The deck is paved with checkered steel plate which is 8mm thick.

A power transmission device with the power of 600kW is used to open the main bridge. The device is installed in the middle of the foot of two pylons. Its balanced rotation function is achieved by steady bearing and rolling bearing equipment. The rotation radius is 12m, and the rotation angle at the end of the beam is 85°. The main advantages of this vertical rotation include higher stability and less operating time. The total time needed to open and close the bridge is 315s and 265s, respectively.

大鹏湾桥
Dapeng Bay Bridge

桥　　名：大鹏湾桥
桥　　型：单塔预应力混凝土梁斜拉桥 / 钢箱梁开启桥
主　　跨：100m
桥　　址：台湾屏东县
完成日期：2011 年
设计单位：台湾世曦工程顾问股份有限公司
施工单位：中华工程股份有限公司

Name: Dapeng Bay Bridge
Type: Single-tower PC girder cable-stayed bridge / Steel box girder movable bridge
Main Span: 100m
Location: Pingdong County, Taiwan
Completion: 2011
Designer(s): CECI Engineering Consultants Inc., Taiwan
Contractor(s): BES Engineering Corporation

大鹏湾桥位于台湾屏东县大鹏湾风景区，跨越大鹏湾出海航道。主桥为独塔混凝土斜拉桥，主跨跨径100m；与主跨相邻的一跨引桥为开启桥，供帆船通行。

主桥斜拉桥采用单塔非对称跨径布置。斜拉索均锚固在桥面中线上。上部结构采用预应力混凝土箱梁，梁高3m；混凝土桥塔高72.9m，采用正面为A形、侧面为风帆造型的空间结构。开启桥为两幅分离单悬臂竖转式结构，上部结构为正交异性桥面板钢箱梁，下部结构包含活动桥座及开启端桥墩。

大鹏湾桥是台湾首座采用开启设计的城市景观桥。风帆造型桥塔的尺寸在三个方向同时变化，造成每一高度的钢筋及模板施工均难以系统化，难度很高。开启桥钢桥面铺装采用10.5mm厚PU环氧树脂掺合金骨材，黏着性及抗弯性好，同时降低了自重。

Dapeng Bay Bridge is located at Dapeng Bay Scenic Area, Pingdong County, Taiwan, across Dapeng Bay sea waterway. The main bridge is a single-tower cable-stayed bridge with a main span of 100m, and the first approaching span is a movable bridge for sailing boats.

The single-tower cable-stayed bridge has two asymmetric spans. The stay cables are anchored along the center line of the girder, which is a PC box girder with a depth of 3m. The pylon is 72.9m high, and the 3D configuration of pylon shows an A shape in the front view and a sail shape in the side view. The movable bridge consists of two isolated single-leaf bascule bridge structure. The superstructure is steel box girders with orthotropic steel decks. The substructure contains a movable bridge seat and an open end pier.

As a landscape symbol, Dapeng Bay Bridge is the first movable bridge in Taiwan. The measurement of the sail shaped pylon changes in three dimensions. Each layer of reinforcement and formwork is different; therefore, the construction cannot be systematized and has high degree of difficulty. The pavement on the orthotropic steel deck in the movable bridge is 10.5mm thick PU epoxy mixed with metal aggregate which has good adhesion, flexural resistance and light weight.

（图片提供者：蔡俊鎧）

九堡大桥
Jiubao Bridge

九堡大桥位于浙江杭州，跨越钱塘江，是国内第一座全桥采用组合结构的大型越江城市桥梁。大桥孔跨布置为 55m+2×85m+90m（北引桥）+3×210m（主桥）+90m+9×85m+55m（南引桥），标准桥面宽度为 37.7m。

主桥采用连续组合拱桥。上部结构为梁—拱组合体系，由钢—混凝土组合结构桥面系和钢拱结构组成。拱肋为钢箱结构，由外倾式主拱肋和空间曲线副拱肋组成空间结构。

九堡大桥位于强涌潮河段，为避免强涌潮对大桥施工的影响，主桥三跨组合拱桥钢结构采用整体顶推法施工。

顶推施工时每跨间设置 1 个临时墩，拱肋与钢系梁间设置临时加强杆件，以满足钢结构顶推施工需要，并充分发挥了钢结构的承载能力。引桥组合箱梁的钢梁采用无临时墩顶推法施工。

Jiubao Bridge is located over the Qiantang River, in Hangzhou, Zhejiang Province. The total length of the bridge is 1855m. It is the first major river-crossing urban bridge which uses steel-concrete composite structure for the entire bridge in China. The spans of this bridge are arranged as 55m+2×85m+90m (north approaching bridges) +3×210m (main bridge) +90m+9×85m+55m (south approaching bridges). The deck width of the standard segments is 37.7m.

The main bridge is a continuous composite arch bridge. The superstructure is designed as a beam-arch composite system, which is composed of steel-concrete composite deck and steel arches. The ribs of the arches have a section of steel box, and are composed of outwardly inclined main arch ribs and spatial secondary arch ribs.

Jiubao Bridge is located in a region with strong surge. To avoid the unfavorable impact brought by the surge, the incremental launching method for the full bridge was adopted for the three main spans.

The arches and steel girder were manufactured in the factories and assembled on-site. During the incremental launching process of the main spans, one temporary pier was built in the middle of each span. Temporary fix members were installed between the ribs and the steel beam, in order to satisfy the construction needs during the incremental launching process of the steel structures and make full use of the bearing capacity of the steel structures. For the approaching bridges, the incremental launching method for the full bridge without temporary piers was adopted.

Name: Jiubao Bridge
Type: Continuous arch bridge
Main span: 3×210m
Location: Hangzhou, Zhejiang Province
Completion: 2012
Designer(s): Shanghai Municipal Engineering Design Institute (Group) Co., Ltd.
Contractor(s): CCCC Second Harbor Engineering Company Ltd.
CRBC International Co., Ltd.

社子大桥
Shezi Bridge

社子大桥位于台北市，跨越基隆河连接北投区及社子区。全桥总长 630m，全宽 41m，设公交专用道、机动车道、摩托车道及人行道，并且为轻轨交通预留 9m 宽度。

主桥为斜塔柱非对称钢斜拉桥，跨径布置为 70m+180m=250m，斜拉索采用双索面。塔柱、底梁、系梁及主梁为钢箱梁，并采用塔、墩分离结构。下部结构采用混凝土墩，ϕ2.0m 桩基。

跨河桥梁施工采用悬臂法。钢箱主梁节段在北投端桥面上完成组装后浮运，再用 400t 吊机吊装就位。

Shezi Bridge over the Jilong River with a total length of 630m is located in Taibei, linking the Beitou District and the Shezi District. The deck width is 41m, including bus lanes, traffic lanes, motorcycle lanes, sidewalks for both pedestrian and bicycles, and a 9m width reserved for future light rail traffic.

The main bridge, having a span arrangement of 70m+180m=250m, is an asymmetrical cable-stayed bridge with single inclined steel tower. The stay cables are using double-sided configuration, and all the tower, bottom beam, tie beam and main girder are using steel box structures. The substructure consists of concrete piers and ϕ 2.0m pile foundations.

The cantilever construction method was used for the cross-river part. After the components were assembled on the deck of the Beitou side, the steel girder segments were shipped with a floating platform and then installed with 400t overhead moving cranes.

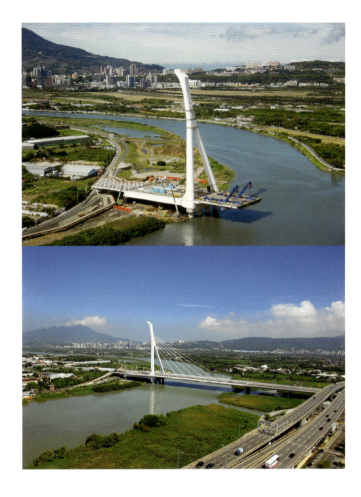

桥　　名：社子大桥
桥　　型：独塔钢箱梁斜拉桥
主　　跨：180m
桥　　址：台北市
完成日期：2012 年
设计单位：台湾世曦工程顾问股份有限公司
施工单位：春原营造股份有限公司

Name: Shezi Bridge
Type: Single-tower steel girder cable-stayed bridge
Main Span: 180m
Location: Taibei
Completion: 2012
Designer(s): CECI Engineering Consultants Inc., Taiwan
Contractor(s): Chunyuan Construction Co., Ltd.

东水门长江大桥
Dongshuimen Bridge over the Yangtze River

　　东水门长江大桥位于重庆市嘉陵江和长江的交汇处，连接渝中区和南岸区。东水门长江大桥采用"公路＋轨道"交通模式，分为上、下两层，上层设置人行道及双向四车道，下层是双向轨道线，是重庆市轨道交通系统的重要节点。

　　东水门长江大桥为双塔单索面钢桁梁斜拉桥，全长858m，跨径布置为222.5m+445m+190.5m。主塔塔高182m，桥面以上高109m，主塔两侧设置9对斜拉索，索面位于桥面中心线。桁架梁为双层布置，主桁高13m，主桁主要杆件均为焊接箱形截面，上下层桥面均采用正交异性钢桥面板。桁架结构的主梁不仅为乘坐轻轨的旅客提供更好的视野，还使大桥本身更具有通透性。

　　该桥桥塔的外形看上去像一把天梭，造型独特。桥塔的外部轮廓具有相同半径的圆弧，并且桥塔厚度从上到下保持不变，桥塔的上塔柱线形接近于直线，这样的外形大大方便了施工，大部分模板可以重复使用。

Dongshuimen Bridge over the Yangtze River is located at the meeting point of the Jialing River and the Yangtze River in Chongqing. It connects the Yuzhong District and the Nan'an District and is a critical project in the urban rail transit system of Chongqing. The bridge has double decks in vertical including highway and railway. The upper deck is designed as four traffic lanes in dual direction and two sidewalks, while the lower deck is designed as dual-way railway, through which the Line 6 crosses both the Yangtze River and the Jialing River.

The Dongshuimen Bridge over the Yangtze River is a steel truss girder cable-stayed bridge with two pylons and single cable plane. The total length is 858m and the spans are arranged as 222.5m+445m+190.5m. The main pylons are 182m high, and 109m above the deck. 9 couples of stay cables are anchored to the pylon, and the cable plane is located along the centerline of the deck. The truss girder is designed as two layers and is 13m high. Main members of the truss girder are of the welded box section. Both upper and lower decks adopt orthotropic steel plate. The use of the truss girder not only provides the railway passengers with better and broader views but also makes the bridge itself more transparent.

The pylon of this bridge is uniquely designed in the shape of spindles. External contours of the pylons adopt arcs with the same diameter. Also the thickness of the pylons keep the same from bottom to top, thus the upper region of the pylon is almost a straight line. This concise design style greatly saves the quantity of construction formworks.

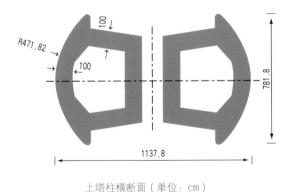

上塔柱横断面（单位：cm）
Cross section of upper pylon

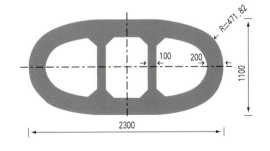

下塔柱横断面（单位：cm）
Cross section of lower pylon

桥　　名：东水门长江大桥
桥　　型：双塔钢桁梁斜拉桥
主　　跨：445m
桥　　址：重庆市
完成日期：2013年
设计单位：林同棪国际工程咨询（中国）有限公司
施工单位：中铁大桥局集团有限公司

Name: Dongshuimen Bridge over the Yangtze River
Type: Double-tower steel truss girder cable-stayed bridge
Main span: 445 m
Location: Chongqing
Completion: 2013
Designer(s): T. Y. Lin International Engineering Consulting (China) Co., Ltd.
Contractor(s): China Railway Major Bridge Engineering Group Co., Ltd.

千厮门嘉陵江大桥
Qiansimen Bridge over the Jialing River

桥　　名：千厮门嘉陵江大桥
桥　　型：单塔钢桁梁斜拉桥
主　　跨：312m
桥　　址：重庆市
完成日期：2013年
设计单位：林同棪国际工程咨询（中国）有限公司
施工单位：中交第二航务工程局有限公司

Name: Qiansimen Bridge over the Jialing River
Type: Single-tower steel truss girder cable-stayed bridge
Main span: 312m
Location: Chongqing
Completion: 2013
Designer(s): T. Y. Lin International Engineering Consulting (China) Co., Ltd.
Contractor(s): CCCC Second Harbour Engineering Company Ltd.

千厮门嘉陵江大桥位于重庆市嘉陵江和长江的交汇处，与东水门长江大桥形成"双桥"通过渝中区连接南岸区和江北区，同样为"公路＋轨道"交通模式，分为上、下两层：上层设置人行道及双向四车道，下层是双向轨道线，是重庆市轨道交通系统的重要节点。

千厮门大桥为单塔单索面钢桁梁斜拉桥，全长720m，桥梁造型与东水门长江大桥类似，跨径布置为88m+312m+240m+80m。两座相似的斜拉桥坐落于渝中区的两侧，形成隔岸相望的"双子桥"，在嘉陵江和长江的交汇点形成了协调统一的视觉效果。

该桥具有东水门长江大桥相同外形的桥塔，外部轮廓具有相同半径的圆弧，并且桥塔厚度从上到下保持不变，桥塔的上塔柱线形接近于直线，这样的外形大大方便了施工，大部分模板可以重复使用。

Qiansimen Bridge over the Jialing River is located at the meeting point of the Jialing River and the Yangtze River in Chongqing. It connects the Yuzhong District and the Jiangbei District, and is the critical project in the urban rail transit system of Chongqing. The bridge also has double decks just as Dongshuimen Bridge in vertical including highway and railway. The upper deck is designed as four traffic lanes in dual direction and two sidewalks, while the lower deck is designed as dual-way railway, through which the Line 6 crosses both the Yangtze River and the Jialing River.

The Qiansimen Bridge over the Jialing River is a steel truss cable-stayed bridge with single pylon and single cable plane. The total length is 720m and the spans are arranged as 88m+312m+240m+80m. The form of the bridge is similar with the Dongshuimen Bridge. These two bridges present a landscape of twin structures and delicately reflect the design intention for harmony at the point where the Yangtze River and the Jialing River meets.

The bridge also has uniquely designed in the shape of spindles. External contours of the pylons adopt arcs with the same diameter. Also the thickness of the pylons keep the same from bottom to top, thus the upper region of the pylon is almost a straight line. This concise design style greatly saves the quantity of construction formworks.

出版后记

经过编委会、编写组和出版社三方近一年的共同努力，这本精美的《中国桥梁》画册终于同读者们见面了。

本画册的编写工作于2012年3月启动并成立编辑委员会，5月在武汉召开了编委会议。6月底，经过编委会两轮投票遴选，第一轮从由编委提名的145座候选桥梁中投票产生了67座，第二轮又从79座桥梁中投票产生了30座，编写组经过集体商议补充了3座桥梁（包括2座台湾地区桥梁），共100座桥梁入选本画册。

2012年7月，编写组开始工作，就分工、内容、篇幅、进度等问题召开了两次会议；8月和9月又召开了两次编写组顾问会，顾问们对入选桥梁的增减提出了宝贵意见，并对各篇的初稿进行了精心修改；特约翻译Paul Gauvreau教授对英文前言和各篇引言翻译稿作了认真修改。经过编委会和编写组的辛勤工作，本画册仅历时9个月就完成了定稿，因为大家都在用高效和努力来表达对李国豪老师的怀念和敬意。

国内大桥建设的许多单位和《桥梁》杂志社以高昂的热情支持我们的工作，提供了桥梁照片和背景材料，大大方便了编纂工作。人民交通出版社的工作人员在很短的时间里完成了繁重的编辑、排版和印刷任务，使我们能在李校长诞辰100周年之际献上这份礼物，在此对他们表示衷心感谢！

我们希望这本画册的出版发行，能成为中国改革开放30多年来、特别是近10年桥梁建设事业发展的珍贵记录，让国际桥梁界同行更加了解中国的桥梁建设，并促进中国从桥梁大国走向桥梁强国。

葛耀君　肖汝诚

2013年3月

Afterword

The album of *Bridges in China* was eventually published after about one year's joint effort of the editorial committee, the compilation board and the publisher.

The edition of this album was started in March, 2012. The editorial committee was set up at the same time and then held a meeting at Wuhan in May, 2012. At the end of June, the editorial committee selected 100 bridges after two rounds of voting. In the first round, 67 bridges were selected from 145 bridges nominated by the editorial committee members, and in the second one, 30 bridges were chosen out of 79 recommended bridges. Furthermore, three additional bridges, including two bridges in Taiwan, China, were included after the decision made by the compilation board.

The compilation board started the editing work in July, and held two meetings to discuss the task distribution among the board members, the content and length of the album, and the schedule. Then, the consultants held two meetings in August and September to discuss the selection of bridges and the revision of the first draft of the album. Prof. Paul Gauvreau contributed a lot to the translation of the preface and the introductions in all six chapters. All contributors expressed the commemoration and respect to our beloved tutor, Prof. Li Guohao, through the effort and efficient work, thus this album was completed within only nine months.

Lots of organizations in Chinese bridge circles and Journal *Qiaoliang (Bridge)* gave us their enthusiastic support through offering photos and information that made the editing work much easier. The help also came from China Communications Press. They completed the complicated task of compiling, typeset and print in a very short period that enables us to give this album as a present to commemorate Prof. Li's centennial birthday. We would like to express our heartfelt gratitude for their great contribution.

We wish this album would become a precious record of Chinese bridge constructions in the past thirty years of reform and opening-up, especially in the recent decade. Furthermore, this album could acquaint our foreign colleagues with Chinese bridges and promote China to a "Strong Bridge Nation" rather than a "Large Bridge Nation".

Ge Yaojun, Xiao Rucheng

March , 2013

图书在版编目（CIP）数据

中国桥梁 / 项海帆等主编. —— 北京：人民交通出版社，2013.4
ISBN 978-7-114-10417-6

Ⅰ. ①中… Ⅱ. ①项… Ⅲ. ①桥－中国－画册 Ⅳ. ① U448-64

中国版本图书馆 CIP 数据核字 (2013) 第 041624 号

本书由人民交通出版社独家出版发行。未经著作权人书面许可，本书图片及文字的任何部分，不得以任何方式和手段进行复制、转载或刊登。版权所有，侵权必究。

Copyright © 2013

All rights reserved. No part of this publication may be reproduced, stored in a retrieval system, or transmitted in any form or by any means, electronic, mechanical, photocopying, recording or otherwise, without the prior written permission of the copyright holder. Printed in China.

书　名：	中国桥梁（2003-2013）	
著作者：	项海帆　葛耀君　肖汝诚　杨志刚	
责任编辑：	孙玺　曲乐　王文华　卢俊丽　郭海龙	
出版发行：	人民交通出版社	
地　址：	（100011）北京市朝阳区安定门外外馆斜街 3 号	
网　址：	http://www.ccpress.com.cn	
销售电话：	(010) 59757973	
总　销售：	人民交通出版社发行部	
经　销：	各地新华书店	
印　刷：	北京雅昌彩色印刷有限公司	
开　本：	965×635　1/8	
印　张：	38	
版　次：	2013 年 4 月　第 1 版	
印　次：	2013 年 4 月　第 1 次印刷	
书　号：	ISBN 978-7-114-10417-6	
定　价：	480.00 元	

Book: Bridges in China (2003-2013)
Author: Xiang Haifan　Ge Yaojun　Xiao Rucheng　Yang Zhigang
Editor in Charge: Sun Xi　Qu Le　Wang Wenhua　Lu Junli　Guo Hailong
Publisher: China Communications Press
Address: No.3 Waiguanxie Street, Chaoyang District, Beijing, China
Zip Code: 100011
Website: http://www.ccpress.com.cn
Tel: +86 (0)10 59757973
Fax: +86 (0)10 85285983
E-mail: gongluzhongxin@ccpress.com.cn
ISBN: 978-7-114-10417-6
Price: RMB 480.00

（有印刷、装订质量问题的图书由本社负责调换）